COMPLETE EDITION

MANDOLIN

Beginning • Intermediate • Mastering

GREG HORNE
WAYNE FUGATE

*Alfred, the leader in educational music publishing,
and the National Guitar Workshop,
one of America's finest guitar schools, have joined
forces to bring you the best, most progressive
educational tools possible. We hope you will enjoy
this book and encourage you to look for
other fine products from Alfred and the
National Guitar Workshop.*

CONTENTS

Alfred Music Publishing Co., Inc.
P.O. Box 10003
Van Nuys, CA 91410-0003
alfred.com

ISBN-10: 0-7390-8788-6 (Book & CD)
ISBN-13: 978-0-7390-8788-6 (Book & CD)

Cover photograph by Karen Miller.
Interior photographs: John Black, Knoxville, TN
Thanks to Sound To Earth, Ltd for use of the Weber Fern mandolin on the cover and other Weber models
used for the interior photographs in this book.

BEGINNING MANDOLIN

GREG HORNE

This book was acquired, edited, and produced
by Workshop Arts, Inc., the publishing arm of
the National Guitar Workshop.
Nathaniel Gunod, acquisitions, managing editor
Ante Gelo, music typesetter
Timothy Phelps, interior design
Audio tracks recorded at Grinning Deer Studios, Knoxville, TN

ABOUT THE AUTHOR

PHOTO • JOHN BLACK

Greg Horne is a performer, writer, producer and teacher. He holds a Bachelor of Arts in Music from the College of Wooster, and pursued graduate studies at the University of Mississippi's Center for the Study of Southern Culture. Greg has been an instructor at the National Guitar Workshop's summer campuses since 1990, specializing in songwriting and acoustic courses. He is the author of *The Complete Acoustic Guitar Method*, and co-author of *The Multi-Instrumental Guitarist*, also published by the National Guitar Workshop and Alfred. Greg has produced several albums of his own songs, as well as producing and performing on projects for other artists. He lives in Knoxville, Tennessee. For more information or to contact Greg, visit www.greghornemusic.com.

Greg Horne plays Weber Mandolins made by Sound To Earth, Ltd in Belgrade, Montana (www.soundtoearth.com). They are heard on the audio tracks that accompany this book.

Greg Horne sends his special thanks to Paula Jean Lewis and Bruce Weber of Sound To Earth, David Lovett, Tim Worman, Pick'n'Grin (www.pickngrin.com), Nat Gunod, Wayne Fugate and his students.

CONTENTS

Track 1

An MP3 CD is included with this book to make learning easier and more enjoyable. The symbol shown at bottom left appears next to every example in the book that features an MP3 track. Use the MP3s to ensure you're capturing the feel of the examples and interpreting the rhythms correctly. The track number below the symbol corresponds directly to the example you want to hear (example numbers are above the icon). All the track numbers are unique to each "book" within this volume, meaning every book has its own Track 1, Track 2, and so on. (For example, *Beginning Mandolin* starts with Track 1, as does *Intermediate Mandolin* and *Mastering Mandolin*.) Track 1 will help you tune to this CD.

The disc is playable on any CD player equipped to play MP3 CDs. To access the MP3s on your computer, place the CD in your CD-ROM drive. In Windows, double-click on My Computer, then right-click on the CD icon labeled "MP3 Files" and select Explore to view the files and copy them to your hard drive. For Mac, double-click on the CD icon on your desktop labeled "MP3 Files" to view the files and copy them to your hard drive.

INTRODUCTION

Welcome to *The Complete Mandolin Method,* a comprehensive series of books designed for mandolinists who are either teaching themselves or working with teachers. This method consists of three separate volumes now available in this complete edition. Each of the three volumes (*Beginning Mandolin, Intermediate Mandolin* and *Mastering Mandolin*) covers the styles, techniques and musicianship you need to take your playing as far as you want to go. You have chosen an unusual, exciting instrument that is a lot of fun to play and is becoming more popular than ever. This book is written to help you have fun and play real music you will love as quickly as possible.

WHO IS THE BEGINNING SECTION INTENDED FOR?

The first section, *Beginning Mandolin,* is written to get you started playing mandolin even if you've never touched an instrument before. The early-intermediate player can also benefit from this section, using it to brush up on fundamental skills and lay a solid foundation for further development.

WHAT IS IN THIS SECTION?

This section covers basic musical skills that apply to all styles, but concentrates on old-time, blues, and bluegrass mandolin traditions. Some of the skills and concepts you will learn include:
- How to choose, tune, hold and pick your mandolin
- Strumming basic open chords to accompany songs
- Reading standard music notation and tablature (TAB)
- Playing several traditional fiddle tunes used widely in jams and contests
- Improvising and soloing over blues and bluegrass songs
- Strumming the famous bluegrass "chop" rhythm
- The structure of major scales, keys and chords
- Moveable chord shapes that allow you to play every major, minor and dominant-7 chord
- Specialized techniques that apply to old-time, bluegrass, blues and rock

HOW TO USE THIS SECTION

Each chapter in this section contains a group of lessons that are related by a theme or set of skills. The chapters are progressive, meaning each lesson within a chapter builds on the previous lesson. What makes this section different from other methods is that once you have mastered the basic skills of Chapter 1, you can work on several chapters at once, or skip around. For example, you could work through Chapter 2: Reading Standard Music Notation at the same time you are learning fiddle tunes in Chapter 3. You could work straight through the section in order, if you prefer.

APPENDIX 1: THE ELEMENTS OF MUSIC

This chapter is designed to gather together the basic music theory concepts that underlie the lessons in this book. You can work through this appendix as a series of lessons, and also use it for reference while working through other sections.

DON'T SAVE THE END FOR LAST

As you get into this section, check out the Appendices at the end. They will provide useful tips for practicing and learning, as well as a reference page for chord shapes.

WHERE DO I GO FROM HERE?

Beginning Mandolin is designed to progress directly to *Intermediate Mandolin*, the second section in this method. The skills and techniques you learn here will be developed and expanded in that section, where you will learn more tunes, styles, scales, chords and improvisation techniques. Happy picking!

CHAPTER 1

Getting Started

LESSON 1—GETTING TO KNOW YOUR TOOLS

THE PARTS OF THE MANDOLIN

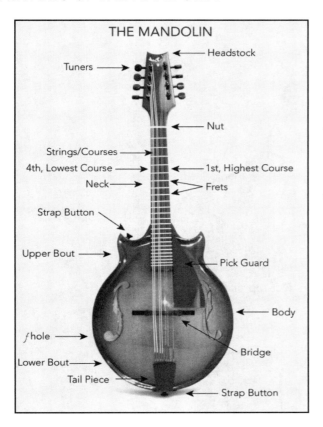

THE MANDOLIN

- Headstock
- Tuners
- Nut
- Strings/Courses
- 4th, Lowest Course
- 1st, Highest Course
- Neck
- Frets
- Strap Button
- Upper Bout
- Pick Guard
- Body
- ƒ hole
- Bridge
- Lower Bout
- Tail Piece
- Strap Button

MANDOLIN HISTORY

Like the guitar, the mandolin is a descendant of ancient plucked instruments found in the Middle East, Asia and Europe. The modern mandolin is descended from the 17th-century Italian *mandola* and *mandolino,* which can be found in the classical music of Vivaldi, Mozart and Beethoven. It remains a popular folk instrument in Italy. Italian mandolins (also called *Neapolitan* mandolins) have a round, convex back. American players nick-named these instruments *bowlbacks* or *taterbugs*.

The mandolin went through a boom of popularity in the early 20th century in America. There were many touring ensembles, and companies like Gibson and Lyon & Healy marketed new instrument designs. Mandolin clubs and orchestras became the hot trend in schools and community groups. These ensembles featured mandolins, mandolas and *mandocellos* (larger, lower-tuned relatives of the mandolin). The music consisted of light classical arrangements, Sousa-style marches and popular songs.

Eventually, the mandolin-ensemble craze died down, but the mandolin had found a new home in Southern American music. Blues and old-time hillbilly string bands had used mandolins for decades. In the early 1940s, Bill Monroe, an ambitious country singer from Kentucky, used the mandolin as the centerpiece of a new string band sound he named *bluegrass*. Bluegrass combined blues scales and forms, Celtic and Appalachian fiddle music and the virtuosic soloing found in jazz. bluegrass mandolin playing incorporates the percussive beat of the snare drum and the melodic range of the trumpet and fiddle.

The mandolin was a fundamental part of the development of Brazilian music, particularly *choro* music. Mandolins appear in modern Celtic music ensembles. Celtic music is the traditional fiddle music of Ireland, Scotland and Britain (and some nearby parts of Europe). Groups such as Led Zeppelin, The Band and R.E.M. brought the mandolin into rock music. In addition, a new enthusiasm for the mandolin is growing among Classical musicians and composers. Contemporary masters combine the influences of jazz, classical, world music, bluegrass and blues to push the mandolin into the 21st century.

WHAT TO LOOK FOR IN MANDOLINS

There are three popular styles of mandolins, plus many variations. The two most common styles are based on the Gibson company's A and F models, which were designed in the early 20th century. A-style mandolins are generally teardrop shaped and may have *f-holes* (holes that are roughly in the shape of the letter "f," as on a violin) or an oval-shaped soundhole. F-style mandolins have a scroll on the upper bout (see photograph below) and may have F-holes or a soundhole. The A-style and F-style mandolins generally have a carved, arched top. Another style, called a *flat-top* or Celtic mandolin, has a teardrop shape, a flat top and a round soundhole. All three styles can sound great. You should look for a mandolin that has a straight neck, comfortable action (easy to fret), working tuners and no sinking spots in the top.

PHOTOS * ROB WILKE/COURTESY WEBER MANDOLINS

A-style mandolin   *F-style mandolin*   *Flat-top or Celtic mandolin*

HOLDING THE MANDOLIN

The mandolin can be held in the lap, but using a strap can help place this small instrument in a better playing position. The strap (even a shoe string will work) is attached at the endpin and can then be tied in a loop around the scroll (on f-styles) or headstock (on any mandolin). The strap may go over your head (around your neck and shoulder) or simply over one shoulder. As an alternative way to attach the strap, you can have a repair shop install a strap button at the heel of the neck (where it joins the body). Many players simply hold the mandolin to their body using the right forearm, but this can restrict movement and cramp your muscles.

Your position should follow the natural, relaxed curves of your body. Your hands and arms should be free to move. Be careful not to hunch up your shoulders, as this may cause discomfort.

Suggested standing position

Suggested sitting position

THE LEFT-HAND POSITION

Your left-hand thumb should be behind the neck, resting lightly and allowing the palm to be open. You may also allow the lowest joint of your index finger to lightly touch the neck. This position resembles the left-hand position used by violinists and fiddlers. You may sometimes need some extra leverage, which may require you to squeeze with both your thumb and the palm of your hand. Try not to bend your wrist too sharply either forward or backward. Stay as relaxed as possible.

Proper left-hand position

LEFT-HAND FINGERS

Your left-hand fingers are numbered as follows:

Index	=	1
Middle	=	2
Ring	=	3
Pinky	=	4

STRINGS AND COURSES

The mandolin has eight strings, arranged in four *courses*. A course is a set of two strings that are tuned to the same pitch and played simultaneously. Since the strings of a course are fretted and plucked as if they were one string, many players refer to the 1st course as "the 1st string," the 2nd course as "the 2nd string," and so on. In this book, the terms *string* and *course* are used interchangeably.

FRETTING NOTES

To fret a note, press your finger just to the left of the fret you want to play. Press down both strings of a course. Do not press down directly on top of the fret. Your finger should press the course down so that it is pressed securely against the metal fret to form a clean, clear note.

THE PICK

The mandolin strings are made to vibrate by the *pick* (also called a *flatpick* or *plectrum*). Picks are available in a wide variety of shapes and sizes. As you begin, try using a standard, teardrop-shaped pick in a medium or heavy gauge. You could also use the larger "rounded triangle" style pick. Stiffer picks allow a great deal of control and more tone from the mandolin than thinner picks. Later, you may want to experiment with different picks.

Top

Actual size

Point

HOLDING THE PICK

Place your right-hand thumb across the top of the pick, with the point at a 90-degree angle from your thumb. Then, curve your index finger behind the point of the pick, holding it between the thumb and side of the first joint of your index finger. The pick should balance comfortably in this spot. Your other fingers should be relaxed, curling into your palm or hanging loosely.

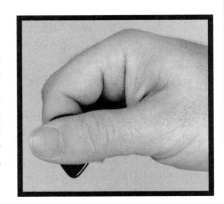

TUNING

Tuning your first stringed instrument is not easy, and you are encouraged to enlist the help of a teacher, store or experienced player. The following suggestions will help at home. Tuning will get easier as you learn more about the instrument.

The strings can be tuned to Track 1 on the CD available with this book. You can also tune the strings to a piano. To tune to a piano, match the courses to the keys as shown.

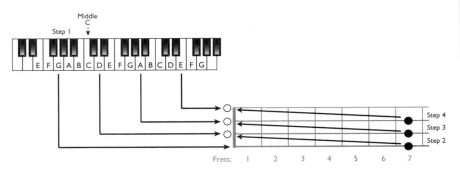

The steps shown here correspond to the procedure described below.

You can also use a guitar tuner, a chromatic tuner or a pitch pipe to get a reference tone for one string, then tune the other strings to it. For example:

Step 1. Tune a single string of the 4th course to G from a reference and match the other single string of the 4th course to that. Listen carefully and turn the tuner gradually while you pick the single string until you get a perfect match. This perfect match is called a *unison*.

Step 2. Play the 7th fret of the 4th course. This is the D note to which you will tune the 3rd course. First match a single string of the 3rd course to the 7th fret of the 4th course, then match both strings (unisons) of the 3rd course together.

Step 3. Play the 7th fret of the 3rd course. This is the A note to which you will tune the 2nd course. Tune a single string of the 2nd course to the 7th fret (A) of the 3rd course, then match the unisons of the 2nd course.

Step 4. Play the 7th fret of the 2nd course. This is the E note to which you will tune the 1st course. Tune a single string of the 1st course to the 7th fret (E) of the 2nd course, then match the unisons of the 1st course.

USING A TUNER

There is nothing better than training your own ears to tune the instrument. A tuner can help you on the way and provide some reassurance that you're getting it right. Tuners are also great for keeping a whole band tuned to one stable reference point, making jamming much more fun (and pleasant for the family).

The trick to learning the notes on the fretboard is understanding the musical alphabet. This is easy. You only need to remember four things:

1. **The musical alphabet goes from A to G, then starts over again with A:**

A	B	C	D	E	F	G	A	B	C	and so on

    This series of seven notes, called *natural notes*, repeats in a continuous cycle.

2. **The shortest distance between two notes is a half step.**

The closest one note can be to another is the distance of one fret. The distance between two notes that are on adjacent frets is called a *half step*. For example, from the 1st fret to the 2nd fret is a half step. The distance of two frets is called a *whole step*. For example, from the 1st fret to the 3rd fret is a whole step.

> Half step   =   One fret
> Whole step   =   Two frets

3. **In the musical alphabet, two sets of notes are only one half step apart.**

> B to C is a half step
> E to F is a half step

There is no note between B and C, or between E and F. All the other natural notes are separated by one whole step.

4. **Special symbols called *accidentals* are used to name the notes between the natural notes.** Remember, there are no notes between E and F, or B and C.

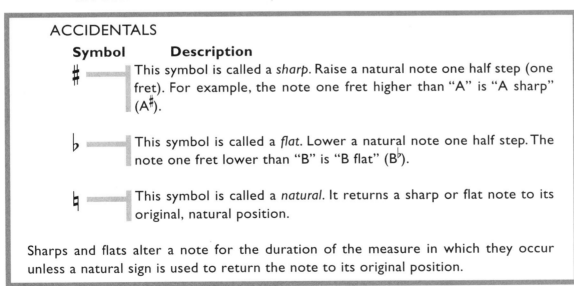

ACCIDENTALS

Symbol	Description
♯	This symbol is called a *sharp*. Raise a natural note one half step (one fret). For example, the note one fret higher than "A" is "A sharp" (A♯).
♭	This symbol is called a *flat*. Lower a natural note one half step. The note one fret lower than "B" is "B flat" (B♭).
♮	This symbol is called a *natural*. It returns a sharp or flat note to its original, natural position.

Sharps and flats alter a note for the duration of the measure in which they occur unless a natural sign is used to return the note to its original position.

All sharp notes can have a flat name, and all flat notes can have a sharp name. For example, A♯ and B♭ fall on the same fret. Two notes that have different names but have the same sound are called *enharmonic equivalents*.

What is the pitch between A and B called?   A sharp (A$^\sharp$) or B flat (B$^\flat$)

What is the pitch between C and D called?   _____

Fill in the note names:

A ___   A$^\sharp$B$^\flat$ B ___   C ___ ___   D ___ ___   E ___   F ___ ___   G ___ ___
              Example

Check your answers by looking at the 2nd string on the chart at the bottom of this page.

Practice saying the music alphabet forward and backward. Remember that as you go forward through the alphabet, the notes get higher in pitch. As you go backward, the notes get lower in pitch.

THE STRINGS

Your strings are tuned to the following pitches, low string to high:

Note:	G	D	A	E
String:	4	3	2	1

One fun way to remember this is to use the first letter of each word in this sentence:

Great **D**anes **A**re **E**normous

Start on any open string and follow the alphabet series up the neck. Check your answers on the chart at the bottom of the page.

For example: Ascending the 1st (E) string:

Open   = E
1st fret = F
2nd fret = F$^\sharp$ or G$^\flat$ 7th fret   =
3rd fret = G   8th fret   =
4th fret = G$^\sharp$ or A$^\flat$ 9th fret   =
5th fret =   10th fret =
6th fret =   11th fret =
                                        12th fret =

Note:

Notice that the 12th fret brings you back to where you started. You have gone an *octave* (distance of twelve half steps)—one cycle through the alphabet! This is why we say the mandolin neck "starts over" at the 12th fret.

Here are all the notes on the mandolin from the open string to the 12th fret:

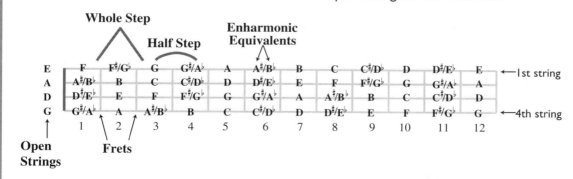

Now that we've covered the basics, it's time to play!

TABLATURE

Mandolin *tablature,* called TAB for short, is a system of writing music just for the mandolin. It tells you what fret to play, and what course to play it on.

The long horizontal lines represent the four string courses. The top line is the 1st course (E) and the bottom line is the 4th course (G). The numbers indicate which fret to play. Try fingering the notes indicated using any left-hand finger.

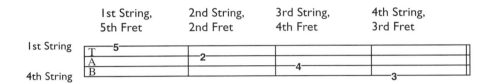

SECRETS OF THE MASTERS

The dots, or fret markers, on your mandolin neck will help you keep track of the frets. The dots are usually on frets 3, 5, 7, 10 and 12. Look at your mandolin and familiarize yourself with where the dots are. Often there is a "double dot" at the 12th fret.

TAB is often attached to written music, so the player will know how long the notes last and when they occur. As you become accustomed to reading standard music notation (see Chapter 2), this will be more and more helpful. The following examples show TAB and standard music notation. If you do not yet read music, *do not panic.* If you like, you can look ahead to Chapter 2 (page 19) for information about reading standard notation. Or, just play the frets and strings indicated in the TAB in a slow, steady rhythm, giving each note an equal amount of time. The numbers under the TAB indicate the left-hand fingers (see page 9).

RIVER'S UP, CAN'T GO ACROSS

Track 2

Left-hand fingers: 1   2   0   0   2   0   1   1   3   1   0   2   1   1   0   0

If you're looking for a fun challenge (and who isn't?), put down that crossword puzzle and instead try to name the notes you are playing from the TAB. Use the musical alphabet from Lesson 2 (page 11). In "This One's Got Spots," the note names are given. In "Mary Had a Border Collie," you're on your own.

THIS ONE'S GOT SPOTS
Track 3

MARY HAD A BORDER COLLIE
Track 4

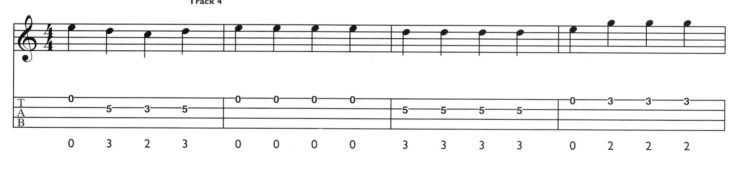

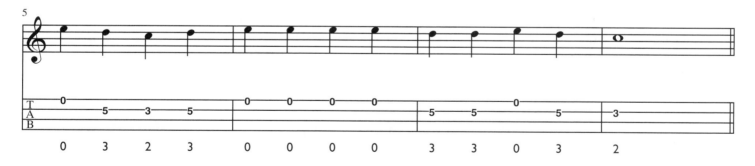

This lesson will get you started playing *chords* that you will use for the rest of your mandolin-pickin' life. A chord is three or more notes sounded simultaneously. Each chord is named for the note on which it is built (the *root,* more on that later*).* The chords in this lesson are known as *open chords* because they use a mixture of open (unfingered) strings and fretted notes. They also occur in the first three or four frets of the fretboard.

SECRETS OF THE MASTERS
During this stage of your learning, it is more important to practice often than to practice for long periods. (For more on practicing, see page 95.)

You will be building new pathways from your brain to your finger muscles. Like mountain trails, these paths need frequent clearing or they grow over and disappear. If you practice for 15–30 minutes every day, you *will* see improvement. On the other hand, if you wait several days between sessions, you will feel like you're starting at the beginning every time. It may take up to a few weeks before these chords start to feel natural (though it may come much sooner). As you work on them, you may also want to begin Chapter 2 to add some variety to your practice.

STRUMMING
One of the most common ways to play a chord is to *strum*. To strum, the point of the pick is moved rapidly across the strings, sounding them nearly simultaneously. A *downstrum* (or *downstroke*), indicated ⊓, is a motion toward the floor. An *upstrum* (or *upstroke*), indicated V, is a motion toward the ceiling.

⊓ = downstroke
V = upstroke

MANDOLIN CHORD DIAGRAMS
Mandolin chords are most often depicted in *chord diagrams*. A chord diagram is like a picture of the fretboard that shows which strings, fingers and frets you will use to make your chord.

Note that a zero (0) over a string means to strum that string open as part of your chord. Here is a chord diagram for the G chord and a photograph for comparison.

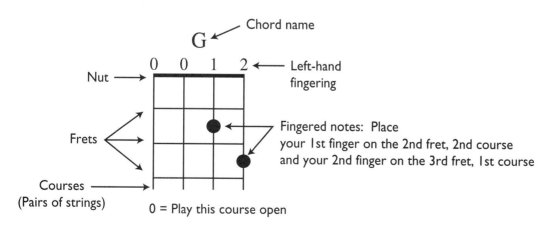

Chord name
G ←
0 0 1 2 ← Left-hand fingering
Nut →
Frets {
Fingered notes: Place your 1st finger on the 2nd fret, 2nd course and your 2nd finger on the 3rd fret, 1st course
Courses → (Pairs of strings)
0 = Play this course open

Here are two more chords for you.

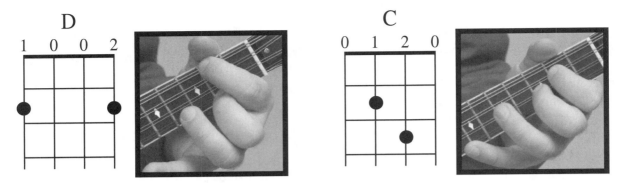

Before you rush into playing your first songs with chords, make sure that each chord is as clean and clear as it can be. While holding a chord with your left hand, pick each string individually from the lowest (4th) string to the highest (1st) string. You may have to move your fingers around slightly to keep them from bumping into adjacent strings or getting too far from or too close to the frets. Keep your fingers curved and your thumb resting comfortably behind the neck (see Lesson 1, page 9).

Once the chords are familiar, try strumming through "Cabbage Seeds." Use downstrokes in time to a slow, even beat. It will help if you tap your foot and count the *beats* aloud. A beat is the basic unit of musical time. When you tap your foot (to a steady rhythm), you are tapping the beats.

"Cabbage Seeds" is written in *slash notation*. Each slash / indicates one beat. The song is divided into groups of four beats called *measures*. Bar lines separate the measures (which can also be called *bars*). Change chords as indicated. For example, in the first measure, start with a G chord, then change to the C chord in the second measure. Count slowly enough to allow for changing chords without stopping the beat.

CABBAGE SEEDS

Track 5

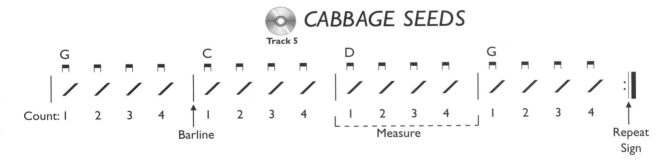

The *repeat sign* at the end tells you to repeat the song from the beginning. Since is a short sequence of chords, you may want to repeat it many times.

There is no need for physical pain or distress when learning the mandolin. If your knuckles are turning white and there are pains shooting through your hands, you may be pressing too hard (or holding a cattle prod). Take it easy and your strength and accuracy (and calluses) will develop in a short time.

LESSON 5: CHANGING CHORDS

Now that you've tried a few chords, here are some techniques to help your fingers learn to get to them faster.

FOUR-STEP FRETTING EXERCISE

This exercise is based on a classical guitar warm-up. Follow the steps slowly and steadily. Once you are familiar with the four steps, try them to the beat of a *metronome* set between 40 and 60 beats per minute. A metronome is an adjustable device used for determining the exact *tempo* (speed) of a piece. It is a great practice tool. (For more information on metronomes, see page 96.)

1. Set   Place your fingers lightly on the strings in the shape of the chord.

2. Press   Press the fingers down on the frets simultaneously and strum the chord.

3. Set   Relax pressure, without lifting fingers off strings.

4. Release Lift fingers off strings about ⅛ inch, holding fingers in the shape of the chord.

Repeat this process several times.

This exercise is a great way to help your fingers learn the different chords faster. Try it every time you practice and with every new chord you learn. Another benefit is that you will learn to use only the minimum amount of pressure needed to play the chord; it doesn't take as much as you may think!

SWITCHING CHORDS

The secret to good chord switching is learning to move your fingers simultaneously from one chord to another. The exercise you just learned will help your fingers get used to acting together to press down a chord.

Moving your fingers precisely, in different directions at the same time, takes practice. It is helpful to look at the switching process closely. Each chord switch is like a tiny dance step for your fingers. Learn the first few steps very carefully and with some concentration, and the whole dance will get easier and easier.

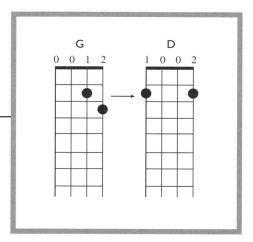

For example, look at the switch from G to D: _____

Make a G chord with your left hand. Now look at your hand and imagine where the fingers will need to go to make the D chord:

- The 1st finger moves from the 2nd to the 4th string, staying on the same fret (the 2nd fret).
- The 2nd finger stays on the 1st string, moving from the 3rd to the 2nd fret. It doesn't even have to lift up from the string!

Now try alternating between G and D using the four-step exercise.

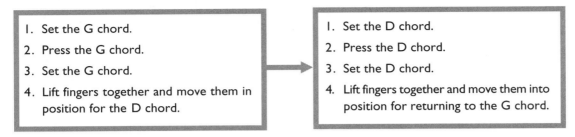

1. Set the G chord.
2. Press the G chord.
3. Set the G chord.
4. Lift fingers together and move them in position for the D chord.

1. Set the D chord.
2. Press the D chord.
3. Set the D chord.
4. Lift fingers together and move them into position for returning to the G chord.

Though this process may seem a little intense, it is actually a shortcut to switching chords cleanly and quickly. A little patience, persistence and focus in the beginning will pay off! Use this technique with each new chord combination you encounter. Try it a few times with G, C and D, then go back to "Cabbage Seeds" and behold the magic.

MAJOR OR MINOR

The chords you have learned so far are called *major* chords. They have a bright, happy sound. As you have seen, chord symbols for major chords are simply the letter name of the root. Any chord that is marked *min* is a *minor* chord. Minor chords have a darker quality. You will learn more about chord structure on page 89.

Here are a few more chords and some songs to try. For more chord shapes, see page 94.

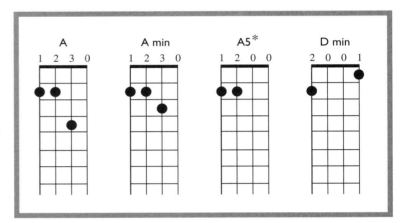

* A5 is a simplified A chord that you can use for either A or Amin.

ROAST THEM RUTABAGAS

Track 6

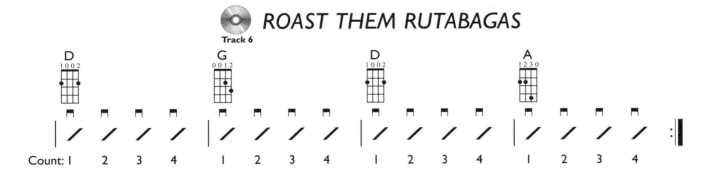

WINDY GROVE

Track 7

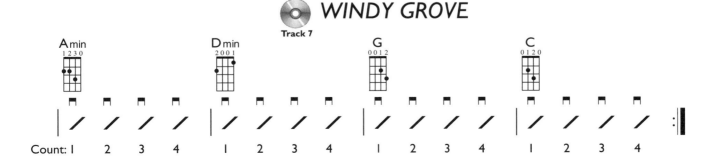

CHAPTER 2

Reading Standard Music Notation

This chapter will provide a quick introduction to reading standard music notation in the first position of the mandolin neck (the first six frets and open strings). You may want to work through this chapter at the same time you are learning to play and strum the chords and melodies in Chapters 1 and 3. This will add variety to your practice and keep things interesting. Also, you will be improving in several things at once, instead of one at a time. Most of the examples in this chapter do not have tablature. TAB is used throughout the rest of the book. You do not have to master reading standard music notation in order to work on the other chapters, since TAB is always available.

Reading standard music notation is a rewarding skill that is easier to develop than most people think. It enhances tablature and chord charts by allowing you to read exact rhythms, vocal melodies and music for other instruments. Even the most basic understanding of the notes of the staff (Lesson 1, below) will give you a point of departure for the concepts introduced later in this book.

Mandolinists also benefit from learning to read music because of the mandolin's similarity to the violin. The range and tuning is the same as the violin. A vast wealth of violin music is available to you to experiment with if you can read standard music notation. For example, there are many traditional Irish, Scottish and American fiddle tune books containing thousands of great tunes.

LESSON 1: THE NOTES AND THE STAFF

We use five horizontal lines as a sort of playing field for our notes. This is called the *staff*. The *natural notes* (notes without sharps or flats) are placed on the lines and spaces of the staff. Lower notes are near the bottom of the staff, higher notes are near the top. A *clef* sign at the beginning of the staff indicates which notes are represented by which lines and spaces. When the *G clef* sits on the second line from the bottom of the staff it is called *treble clef*. The line it encircles is called G.

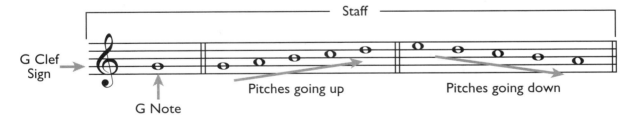

Now that you know the second line from the bottom is G, all the other notes can be related to that line. For example, the space under it is F, the note before G in the musical alphabet. The space above the G line is A, the next note in the musical alphabet.

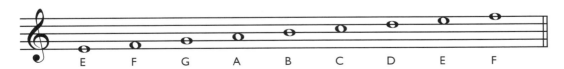

LEARNING THE NOTES ON THE STAFF

There are several memory devices you can use to quickly learn all the notes on the staff. One is to separate the notes on the lines from the notes in the spaces. The notes on the lines give you the first letter of each word of this sentence: "**E**very **G**ood **B**eginner **D**oes **F**ine." The notes in the spaces themselves spell the word "FACE."

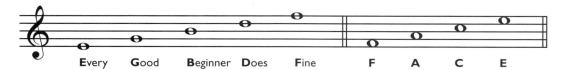

LESSON 2: NATURAL NOTES ON THE 1ST STRING

Reading notes on the staff is easier when you learn a few at a time. Your first notes are on the 1st string, using your 1st, 2nd and 3rd fingers. This example shows where they are on the staff and on the mandolin. Note that the A note appears on a *ledger line*. Ledger lines are additional lines that allow us to extend the range of the staff.

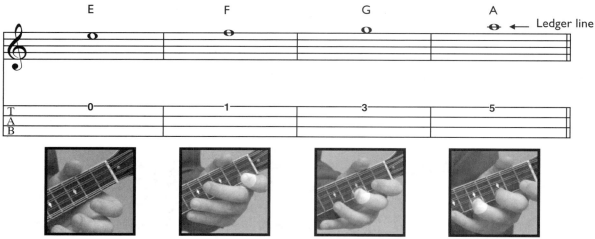

In the photos above, the highlighted finger plays the note.

Here are some practice examples. First, make sure you can name all the notes easily. Then, try to play them in a slow, steady rhythm. Using your pick, play each note with a downstroke. Strive for a good tone right away by using just the point of the pick and not picking too hard. Always pick both strings in a course simultaneously with each stroke of the pick.

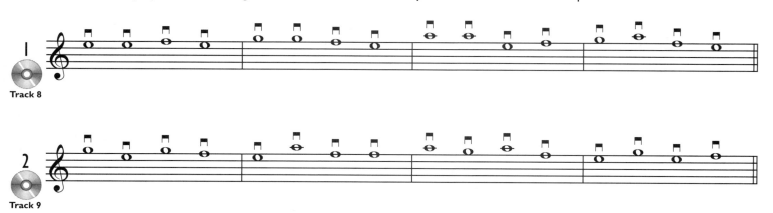

The first part of this lesson is a quick review of material you learned in Chapter I. Read it anyway, as there are important new details.

GET THE BEAT

The *beat* is the steady, even pulse that remains constant throughout a passage of music. It is what the listener's foot taps.

THE MEASURE

Musicians count beats and divide them into small groups. As you know, a group of beats is called a measure. Measures can consist of any number of beats. It is most common to have four beats in a measure. Measures are marked on the staff using bar lines. For this reason, measures are sometimes called *bars*. A double bar indicates the end of a passage of music or short example.

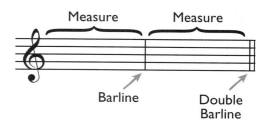

SIGNS OF THE TIMES

The *time signature* tells you how many beats are in a measure and which type of note gets one beat. It is found at the beginning of the piece. The upper number indicates the number of beats per measure. The lower number shows what type of note is one beat.

Like a fraction, the bottom number can be understood as a "quarter," so $\frac{4}{4}$ could be read as "four quarters." This would mean that every measure has the equivalent of four *quarter notes* ♩, with each quarter note equaling one beat. Read on to learn about the different types of notes.

THE LONG AND SHORT OF IT

The *value* of a note is its duration (in beats). The appearance of a note tells us its value. Here are three note values and their durations:

The *whole note* gets four beats. Try playing the following example and counting aloud. Remember to pick the note at the same time you say "one" and let it ring all the way through "two, three, four." Keep the beat steady and even. Tap your foot while you count!

Track 10   Count: I   2   3   4   I   2   3   4   I   2   3   4

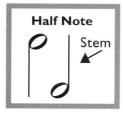

The *half note* lasts for two beats. In a measure of four beats, the half notes start on beats I and 3. Notice that some *stems* go down and some go up. Normally, notes on or above the middle line of the staff have their stems going down, and notes below the middle line have their stems going up.

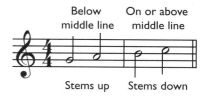

Track 11   Count: I   2   3   4   I   2   3   4   I   2   3   4

Quarter Note

The *quarter note* lasts for one beat. Play along with your counting.

Count: 1 2 3 4   1 2 3 4   1 2 3 4

Here is an exercise to try using E, F, G and A with quarter, half and whole notes.

Track 13

FINGERING ALERT

Most of the music in this book is in the 1st or "open" position. The placement of fingers on the neck is identical to a violin. The fingers stretch out over a position including six or seven frets. Here's how it works for each finger in the open position, depending on the scale or key.

Left-Hand Finger	Frets Played
1st Finger	1st or 2nd fret.
2nd Finger	3rd or 4th fret. The 2nd finger may be held so that it touches the 1st finger or 3rd finger, depending on which frets are being used.
3rd Finger	5th or 6th fret. The 3rd finger may also be used to slide up to the 7th fret.
4th Finger	6th or 7th fret.

Left-hand fingering

A CLOSER FINGER IS A FASTER FINGER!

As you progress through this chapter and in the future, try to keep your fingers spread out in this form, floating just above the frets. You don't want your fingers to have to travel too far to work.

LESSON 4: NATURAL NOTES ON THE 2ND STRING

Here are the natural notes in the *1st position* (first five frets) on the 2nd string.

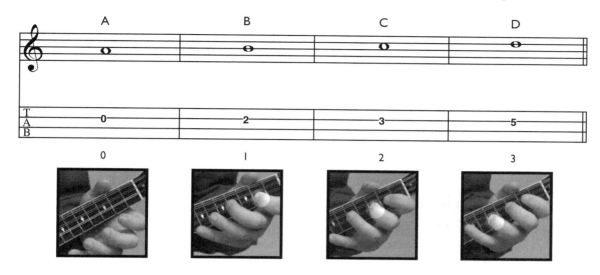

Try these examples. The first one only uses the new notes. "Cumberland Gap" is a traditional tune using notes on the 1st and 2nd strings.

7

Track 14

CUMBERLAND GAP

Track 15

LESSON 5: RESTS

Silence is as important a part of music as sound. The symbols that represent silence are called *rests,* and just like notes, they are divided into wholes, halves and quarters.

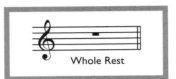

A *whole rest* is four beats of silence. It is a small rectangle that hangs like a full suitcase from the fourth line of the staff.

A *half rest* is two beats of silence. It is a small rectangle that sits like a hat on the third line of the staff.

A *quarter rest* is one beat of silence. It looks a bit like a bird flying sideways.

SECRETS OF THE MASTERS
Rests must be "played" with the same precision and importance as pitches! To play a rest, you must stop the string or strings from ringing by using your right hand or lifting up a fretted note with your left-hand finger to stop the sound.

The following examples use some of the notes and rests you've learned. Enjoy playing them.

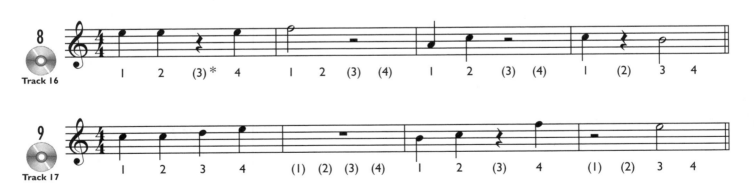

* The numbers in parentheses correspond to rests in music. They are used to assist in counting beats.

Here are the natural notes in 1st position on the 3rd string.

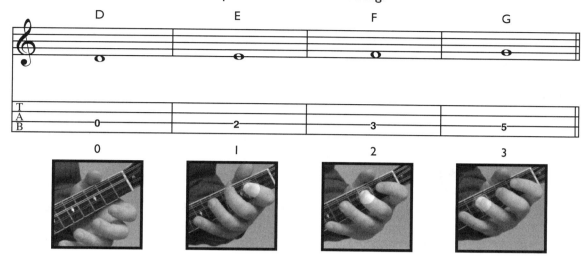

FINGERING ALERT: GUIDE FINGERS

Notice that the fret and finger locations are the same as the natural notes on the 2nd string. You will often use this finger placement, with your 1st finger on the 2nd fret, and your 3rd finger on the 5th fret. Your 1st and 3rd fingers can be thought of as guide fingers to help keep you in a position. For a thorough explanation of guide fingers, see page 93.

Try these examples. The first one uses just the 3rd string, the next adds in the other notes you've learned. Watch out for rests!

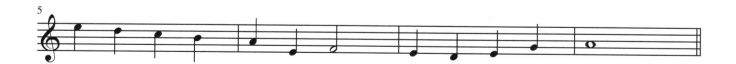

LESSON 7: EIGHTH NOTES

The beat can be divided into smaller subdivisions to allow for faster notes. A quarter note can be divided into two *eighth notes*. Each eighth note lasts half of a beat. Eighth notes can appear alone (with *flags*) or connected in groups (with *beams*). The stems follow the same rules as for other notes: notes on or above the middle line of the staff have their stems going down, and notes below the middle line have their stems going up. An eighth rest looks like a slash with a small flag waving from it and it lasts for half a beat.

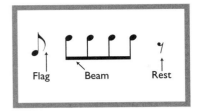

We can organize our note and rest values into a "tree" to help visualize the relationships.

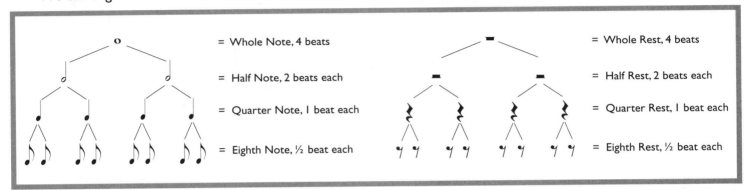

COUNTING EIGHTH NOTES

Eighth notes are counted by dividing the beats (counted "1, 2, 3, 4") into "1-&, 2-&, 3-&, 4-&." Tap on the numbered beats as before. Let's call these *onbeats* (sometimes called *downbeats*). Move your foot up on the "&s" ("ands"). Let's call these *offbeats* (sometimes called *upbeats*). Try clapping or playing this example on one note while you count and tap.

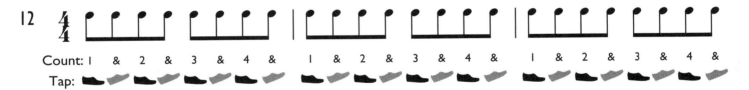

WHAT GOES DOWN MUST COME UP

To play eighth notes, use a downstroke of the pick (⊓) for the onbeat, and an upstroke (∨) for the offbeat. As you play the next example, try to make the upstrokes sound identical in tone and quality to your downstrokes. Notice that your pick moves exactly the same as your tapping foot: down–up, down–up, down–up.

Track 20

SECRETS OF THE MASTERS
Play as steadily as a Swiss watch! By using a consistent down-up motion, you will have an easier time keeping the beat and playing smooth, graceful lines at any speed. Make a lifetime commitment to even down–up picking!

LESSON 8: NATURAL NOTES ON THE 4TH STRING

Congratulations! You've made it to the 1st position of the 4th string. The following example contains the natural notes. These notes incorporate the use of ledger lines below the staff.

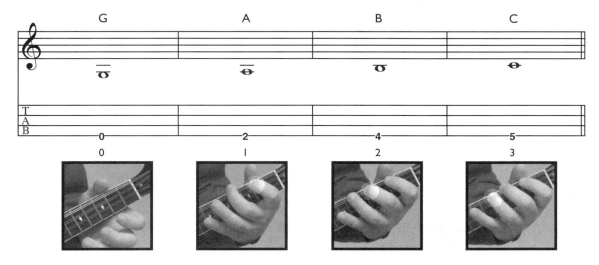

Put a little extra effort into memorizing these notes and their location on the ledger lines. This will help you identify the notes quickly and avoid unnecessary confusion. *Always* avoid unnecessary confusion!

Try this example. The first half is on the 4th string, the second half uses the other strings.

14
Track 21

LESSON 9: DOTTED NOTES

A *dot* placed after a note head increases its duration by half of the note value. For example, a half note equals two beats. Half of that value is one beat so if we add a dot to a half note, it equals three beats (2 + 1 = 3).

Dotted Half Note

The same logic applies to other note values. For example, a quarter note equals one beat. Half of that value is half a beat (an eighth note) so a dotted quarter note equals one-and-one-half beats (1 + ½ = 1½, or a quarter note plus an eighth note).

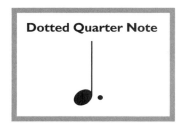

Dotted Quarter Note

Example 15 will give you some practice reading notes with dotted rhythms and eighth rests. To help you with the new rhythms, the counting is shown below the music. Remember, the numbers in parentheses are rests.

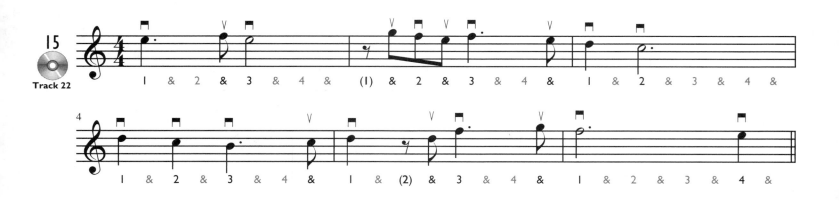

LESSON 10: SHARPS AND FLATS

ACCIDENTALS DO HAPPEN

Now it is time to learn the sharp and flat notes (*accidentals*) between the natural notes you have mastered. To review the accidentals, see page 11.

THINGS TO KNOW ABOUT SHARPS AND FLATS

- A sharp ♯ raises a note by one fret, while a flat ♭ lowers a note by one fret.
- Both sharps and flats are written by placing the proper symbol directly on the line or space before the affected note. The accidental is placed immediately *before* the note. That way, you know what's going to happen.
- Sharps and flats last for the duration of the measure in which they appear. When a new measure starts, the note returns to its natural position, unless a new sharp or flat is written.
- A natural sign ♮ is used to cancel a sharp or flat and return a note to its natural position. Like sharps and flats, naturals last for the duration of the measure in which they appear.

Below are all of the notes on the 1st and 2nd strings, including naturals, sharps and flats, up to the 7th fret. *Pay close attention to the fingering!* Each left-hand finger may be responsible for multiple notes. For example, on the 1st string, the 1st finger may play F at the 1st fret, and F♯/G♭ at the 2nd fret.

Here are all of the notes on the 3rd and 4th strings up to the 6th fret. As you probably know from tuning your mandolin, the 7th frets of the 4th, 3rd and 2nd strings are the same as the next higher open strings, which is why these charts stop at the 6th fret (except on the 1st string).

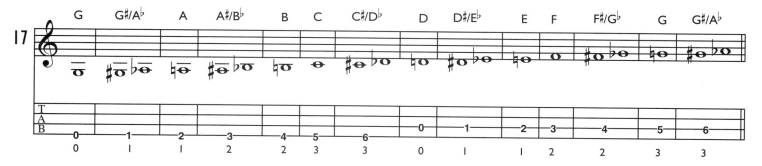

Here is a tune to play incorporating some of the sharps, flats and naturals. TAB has been included to help you locate the right frets and fingers. As you get better reading standard music notation, try covering the TAB with a piece of paper.

 ## OOOOH...CREEPY!
Track 23

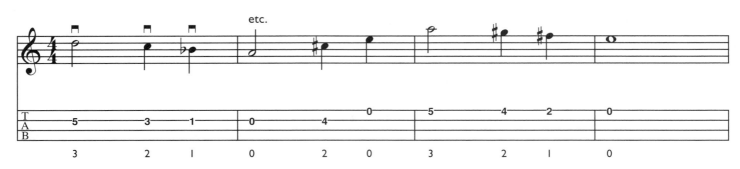

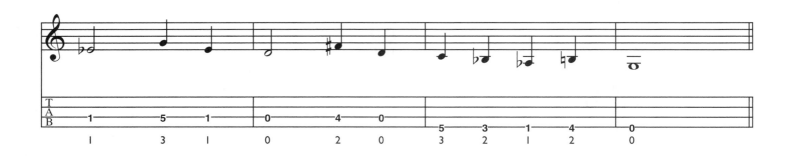

Here's another one to try. This one has no TAB (gasp). It is also in ¾ time, which has only three beats per measure. For more on ¾ time, see page 49. This tune is from a piece by Johann Sebastian Bach (1680–1750), one of the greatest classical composers of all time.

 ## THEME FROM INVENTION NO. 4, BWV 775
Track 24

Johann Sebastian Bach

LESSON 11: KEY SIGNATURES

Most pieces of music have a *key*. A key is the *tonal center*—the note the piece revolves around. For example, in the *key of C*, the note C is the *tonic* or *keynote*. It's like home base for the key. When you learn about the *major scale* (page 81), you'll discover how a key is really composed of a entire set of notes and the relationships between them.

A *key signature* appears just after the clef sign at the beginning of each line of music. It is a set of sharps or flats (never both). The key signature is a form of shorthand that helps prevent the music from getting too cluttered with accidentals.

Reading a key signature is very simple. Look just to the right of the clef sign. Any sharps or flats that appear will affect that pitch throughout the entire piece of music.

For example, the key signature in the example on the right has an F♯ (F-sharp) and a C♯ (C-sharp). This means that *all* of the F notes and *all* of the C notes will be sharped in this piece, unless marked with a natural sign.

> **IMPORTANT NOTE:**
> Accidentals in key signatures affect the notes in every octave, not just the line or space on which the accidental appears.

To learn which key signatures go with which keys, check out page 82.

This tune is in the key of D Major, which uses two sharps (F♯ and C♯). Tablature has been included to help you find the new notes. In this example, the pitches affected by the key signature have been circled.

RAISE A GLASS FOR PYTHAGORAS

Track 25

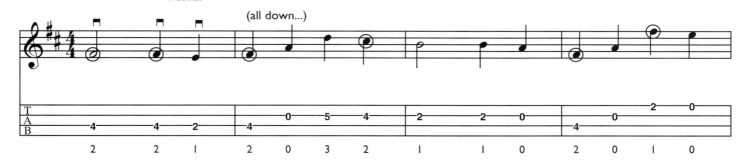

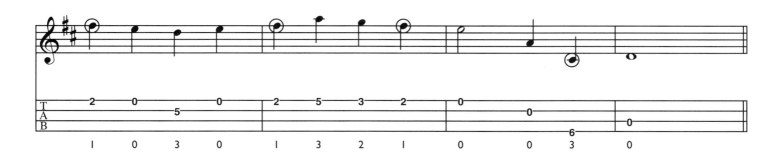

1st and 2nd endings are used to add variety to a repeated passage of music. The first time through, play the 1st ending, then repeat the passage. As you play the repeat, skip over the 1st ending and play the 2nd ending instead. The piece may end at this point, or it may continue on to a new section.

This example is in the key of F Major, which uses one flat (B♭). Try circling the B♭ notes before you play. It also uses dotted rhythms (page 28). As your standard music notation reading improves, try covering up the TAB. Notice the high B♭ (6th fret, 1st string) in the 2nd ending.

 MARCHING OFF TO LITCHFIELD

Track 26

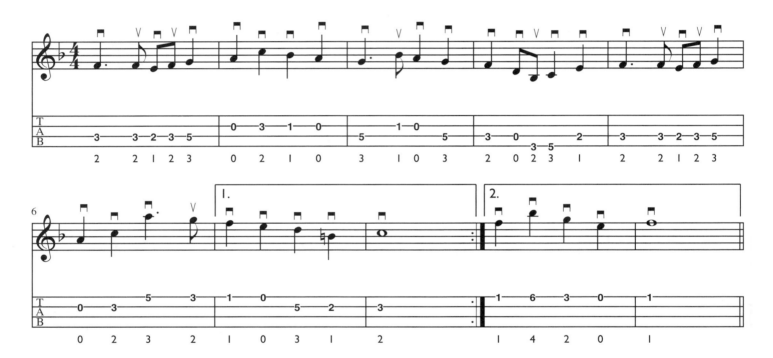

Bill Monroe *(1911-1996), the "Father of Bluegrass," defined the bluegrass mandolin style for many players who came after him. In addition to his classic solos and great rhythm playing, he was one of America's great songwriters.*

PHOTO • MAUREEN DELGROSSO

Now that you are comfortable with at least a few basic chords and can read rhythms, you can shift your attention from your left hand to your right hand and begin refining your strumming technique.

Here are some things to keep in mind when working on your strumming:
- Keep your wrist loose and your arm relaxed.
- Resist the urge to tighten up your muscles as you play faster.
- Work on developing a steady, even beat. You may want to try working with a metronome (see page 96).

> ### SECRETS OF THE MASTERS
> *To become a truly good mandolinist, you must develop an internal sense of rhythm that is steady and predictable. The best way to do this is to tap your foot on the beats and count aloud. Practice slowly and synchronize the movements of your right hand with the tapping and counting.*

RHYTHMIC NOTATION

In the following examples, *rhythmic notation* is introduced. This is a common way to show strumming rhythms when a specific rhythm is called for. The note values are indicated with slashes instead of circles for eighth notes and quarter notes, and with diamond-shaped heads for half notes and whole notes instead of open circles.

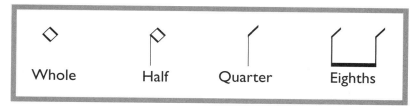

Practice your strumming with the following rhythms:

Strum No. 1: Try this strum with a G chord using a steady down-up motion.

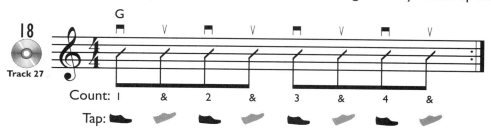

∏ = Strum down

V = Strum up

Strum No. 2: Here's one that mixes together quarter notes and eighth notes.

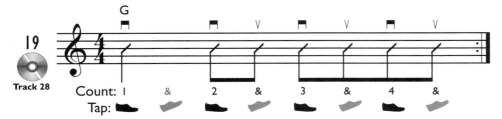

Strum No. 3: This one is great for singing to and for accompanying old-time fiddle tunes (coming up in the next chapter). This strum creates an open, ringing sound and is often used by Norman Blake.

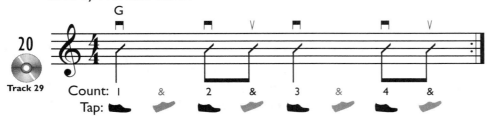

For a brighter, less cluttered sound, try strumming just the *backbeat*. The backbeat is a groove that results from playing just beats 2 and 4. Beats 1 and 3 are silent, and are marked with *quarter rests* (see page 24). Use the heel of your hand to stop the strings between strums on beats 2 and 4.

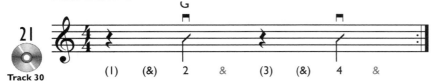

Here's an old bluegrass favorite. It is shown using Strum No. 3, but try them all!

BOIL THEM CABBAGE DOWN

Track 31

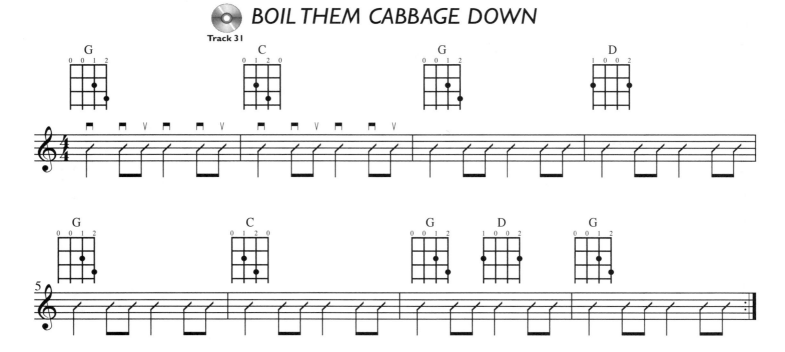

CHAPTER 3

Fiddle-Tune Style: The Roots of Bluegrass

WHAT IS A FIDDLE AND WHY DO I NEED TO KNOW?

Fiddle tunes are short melodies that have been used for centuries as music for dancing. In many European and American traditions, the violin (nicknamed "fiddle") has been the most common lead instrument for dances due to its portability, volume and familiarity. Therefore the huge body of tunes that have grown up around folk dancing, jamming and performing are called "fiddle tunes." The tunes consist of two repeated parts (sometimes three or more). Fiddle tunes can be played on any instrument. The mandolin is particularly good for these tunes because it has the same range and fingering as the fiddle.

WHEN DO I GET TO PLAY BLUEGRASS?

When you learn fiddle tunes, you are learning a major part of the roots of bluegrass. Bluegrass combines the rich tradition of American, Scottish, Irish and British fiddle tunes with African-American blues and jazz influences (Chapter 4, page 53, will introduce blues, and Chapter 5, page 61, will put it all together as bluegrass).

Learning fiddle tunes will help you:

1. Build a repertoire of songs you know by heart to play for fun, or at jams, parties and in bands.

2. Learn many of the kinds of finger moves and melodies that pop up in other tunes and in improvisations. Real tunes are way more fun than exercises!

3. Learn the techniques and structures of tunes, making it easier to pick up new ones by ear. You can even write new tunes of your own!

LESSON 1: D MAJOR SCALE; YOUR FIRST D TUNE

A great place to start your fiddle-tune collection is with tunes in the key of D, called *D tunes* by many musicians. To play D tunes, you need to know your *D Major scale*. A *scale* is a series of notes in a specific arrangement of whole steps and half steps. The major scale is a special sound associated with "Do, Re, Mi," a big hit song from the musical show *The Sound of Music*. Below is a D Major scale that covers two strings. Memorize it. For more on Major scale structure, see page 81.

THE D MAJOR SCALE

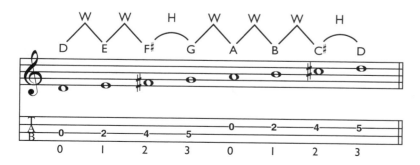

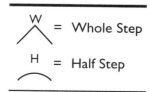

W = Whole Step

H = Half Step

Here is a simplified version of a traditional tune called "Old Liza Jane." It comes from the American tradition called *old-time* music. Old-time music seeks to preserve the sounds, songs and styles of string-band music of the late 1800s and early 1900s. Though it is an ancestor of bluegrass, old-time music is constantly evolving and gaining new tunes and masters. "Old Liza Jane" represents one of the quirky things about old-time music in that one name (like "Liza Jane") may be used for several completely different tunes. Apparently Liza was very well-travelled and highly thought of. This is just one of many tunes that carry her name.

OLD LIZA JANE

Track 32

* Right-facing repeat

* Left-facing repeat

PRACTICE TIPS:

- Use all downstrokes.
- Notice that there are two parts to this tune, "Part A" and "Part B." Each part must be repeated (played twice) before going on to the next part. The tune can be played over and over this way.
- Every time you learn a tune, learn to strum the chords too. They are indicated above the music. This way you can play chords while someone else tries the melody, then trade. Use a simple strum rhythm like the ones you learned on pages 33–34.

- If you like the sound of a tune, try to learn it by heart. That way you won't need to have the music with you to play it at Part Ay or a jam.
- Now would be a great time to check out APPENDIX 2 on page 93, for tips on guide fingers and good fingering.

*When you get to the left-facing repeat sign at the end, go back to this right-facing repeat and play the section again.

LESSON 2: ALTERNATE PICKING

Alternate picking (or "down-up" picking) is crucial to developing the speed and agility you will need for fiddle tunes and everything else. Your picking hand should move with a consistent, standardized motion that locks in with the basic pulse of the song. You have already learned about eighth notes (page 26). Here's a review of how to count and pick eighth notes. Try this on any note.

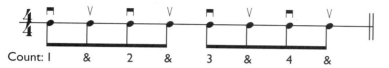

Count: 1   &   2   &   3   &   4   &

THE FIVE RULES OF ALTERNATE PICKING

- Pick down (downstroke) on the numbered beats, also called onbeats (1, 2, 3, 4).
- Pick up (upstroke) on all the "&'s," also called offbeats or upbeats.
- Always move your hand in a down-up pattern, even if the pick doesn't hit the strings. This way, you will always be in the right place at the right time.
- Count aloud whenever you can. This will help train your hand to move in the right direction and in rhythm. This really works. No kidding. Seriously, it does work.
- Try to get your downstrokes and upstrokes to sound as similar as possible, and hit both strings of a course with each stroke.

> ### SECRETS OF THE MASTERS
> *It cannot be stressed enough how important good, strict alternate picking will be to your future as a musician. Some patience and care now will pay off later. With good picking skills, you will be able to build as much speed, fluidity and rock-solid rhythm as you want in the future.*

Here are some exercises using notes from the two-string D Major scale (page 35).

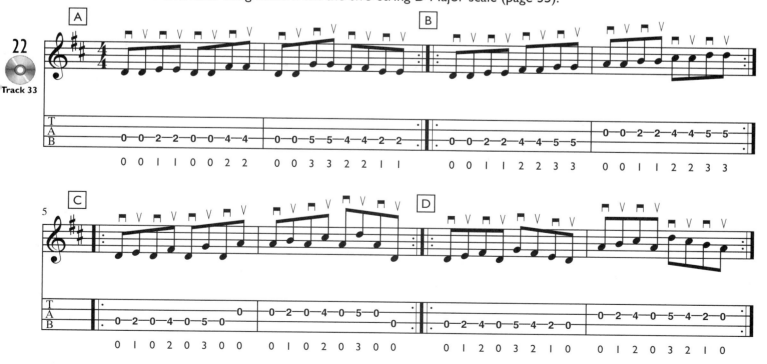

Track 33

This is one of the oldest and most well-known old-time and bluegrass jam tunes. Even many Celtic players know this one. It has been traced back to the British Isles as far back as the 1700s and is so important that it will show up in the *Mastering* section, too. As in "Old Liza Jane," Part A and Part B have been indicated. You may want to work on it one part at a time and memorize as you go. Don't forget to learn the chords! On the recording for this book, they are played on a guitar.

Notice that this tune has two notes before the first full measure. This is called a pickup. Count 1–2–3 and play on beat 4. The value of the pickup measure is then subtracted from the final measure of the tune.

SOLDIER'S JOY
Track 34

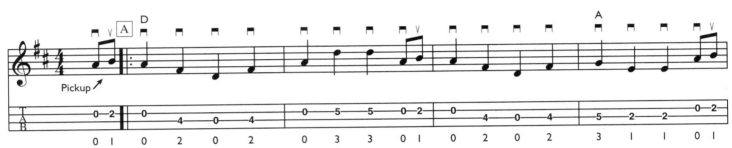

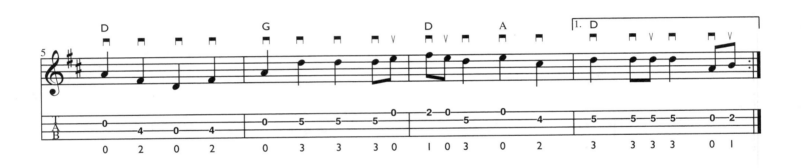

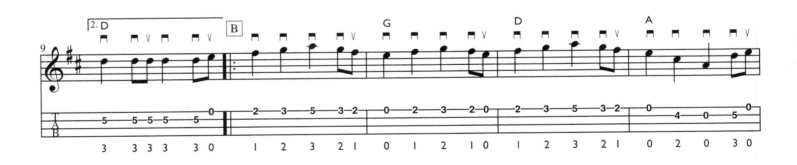

LESSON 3: CONNECTING THE DOTS WITH PASSING TONES

Here is a question you may want to ask once you've heard several people play a tune you've learned.

QUESTION: Why does "Soldier's Joy" sound slightly different each time I hear a new person play it?

ANSWER: *Variation.* Fiddle tunes are part of an oral tradition. This means that for hundreds of years, people have learned the tunes by copying what they hear others play. In the translation from one person to another, changes or variations are bound to occur. These variations are treasured as part of the individual player's personal "stamp" on the tune. Advanced pickers work very hard to put in small new variations nearly every time they play a tune.

In the previous lesson, you learned a simple, solid version of the melody for "Soldier's Joy." One way to add variations to a tune is to add new notes to the basic melody. These are called *passing tones*, and serve to connect the main melody notes. A more traditional definition of passing tones is that they are *non-chord tones* (notes not in the chord) that connect chord tones. Passing tones usually come from the same scale as the melody.

The following example shows the first phrase of "Soldier's Joy." First, you see it as you learned on page 38. In the second part of the example, passing tones have been added as new eighth notes between the main melody notes. The passing tones are circled.

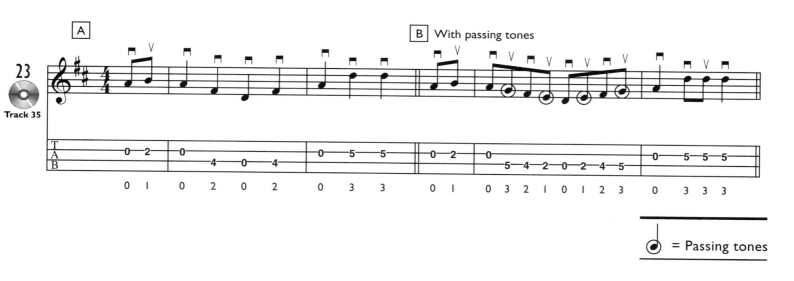

= Passing tones

Here is a variation of "Soldier's Joy" that incorporates passing tones. Note that there are a lot more eighth notes, which means more alternate picking! Play slowly and be sure everything is smooth and clean before you try to speed up. After you've mastered this version, try finding your own ways to vary the tune with passing tones.

 SOLDIER'S JOY (VARIATION WITH PASSING TONES)
Track 36

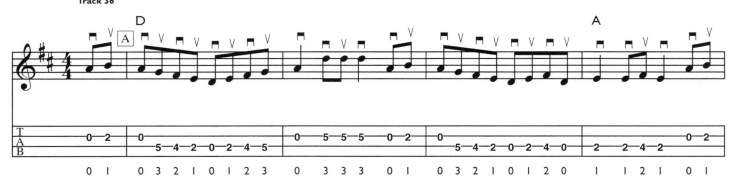

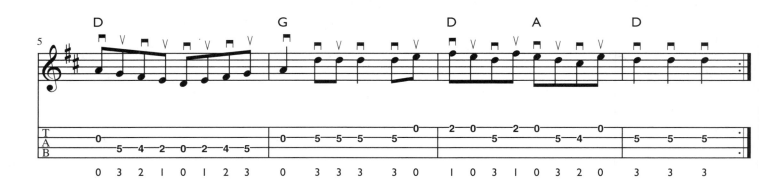

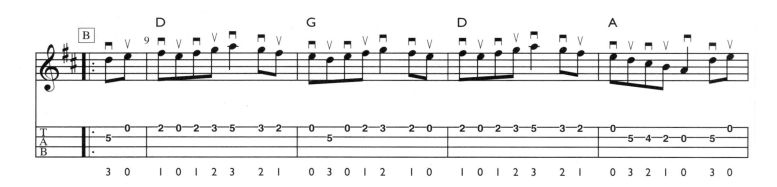

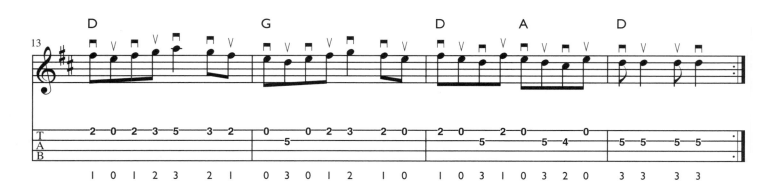

LESSON 4: DRONES AND SHUFFLES

DRONES

When you play more than one note at a time, as in a chord, you create *harmony*. Adding harmony notes along with the melody is another way to spice up your playing. Fiddlers often do this by playing a *drone* note on an adjacent string. A drone note is an open string, adjacent to the melody string, either above or below, whose note fits with the chord for that part of the tune. Drones imitate the sound of Scottish and Irish bagpipes, where one pipe plays the melody and the others play unchanging drones.

For example, in the tune "Soldier's Joy," the first two full measures of Part B are on the 1st string (see example A below). The open 2nd string, an A note, goes nicely with the main melody (see example B below.)

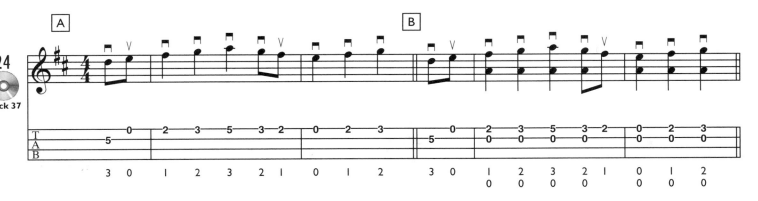

FIDDLE SHUFFLES

You may have noticed that mandolin notes don't sustain very long after they are picked. Unlike notes played with a fiddle bow, which can keep a note going and going, picked notes decay quickly. Mandolinists sometimes compensate for the lack of sustain by playing steady eighth notes when a pitch is to be held for a beat or more. Rhythms that imitate fiddle bowing are also used. These are called *shuffles*, after the "shuffling" effect of the bow. Here is a simple fiddle shuffle rhythm on one string and two strings. This rhythm is the same as Strum No. 3 on page 34.

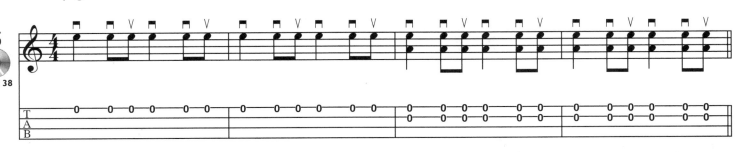

This kind of shuffle is not to be confused with the way the word shuffle is used in the blues tradition. In the blues, a shuffle is a kind of rhythm pattern based on *swing 8ths*. Don't worry about this yet (if it keeps you up at night, see page 55 and all shall be revealed). It may seem odd to have one word mean two different things, but the fiddle *shuffle* and the blues shuffle are very common concepts. It's kind of like the way the word toast can mean burnt bread or a speech made by someone at a birthday party.

Here is another old traditional tune for jamming. Notice that it uses drones and the fiddle shuffle rhythm. In the second bar, the drone note (the open A string) changes to the 2nd fret (B), making the high notes of the old familiar G chord. This fits with the harmony of the tune (note the G chord over the second measure).

In Part B, the melody notes are mostly on the 3rd and 4th strings, while the drones are all above on the 2nd string.

MISSISSIPPI SAWYER

Track 39

As tunes in D Major are called "D tunes," guess what tunes in A Major are called! When we move to the key of A Major, we see some of the beauty in how the mandolin is laid out. Below is the A Major scale. Note that the 1st, 2nd and 3rd strings have the same fret arrangement as the 2nd, 3rd and 4th strings did in the key of D Major. In other words, the fingerings for the key of A Major are simalir to D Major, only moved one string higher.

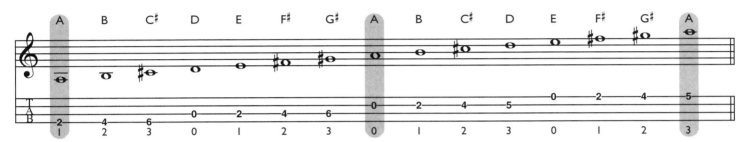

The key signature of A uses three sharps (F♯, C♯ and G♯).

UNISON DOUBLES

Another sound borrowed from the fiddle is the *unison double*. A unison double occurs when playing a melody note on an open string. If your melody note is on an open string and you want to make it really pop out, you can double that note on the 7th fret of the adjacent lower string. This is called a *unison*, which means "one sound," or the same note.

This example shows an open A note, then the unison double.

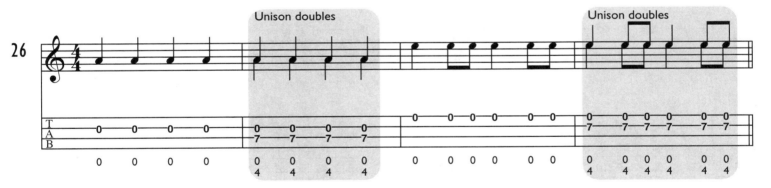

26

NEW CHORD: E

To play A tunes, you will often use A, D and E chords (among others). Here are the chords you will use in the next tune, "Old Joe Clark." Note that the E chord looks like the A chord, moved one string higher.

TIES

"Old Joe Clark" uses a device called a tie. A tie is a curved line ⌣ that connects two notes of the same pitch. The value of the second note in a tie is added to that of the first; it is not plucked. The two notes are added together to make one longer note. For example, a half note (two beats) tied to a quarter note (one beat) lasts for three beats (2+1=3). This is a great way to extend the length of a note beyond one measure and into the next.

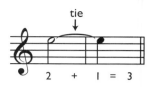

"Old Joe Clark" is another very well-known bluegrass and old-time fiddle tune. It sometimes uses a G♮ note instead of the G♯ found in the A Major scale. This gives parts of the melody a bluesy sound. This version incorporates drone notes, unison doubles, occasional alternate picking and some other harmony notes.

OLD JOE CLARK
Track 40

LESSON 6: THE MODAL SOUND OF THE A MINOR PENTATONIC SCALE

In the old-time fiddle tune tradition, a *modal tune* is any tune that uses a minor scale or a mix of major and minor scales. There are many types of minor scales, and they each have a minor 3rd (also called *flatted 3rd*, or $\flat$3). This means that the third note of the scale is one half step lower than it would be in a major scale. Modal tunes also use a *minor 7th*, or flatted 7th ($\flat$7).

A very simple scale that gives us the modal sound is the *minor pentatonic scale*. *Pentatonic* means "five notes." In an A Minor Pentatonic, the five notes are A–C–D–E–G. Compare this with the A Major scale on page 43 and notice that you now have a $\flat$3 (C) and a $\flat$7 (G).

THE A MINOR PENTATONIC SCALE

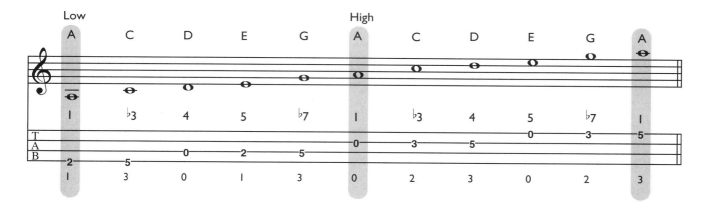

CHORDS IN THE KEY OF A MINOR

The next tune you will play, "Cluck Old Hen," uses the main chords of the key of A Minor. These are Amin, Dmin, Emin and G.

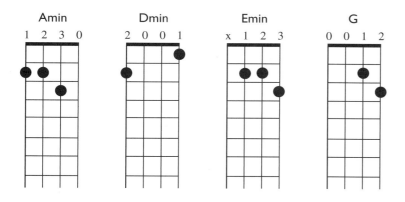

Here is an easy traditional tune that uses the A Minor Pentatonic scale. The melody only takes up two strings. This makes it easy to learn in both high (on the 1st and 2nd strings) and low positions (on the 3rd and 4th strings) of the A Minor Pentatonic scale.

CLUCK OLD HEN (HIGH)

Track 41

CLUCK OLD HEN (LOW)

Track 42

LESSON 7: THE KEY OF G MAJOR; HAMMER-ONS AND PULL-OFFS

Now it's time to try the key of G Major. G tunes are fun because their melodies often cover a wide range of notes through the scale. Learning G tunes will help you get ready for some of the most popular bluegrass songs. Here is the G Major scale.

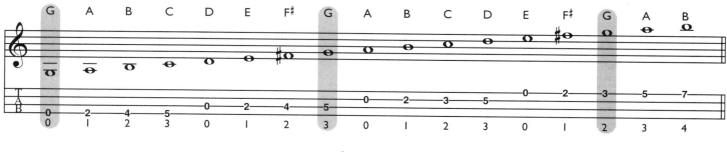

The key signature of G uses one sharp (F♯).

Notice that the low part of the scale (the 3rd and 4th strings) has the same fingering as the D Major scale (page 35, 2nd and 3rd strings). It is also the same fingering as the high A Major scale (page 43, 1st and 2nd strings).

HAMMER-ONS AND PULL-OFFS

Hammer-ons and *pull-offs* are special techniques that add smoothness (*legato*), fluidity and speed to melodic playing. Both techniques allow you to play multiple notes on one string with only one stroke of the pick. In musical terms, this is called a slur and is denoted by a curved line connecting notes of different pitches. Be careful not to confuse this with a tie (page 44), which connects notes of the same pitch.

To play a hammer-on, pick a note and bring a higher-numbered finger down on a higher fret quickly and firmly. You should hear the note change without having to pick again. It may help to imagine that your finger is going to keep going right through the neck. Practice hammer-ons on every string, with every finger, many times.

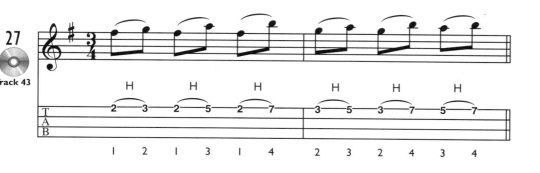

H = Hammer-on

This example shows pull-offs. A pull-off happens when the slurred note is lower than the starting note. To play a pull-off, you must start with both notes fretted. Pick the first note, then pull that finger off the string, leaving the second note fretted. You will need to give the pull-off a little "snap" by pulling your finger in towards your palm as you come off the high note. Imagine you are plucking the string with your left-hand finger.

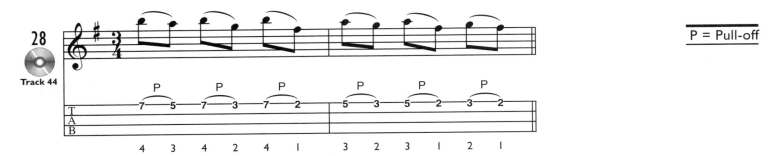

P = Pull-off

Here is a traditional fiddle tune that uses the G Major scale, hammer-ons and pull-offs. This tune is very old and is found in the American old-time and Scottish/Irish traditions. It has many names and variations. Celtic musicians call it "Miss McLeod's Reel." American pickers know it as "Hop High Ladies," or "Uncle Joe."

MISS MCLEOD'S REEL/HOP HIGH LADIES/UNCLE JOE

Track 45

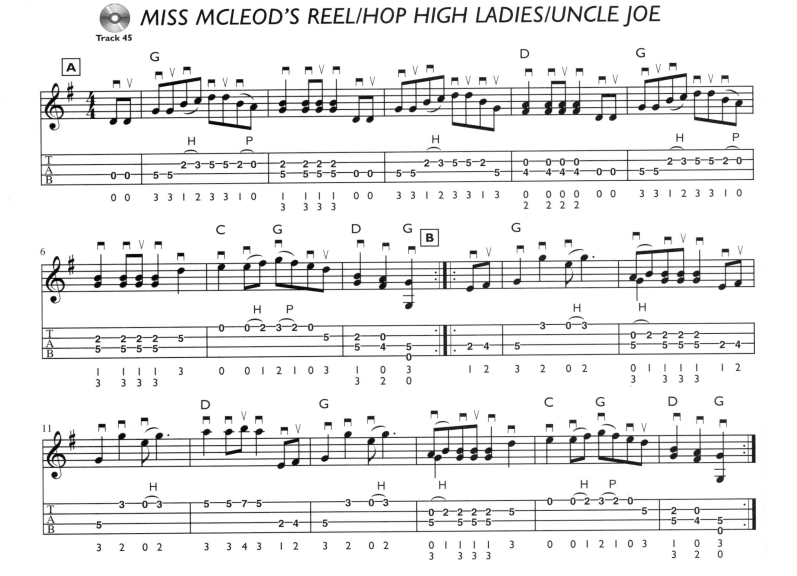

Waltz time is another name for $\frac{3}{4}$ time (page 30). This means there are three beats in every measure and the quarter note gets one beat. First, familiarize yourself with the feel of three beats per measure by counting and tapping your foot for a few bars.

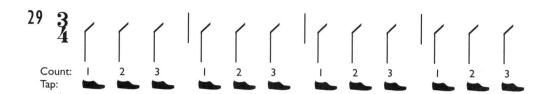

There are a variety of ways to strum in $\frac{3}{4}$ time.

Waltz Strum No 1:
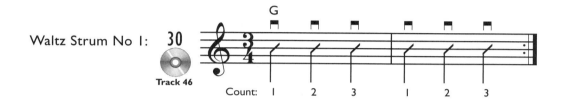

Waltz Strum No. 2: Simple Bluegrass
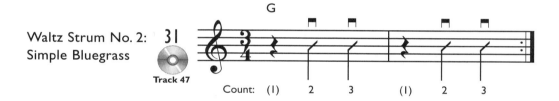

Waltz Strum No. 3:
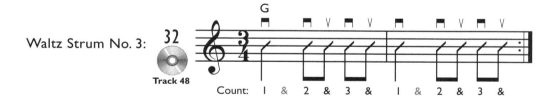

Waltz Strum No. 4: Country/Bluegrass (also known as "oom-pah-pah"):

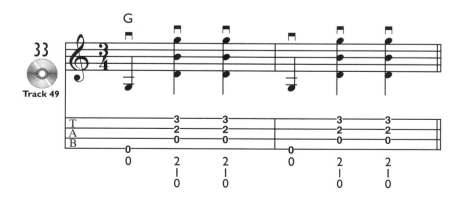

The gentle roll of waltz time can be particularly beautiful and lyrical. One of the most famous songs in $\frac{3}{4}$ is the traditional tune, "Amazing Grace." While it is not exactly a fiddle tune, it is popular in both the Celtic and American traditions. Try the chords using any of the strums on page 49, then try the melody.

AMAZING GRACE

Track 50

LESSON 9: SIXTEENTH NOTES; TREMOLO

So far, the quickest notes you have played have been eighth notes (page 26). The next smaller subdivision is the *sixteenth note*. A sixteenth note has a double flag or double beam. Sixteenth notes are eighth notes divided in two. There are four sixteenth notes per beat. A good way to count them is "1-e-&-a, 2-e-&-a," and so on. They are picked in strict down-up alternation.

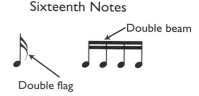

Sixteenth Notes

Tremolo picking is a technique that has been associated with the mandolin for hundreds of years. When a note is picked on the mandolin, it decays (gets softer) fairly quickly. Tremolo is used to create the impression of sustain.

On the mandolin, tremolo is achieved by repeating a note very rapidly with alternate (down-up) picking. The note is given a shimmering or "trembling" sound. Tremolo is also the only way mandolinists can change the volume of a note after it has been struck.

Here is an exercise on one string that will help you work on the tremolo technique. First you will pick slow quarter notes, then eighth notes, then sixteenth notes, then tremolo, which will be even faster (as fast as you can!). The tremolo is indicated by three diagonal slashes above the note head. Practice this exercise on each string. You may want to repeat each bar many times before moving to the next.

34
Track 51

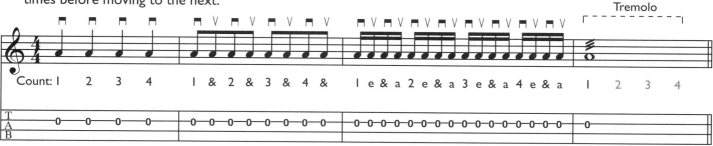

TREMOLO TIPS

- Hold the pick lightly between your thumb and index finger. As you slowly pick down and up on a single string, allow the pick to "flop around" a bit. This will help you find the point at which the pick is balanced in your grip.

- Tighten your grip a little so that the pick doesn't move as much, but stay relaxed. As you pick down, allow the pick to travel almost all the way to the next higher string. As you pick up, travel almost to the next lower string. This will help you find the range of motion for your tremolo. Try this with each open string.

- Try to keep the sound smooth and even, in terms of rhythm and volume.

- As you build speed, try to stay relaxed, feeling the balance of the pick and the range of motion. Many players keep their wrist fairly stable and move from the arm or elbow when playing tremolo. Some also use just the very point of the pick, or even use a part of the pick with a rounder edge. See what works for you.

- Practice tremolo several minutes every day. Be patient, and persistent. It may take a long time before you master this technique, but keep trying.

> ### SECRETS OF THE MASTERS:
> *Mandolinists use tremolo as a way to express their personality and emotions on the instrument. Once you can do a steady, even-sounding tremolo, try varying the speed of the tremolo (fast and slow) on different notes. This is called an unmeasured tremolo. You can even vary the speed during the sustain of one note. You can also vary the volume (loud and soft). Many players increase the speed of the tremolo as they increase the volume, and vice versa.*

This tune may be the oldest one you've learned yet, as it is from the 16th century (some say by none other than Henry VIII). Play it slowly and expressively using unmeasured tremolo. This tune is in D Minor, using a D scale with minor 3rd (F♮ instead of F♯) and sometimes a minor 7th (C♮ instead of C♯). Some of the chords may be new to you. They can be strummed using any of the waltz-time strums.

GREENSLEEVES

Track 52

CHAPTER 4

The Blues

THE OTHER ROOTS OF BLUEGRASS

The blues is the "blue" in bluegrass mandolin. Bill Monroe in particular was influenced by blues musicians and incorporated the blues deeply into his style. There are also many blues mandolin players who are documented in recordings, including Yank Rachell, Carl Martin, and Howard Armstrong, plus Vol Stevens and Charlie Burse of the Memphis Jug Band.

The blues is so much a part of American music that its influence is felt in nearly every style. Far more than just the feeling of good times that done gone bad,

> ### the blues is:
> - *A musical style*
> - *A form of poetry*
> - *A type of scale*
> - *An attitude*
> - *A specific musical form and chord progression*
> - *An incurable, infectious human condition that is both miserable and joyful at the same time*

LESSON 1: BASIC BLUES THEORY

The chords we use to play the blues are derived from the major scale. Remember that a chord is three or more notes played together. We create a triad, the most basic kind of chord, by simply using every other note in a major scale. For example, here is how we build a G Major chord:

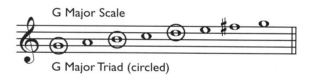

In the blues, we usually need only three chords for any tune: a chord built on the first note of the scale (called I—musicians all over the world use Roman numerals to communicate about chords), a chord built on the fourth note (called IV) and a chord built on the fifth note (called V). These are called the primary chords. Here they are in G Major:

For more information on this subject, see pages 89 and 90.

LESSON 2: THE 12-BAR BLUES

The *12-bar blues* is one of the most basic song *forms*. The form is the organization or structure of a piece. The 12-bar blues derives its name from the number of measures (also called bars) in the form. On the top of page 54 is a common version of the 12-bar blues in the key of G. Included are chord symbols and Roman numerals indicating the analysis of the harmony. Try it with either simple downstrokes or a strum pattern from pages 33–34.

Try to memorize the progression using Roman numerals. That way, you will learn its structure without being limited to the key of G. Soon, you will be able play the blues in any key, as long as you know what the I, IV and V chords are for that key. To make it easier, memorize one line at a time.

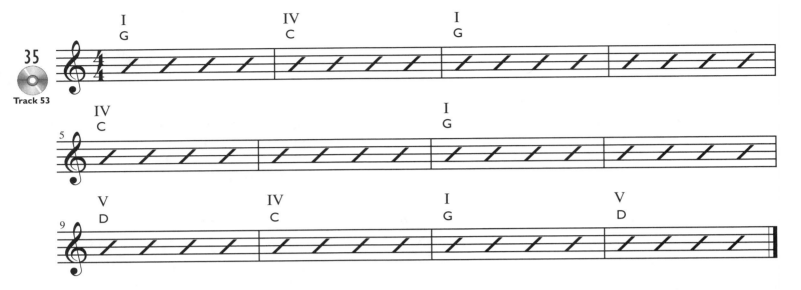

LESSON 3: MEMORIZING THE 12-BAR BLUES

WHY MEMORIZE IT? TO JAM, OF COURSE

There may be times when you want to play with other people who don't know the same songs you do. The 12-bar blues is widely known by musicians at all levels of experience. A working knowledge of how to play through the *progression* (a series of chords) can give you an "ace up your sleeve" in those difficult situations when you and your fellow musicians can't decide what to jam on.

BLUES POETRY

Understanding the blues poetry form will help you memorize the musical form. The 12-bar blues is organized in three lines of four measures each. This mirrors the poetic form of many blues lyrics. A common form of blues lyric consists of a statement (line 1), a repetition of the statement (line 2) and a sort of "clincher" (line 3). Check out these blues verses in the common blues form:

My baby just left me, and man I feel so bad
My baby just left me, and man I feel so bad
Since my baby left me, I lost everything I had

I'd rather drink muddy water, sleep in a hollow log
I'd rather drink muddy water, sleep in a hollow log
Than stay in this city, treated like a dirty dog

PLAY IT IN YOUR SLEEP

Learn to play the blues progression over and over without losing your place in the form. This will make it much easier to jam with other players. You will be able to enjoy the musical interaction of the moment without worrying about whether you brought your music, or whether you are on bar 10 or bar 6.

In addition, you should know that there are many, many variations possible on the 12-bar blues form. Some have more chords, some have fewer, some have different chords substituted for the common ones. By burning a specific, basic version of the pattern into your memory through repetition and study, you will have an easier time compensating for slight variations from song to song.

THE ALMIGHTY BLUES SHUFFLE—SWING EIGHTHS

While the blues progression can be played with any rhythm (from bluegrass to punk to reggae and beyond), the *swing shuffle* is the most recognizable blues rhythm. It is very easy to play and has a propulsive, rocking sound that feels good at any speed.

The first step to learning the shuffle is to learn a new counting rhythm. Until now, you have been counting eighth notes in a steady, even beat like this:

These are known in musical lingo as *straight eighths* because each eighth note is the same length. *Swing eighths* are heard in jazz, blues, rockabilly and folk music. In swing eighths, the onbeat is given longer emphasis while the offbeat ("&") is made shorter.

The best way to understand the swing rhythm is to relate the eighths to *eighth-note triplets*. These are groups of three eighth notes that are played in the time of two (one beat). To get the feel, try saying this aloud to a steady beat: "trip-pul-let, trip-pul-let."

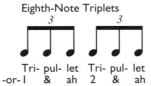

In swing eighths, the first two notes of the triplet are tied together.

Swing eighths are usually designated in music in one of two ways:

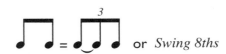

In this method, we use the latter of the two, *Swing 8ths*. Often, out there in the real world, there is no indication given at all; blues and jazz players just automatically swing the eighths. *And the real kicker is that swing eighths look just like straight eighths!*

7TH CHORDS AND THE SHUFFLE STRUM

> ### HOLD IT! DID YOU SAY "SHUFFLE"?
> *Yes, the word "shuffle" has two different meanings that are both important to the mandolinist. A fiddle shuffle (described on page 41) is a rhythm imitating a fiddle bowing pattern. A swing shuffle, also called a blues shuffle, is a rhythm pattern based on swing 8ths.*

Here are three new chords. When a 7 is added to the name of a major chord, it becomes a *dominant-7th chord*. Dominant-7th chords have an unsettled sound that has come to be associated with the blues.

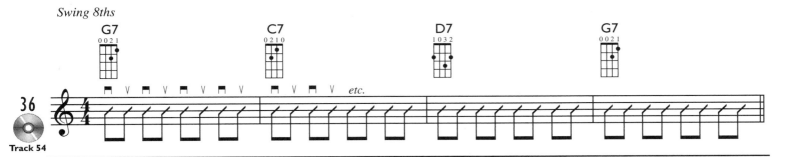

THE BOOGIE-WOOGIE

Blues accompaniments, also called *rhythms*, on the mandolin can use strummed chords or short melodic ideas called *riffs*. The following riffs imitate a boogie-woogie bass line that a pianist might play. Here is the riff you would use for each chord in a blues in G.

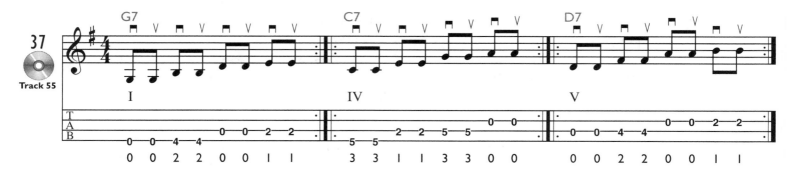

Here's a 12-bar blues boogie in G. On the recording for this book, you will first hear the chords strummed in swing 8ths and then the boogie-woogie riff.

BLUES BOOGIE IN G

Track 56

On page 45, you learned the A Minor Pentatonic scale. To review, the minor pentatonic scale is a five-note scale made up of the *tonic* or first note of a major scale (or 1), ♭3, 4, 5 and ♭7. The minor pentatonic scale is a great for blues soloing. Here is a G Minor Pentatonic scale. The scale degrees are indicated so that you can see how it differs from the G Major scale on page 47.

THE G MINOR PENTATONIC SCALE

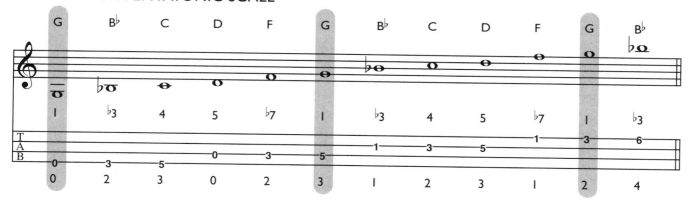

Compare it to the A Minor Pentatonic on page 45. Notice that the fingering for G Minor Pentatonic scale on the 3rd and 4th strings is the same as the fingering for the A Minor Pentatonic on the 1st and 2nd strings.

BLUE NOTES

When a scale has a lowered 3rd degree (♭3), it is said to be a *minor scale*. The cool thing about the blues is that, while the chords are often major, the melody is often minor. This creates a funky, slightly *dissonant* (clashing) sound between the chords and the blue notes in the melody and gives the blues its melancholy, expressive sound.

The minor pentatonic scale contains both the ♭3 and the ♭7. These notes help us approximate the sound of old African scales that lie at the core of the blues. When these minor scale notes are played against major chords, they are called *blue notes*.

EXPERIMENTING WITH THE SCALE—IMPROVISATION

The first step to improvising a blues solo is learning to get around in the minor pentatonic scale. Try to create melodies that use the notes in the scale. Go up a few notes, go down a few notes. Play long and short notes. Skip around. Don't worry about whether it's "right" or "wrong" — just try to stick to the notes in the scale. Above all, have fun and let your ear be your guide. This spontaneous creation of melodies is called *improvisation*.

GET IN YOUR LICKS

A *lick* is a small idea or figure that can be used as a building block for a solo. A lick can be repeated, altered or strung together with other licks. The following page contains some licks to get you started.

BLUES DOWN-PICKING

The pioneers of blues mandolin, from Yank Rachell to Bill Monroe, drew on a wide variety of textures and *dynamics* (degrees of loudness and softness). One way to add some blues feel to your playing is to use aggressive down-picking in some passages of your solo. While this may cut down on your speed, it makes up for it in emotional intensity. Often, down-picking is used when adding triplets (page 55) to the melody.

Here are a few licks to try. Learn them, make variations and then try soloing over the blues progression on page 56.

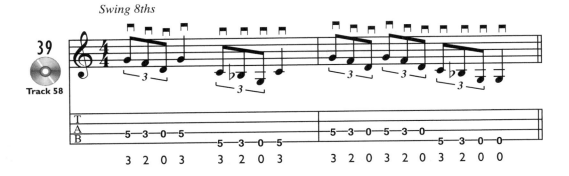

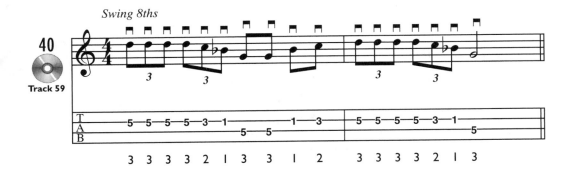

LESSON 6: BLUES IMPROVISATION WITH THE G BLUES SCALE AND SLIDES

In blues and bluegrass soloing, most mandolinists use a scale that brings together elements of the minor pentatonic and major scales. This creates a hybrid called a *blues scale*. The following blues scale also adds one more *blue note*, the lowered 5th or ♭5. This note is one half step lower than the fifth note of a major scale.

G BLUES SCALE

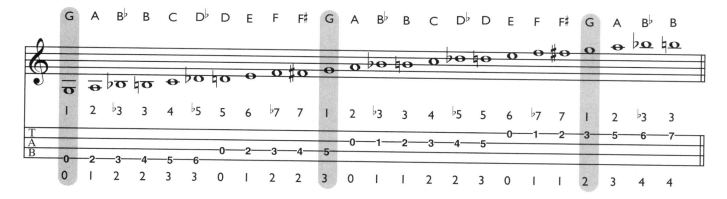

SLIDES

In the G blues scale there are several places where you use one finger to play two notes (such as the B♭ and B natural on the 2nd string with the 1st finger). This provides opportunities to *slide* from one fret to the next using the same finger. You must keep the pressure constant as you slide to keep the string singing so that you hear the sliding sound. Try these licks using the scale and some slides. Notice that a slide is indicated with a slur, a diagonal line and the letters "SL" above the TAB.

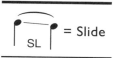

= Slide

Track 60

Slides can connect two notes in rhythm or they can be *grace notes* (small, quick notes ♪ that occur before the main note). Grace-note slides allow you to swoop up or down to the main note from another fret on the same string without changing the rhythm. Try these licks using slides both in rhythm and as grace notes.

♪ = Grace note

Track 61

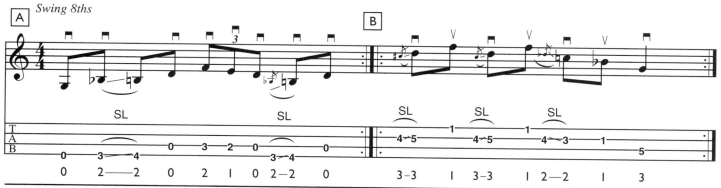

Here's a sample solo using down-picking, alternate picking, slides, triplets and tremolo. Try it and then make up your own solos! This one's named after Howard Armstrong (nicknamed "Louie Bluie") and Yank Rachell. On the recording for this book, you will first hear the mandolin solo with guitar accompaniment. Then the guitar will repeat the blues progression so you can improvise your own solo.

LOUIE'S GOT THE BLUIE AND YANK'S AT THE BANK

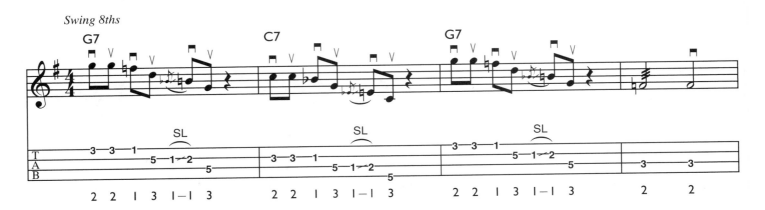

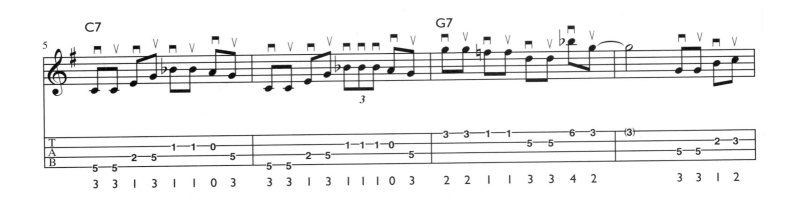

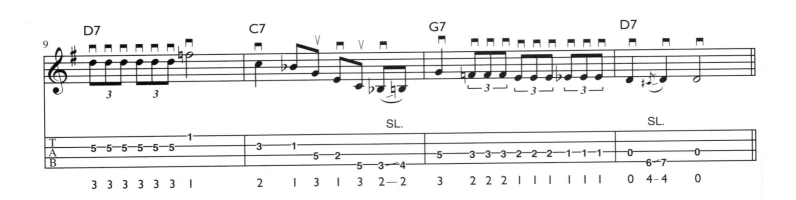

CHAPTER 5

Bluegrass

Bluegrass mandolin owes its history to a long string of innovators, from Chris Thile, Mike Marshall and Sam Bush, back to Bobby Osborne, John Duffey, Jesse McReynolds and many more. The father of the style is Bill Monroe, who combined aggressive blues, fluid fiddle tunes and the "chop" style of rhythm. If you've come straight to this chapter for bluegrass, you've come to the right place. But don't forget to go back through the Chapters 3 and 4, as fiddle tunes and the blues are fundamental parts of bluegrass too!

LESSON 1: BLUEGRASS RHYTHM

MOVEABLE CHORDS

Most bluegrass mandolinists use moveable chords to play rhythm (remember, in this context, *rhythm* means accompaniment). Moveable chords allow you to play in any key with just a few chord shapes. They also eliminate open strings, which will help you achieve the percussive "chop" later in this lesson.

Find the Root

The root of a chord is the note it is named for. In the following lessons, the roots of the chords have been noted on the diagrams using the letter "R." To find any chord you might need, locate the root note you need on the proper string, and build the chord shape using the fingering shown. For more on chord structures, see page 89.

Moveable Chord Shape No. 1

This shape is used heavily in bluegrass rhythm playing because the notes of the chord are *voiced* (arranged) fairly close together. This provides more density and punch. This voicing can have its root on the 3rd string for a four-note version of the fingering, or on the 4th string for a three-note version. Major and minor fingerings are shown for G, C and D.

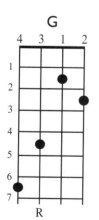 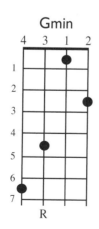 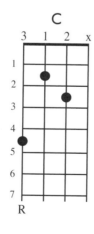 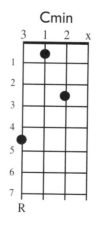 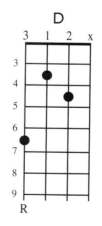 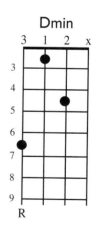

> **SECRETS OF THE MASTERS:**
> *You may need to use the palm of your left hand on the back of the neck to help you squeeze the notes on the moveable chords. They need more pressure and leverage than open chords.*

THE ALMIGHTY CHOP—IT'S ALL IN THE WRIST

One of the most famous sounds of the mandolin is the short, percussive, rifle-shot chop heard in bluegrass. Using the chop sound on the backbeat (beats 2 and 4, page 34), the bluegrass mandolinist joins in a melding of the minds with the bass player (who plays on beats 1 and 3) to form a single, unified rhythm section.

The chop sound is made by fingering a moveable chord and strumming it with a brisk flip of the wrist downward (a downstroke). Then immediately relax the left-hand fingers, keeping them on the strings, to cut off the notes. This is called playing staccato and is marked in the music with a small dot above or below the note head. Try the chop using a G Major chord as shown.

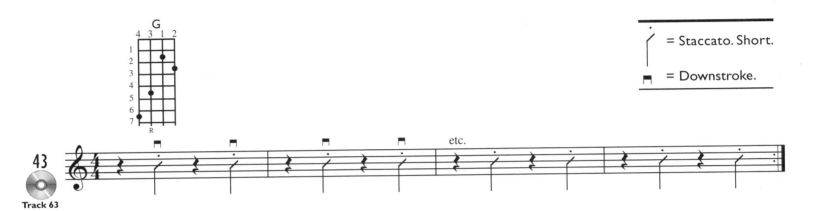

CHOP TIPS

- Stay relaxed, keep your strumming wrist and hand loose and bouncy!
- When "flicking" the wrist, think of the motion used to throw a dart or one of those flying discs dogs love. It's a bouncy, springy motion, not a stiff motion.
- Let your left-hand fingers "pulse" the chord on the strings. Try pulsing (fretting the chord) for different durations and pressures.

Here's a progression to try using the G, C and D chords you learned in this lesson. It's based on a standard bluegrass progression heard in songs like "9-Pound Hammer" and "Roll on Buddy." Use the chop strum.

THIS HAMMER'S TOO HEAVY

Track 64

Unlike old-time fiddle music, where all the melody instruments play the same tune at the same time, bluegrass calls for some separation of the *lead* (melody) and rhythm roles. Bluegrass bands may include mandolin, guitar, fiddle, banjo, resonator guitar (Dobro), bass and a few other instruments for variety. Each instrument may have spots in a song where it is the lead, or solo instrument. A full solo is called a *break*, while little melodic responses are called *fills*. On the mandolin, if you are not playing breaks or fills, you are probably playing chop rhythm.

WHAT IS A BREAK?

A traditional bluegrass break is generally an improvised variation on the melody of the tune. A break may include:
- Passages of the melody, sometimes with passing tones
- Licks—short melodic figures borrowed from blues or fiddle tunes
- Chords strummed or broken into single-note *arpeggios* ("broken chords")
- Anything else you think might sound good

HOW DO I GET GOOD AT PLAYING BREAKS?

To get better at playing breaks:
- Learn a simple, clear version of the melody of the tune (it may be a vocal tune or a fiddle tune). This is always the best place to start.
- Practice fiddle tunes and incorporate the alternate picking and passing tones you learn into your soloing.
- Practice blues and other styles to pull in new licks and sounds.
- Study the breaks of your favorite players and learn how to play them.
- Play lots of tunes with other people. There is no better way to get your brain and ear "up to speed" than playing in a group!

On the following page you will find a chord progression and an easy Bill Monroe-style break based on the old standard "Sittin' on Top of the World," which is also the melody of the blues song "Come on in My Kitchen." It uses the G Blues scale, which is the scale you used to improvise on the blues in G. Here it is again for review. Learn this break, then use it to make up your own breaks on the same tune.

G BLUES SCALE

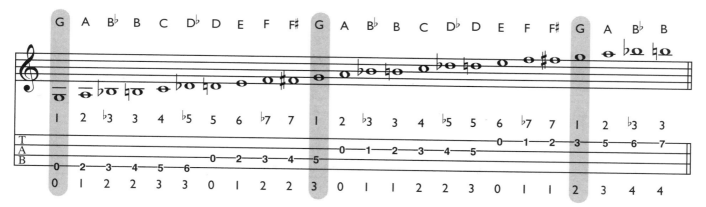

Here's a sample break and chord progression to solo over. Use the chop rhythm and the chords you learned on pages 61–62.

Track 65

COME ON AND SIT ON TOP OF MY KITCHEN COUNTER

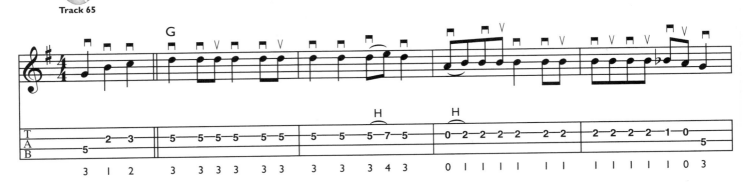

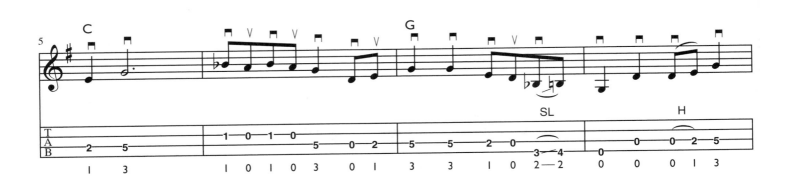

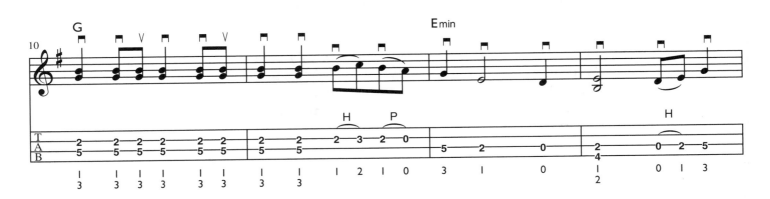

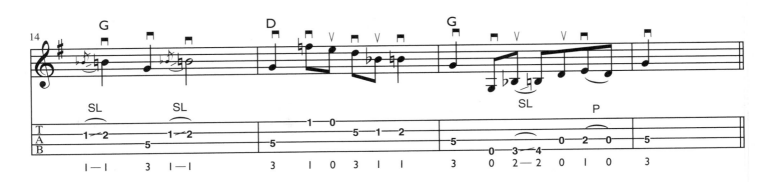

Transposing means changing the key of a song.

WHY TRANSPOSE?

The most common reason for transposing a song to a new key is to better fit the vocal range of a singer. For example, imagine a song in the key of G Major. If this key is too low, you could transpose up to A or even B. Another reason to transpose is to make a melody easier to play on the mandolin.

THE SUBSTITUTION METHOD

This method of transposition is the easiest to learn, but not the most efficient. First, consider this progression in G Major. Use simple downstrokes or the chop rhythm.

Transposing From G Major to D Major

First, you must know how far the new key is from the original key. The key of D is an *interval* (distance) of a *perfect 5th* (P5, seven half steps, seven frets) higher than the key of G (for more on interval distances, see page 83). To transpose the song, substitute each of the original chords with the chord a perfect 5th higher:

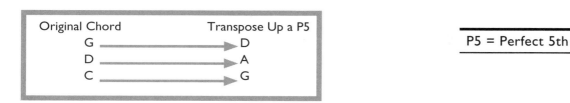

P5 = Perfect 5th

Here is the above progression transposed to D Major.

Transposing From G Major to A Major

Try using this method yourself. The answers are at the end of the lesson on page 66.

1. How far above G is A?
2. What is the new chord progression?

Transpose this example to the key of A (write in your answers):

THE CHORD ANALYSIS METHOD

At first, this method takes more practice and thought, but eventually you will be able to transpose songs without having to write out the new chords.

Here is an example progression in the key of D Major.

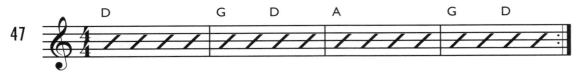

Transposing From D Major to G Major

First, analyze the chord progression with Roman numerals (page 53, you may also want to study pages 89 and 90).

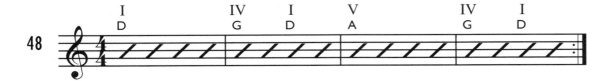

Now you are ready to transpose to any key. Try the key of G Major.

Key of G: I = G   IV = C   V = D

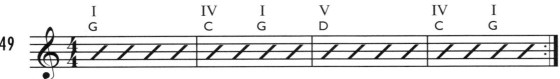

Transposing From D Major to A Major

Try this one yourself (the correct answer is at the bottom of this page).

1. What are the primary chords in the key of A Major? I = _____   IV = _____   V = _____

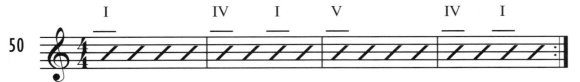

ANSWERS TO EXAMPLES 46 AND 50:

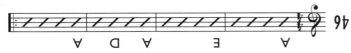

First, let's see how you do combining transposition and moveable chord shape No. 1 (page 61). Here is "This Hammer's Too Heavy" transposed from G Major (page 62) to the key of A Major. Notice that you simply move the chord shapes from the key of G Major up one whole step to A Major. For a challenge, try moving the whole thing up to B Major.

Original key:	G Major	I = G	IV = C	V = D
New key:	A Major	I = A	IV = D	V = E

 THIS HAMMER'S TOO HEAVY (IN A)

Track 66

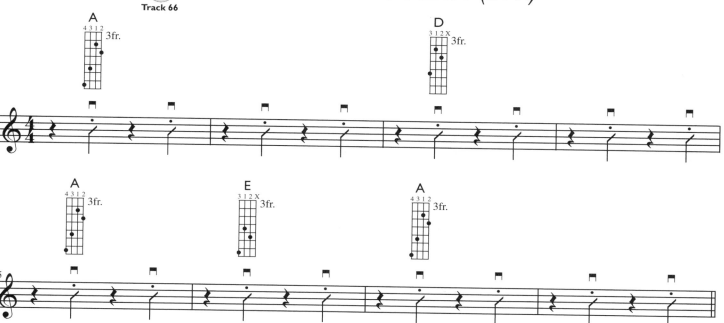

MOVEABLE CHORD FINGERING NO. 2

This is a more open-sounding voicing. Note that its shape is based on the open G Major chord you learned way back on page 15! It is very easy to finger both the major and minor versions of this voicing. You do have to fret two strings with one finger (this is called a *barre*). To make the barre, flatten your finger across the strings instead of playing up on the tip of your finger. Remember that you can use your left-hand palm for extra squeezing power.

This voicing can have its root on both the 1st and 4th string (see A chords below), or have its root on the 2nd string (see D chords below).

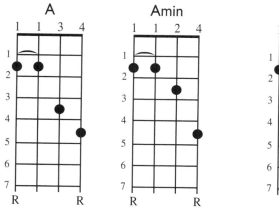
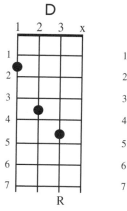
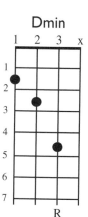

MOVEABLE CHORD FINGERING NO. 3

This shape is based on the shape of the open D Major chord. This one is also easy to finger in major and minor voicings. Note that the root is on the 3rd string.

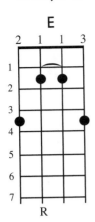

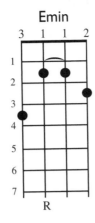

MOVEABLE 7TH CHORDS

Here are some moveable voicings for dominant-7th chords. Learn the locations of the roots so that you can move them to any chord you need.

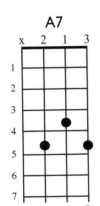

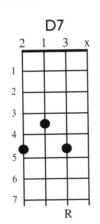

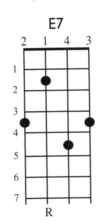

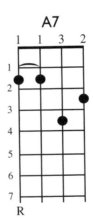

This lesson brings together transposition and some new rhythm and lead techniques. First you need a 12-bar blues progression in the key of A Major. Review the basics of the 12-bar blues on pages 53–56. To transpose the blues to the key of A, think of the primary chords. Notice that in the blues, dominant-7th and major chords are interchangeable.

I= A or A7   IV=D or D7   V=E or E7

Here is a 12-bar blues in A Major using some of the fingerings you have learned in the last few lessons. The strum is based on the chop, but adds single bass notes on beats 1 and 3. These should be played very lightly, while the chops on 2 and 4 are *accented* (played louder). This "boom-chick, boom-chick" type of rhythm will help you keep time and makes a nice variation on the chop rhythm.

> = Accent

BLUEGRASS 12-BAR BLUES IN A

Track 67

Here is a blues scale in A Major that you can use to improvise on "Bluegrass 12-Bar Blues in A." You could use the A Minor Pentatonic found on pages 45 and 71 as well. Following is a sample bluegrass-style lead break. Many blues breaks in bluegrass are made up of short licks and improvisation, rather than sticking to the melody of the song.

BLUES SCALE IN A

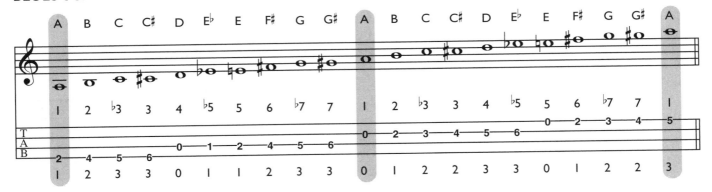

After you learn the solo below, try improvising your own over track 67.

 BLUEGRASS 12-BAR BLUES IN A (LEAD BREAK)

Track 68

Bluegrass songs come in many tempos (speeds), moods and grooves. Some are hot breakdowns and some are weepy ballads. Some are major, some are bluesy, and some are down-and-out minor.

To play bluegrass breaks in a minor key, you can almost always use the minor pentatonic scale. Here is an A Minor Pentatonic that you learned for "Cluck Old Hen" on page 45.

A MINOR PENTATONIC SCALE

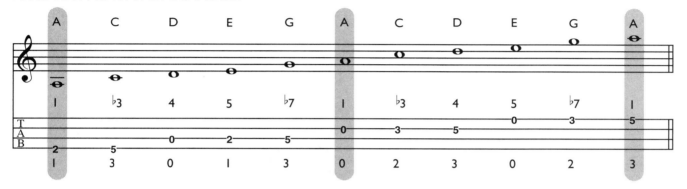

You can also use a full A Minor scale. This scale is also known as the *natural minor scale* (in the future you may even learn it as the *Aeolian mode*, pronounced "ay-OH-lee-yun"). Compare the A Natural Minor scale to the A Major scale (page 43). The natural minor scale has a ♭3, ♭6 and ♭7.

A NATURAL MINOR SCALE

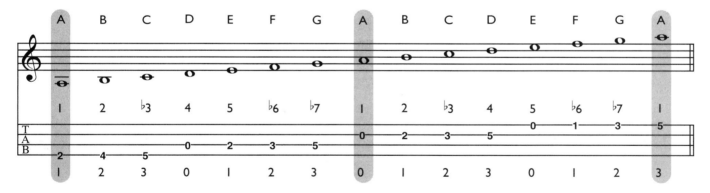

Here is a bluegrass style tune in the key of A Minor. Use the moveable chords shown and a chop strum for the rhythm. Try the lead break shown, then make up your own using the A Minor Pentatonic and the A Natural Minor scale. On the CD, you will hear the melody first and then the chords will continue so you can improvise your own break.

This break incorporates another technique used by Bill Monroe and countless other mandolinists: Steady eighth notes are maintained throughout most of the solo, using strict alternate picking. This creates a feeling of drive, emotional intensity and tension in the music.

DARK ON THE DRIVE HOME

Track 69

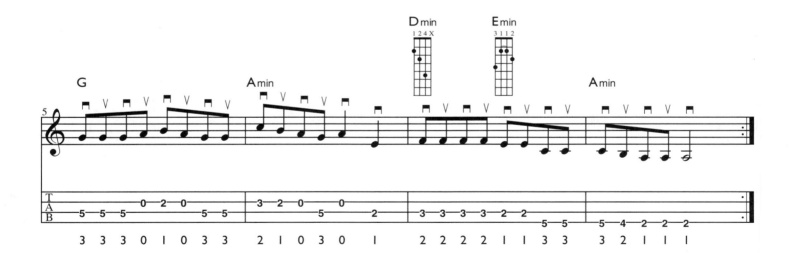

LESSON 7: KICKOFFS AND TAGS

Now that you know how to fly your airplane of bluegrass, you should learn a few takeoffs and landings. A *kickoff* can be used as an introduction to a song or a lead break. Likewise, a *tag* can either end a break or a whole song. There are infinite ways to kickoff and tag. The ones you create or use become part of your individual musical voice.

POTATOES

The easiest kickoff is called *potatoes* because it sounds like "one 'tato, two 'tato, three 'tato, four 'tato." This one is used by fiddlers to kickoff tunes. It uses the simple fiddle shuffle rhythm for two bars to set the tempo for the whole band.

Potatoes are always played in the key of the tune. For example, a D tune will use potatoes made up of notes from a D Major chord. Here are some typical potato chords for the keys of D, A and G Major.

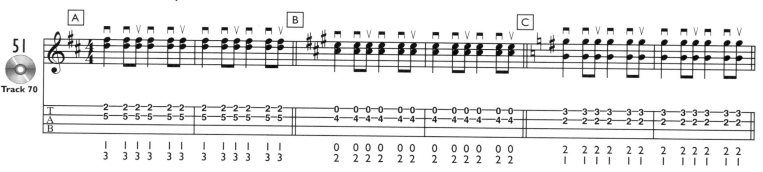

51 Track 70

WALKUP KICKOFF

Another way to kickoff a tune or break is to *walk-up* (move in a stepwise manner) some notes of the scale that lead to the starting note of the melody. Below is a simple walk-up that can set-up almost any melody note for the keys shown. This kickoff works if the melody or break starts on the first beat of the measure. In other words, this kickoff is a pickup (page 38). If the tune already has pickup notes (like "Soldier's Joy" on page 38), then you would not use this kickoff. Here are some walkups for D, A and G Major.

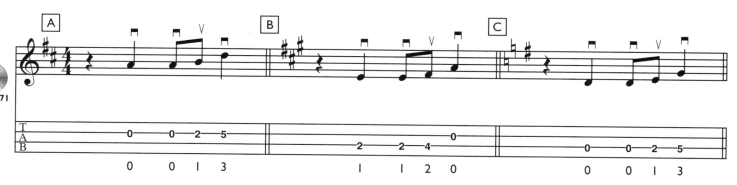

52 Track 71

SHAVE-AND-A-HAIRCUT TAG

The most common tag is the old "shave and a haircut, two bits" (which is the rhythm you use for that "secret knock" you used to get into the neighbor kid's treehouse). You would use this tag after the end of the tune as an extra flourish. Here is the shave-and-a-haircut tag for the keys of D, A and G Major. Look for other keys and ways to play it, too.

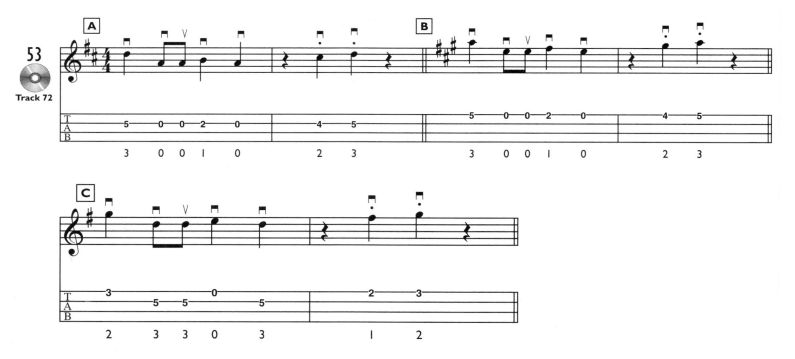

THE BILL MONROE BIG FINISH

This one shows up in a lot of Bill Monroe songs and traditional bluegrass tunes. It sounds great on the mandolin. To play it, just strum the chord of the key in the rhythm shown below. Play it strongly and cut the chords off (staccato) as shown. You can make up new versions of this, but this rhythm is very widely known. The whole band hits it all together, like a 21-gun (or string) salute. Here it is for D, A and G Major.

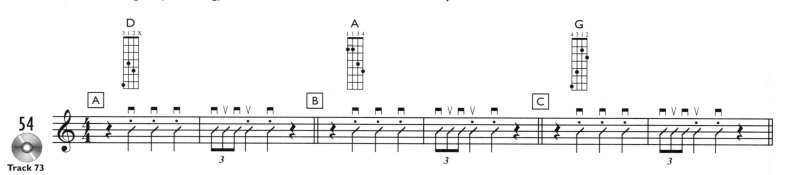

CHAPTER 6

Rock Mandolin

When you think of rock music, do you think of mandolin? The mandolin has been used since the early days of rock to add a distinctive, chiming color to the standard guitar-bass-drum-keyboard band. Some rock mandolin pioneers and bands include Jimmy Page (Led Zeppelin), Levon Helm (The Band), Peter Buck (R.E.M.), Steve Earle (solo and with many bands), Max Johnston (Wilco) and Ry Cooder (solo and with many bands, including the Rolling Stones).

LESSON 1: ROCK 'N' ROLL FOLK STRUMMING

THE SYNCOPATED STRUM

Syncopation means to shift the emphasis to the offbeat. To show syncopation in written music, dotted rhythms, rests and ties are sometimes used.

The strum shown below is the Swiss Army knife of strum patterns. It is the universal folk-rock-alternative-swing-funk-campfire strum. This one is good at any speed, fast or slow, swinging or straight. Note the tie that connects the "&" of beat 2 to beat 3, creating a syncopation. Be sure to tap your foot and count aloud.

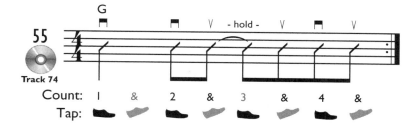

If you find this rhythm to be a little confusing, break it down into one- or two-beat segments:

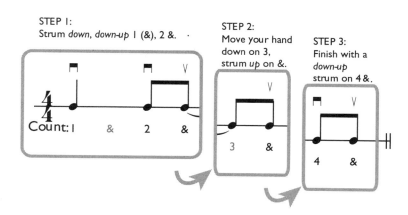

STEP 1:
Strum *down, down-up* 1 (&), 2 &.

STEP 2:
Move your hand down on 3, strum *up* on &.

STEP 3:
Finish with a *down-up* strum on 4 &.

Here are a couple of tunes to try, one in a major key and one in a minor key.

THE LONG FORGOTTEN DAZE OF MY YOUTH

Track 75

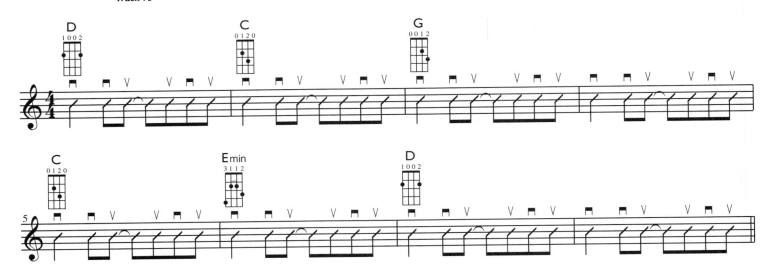

THE BATTLE OF THE ELVES, DRAGONS AND ROCK VOCALISTS

Track 76

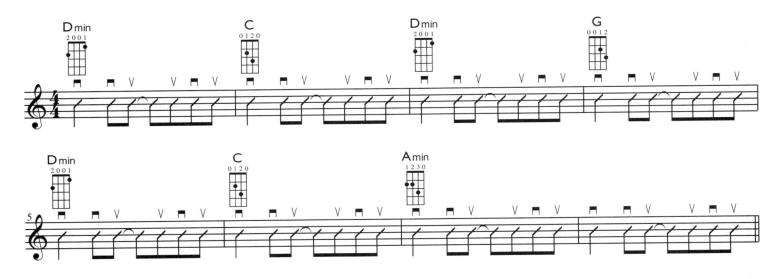

LESSON 2: ARPEGGIATING CHORDS

Arpeggios are "broken chords," or chords played one note at a time. Mandolinists use arpeggios to accentuate the chiming, jangly quality of the instrument. This works especially well in a song that already uses acoustic guitars. The mandolin arpeggios blend into the other instruments, and also cut through in the upper ranges of the harmony.

Here is a simple pattern to get you started. It is shown with G, C and D chords, but you should practice it with lots of chords. Use alternate picking. This may take some practice because you have to pick down on one string and up on the next.

Hold down the chord the whole time and let the notes ring throughout.

ARPEGGIO PATTERN NO. 1

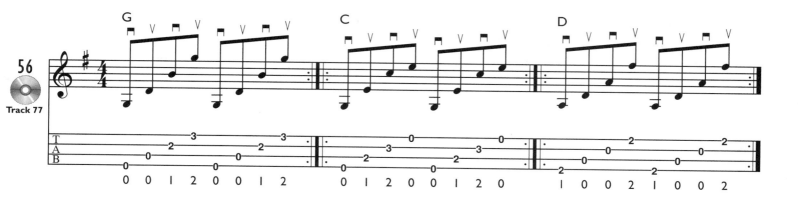

ARPEGGIO PATTERN NO. 2

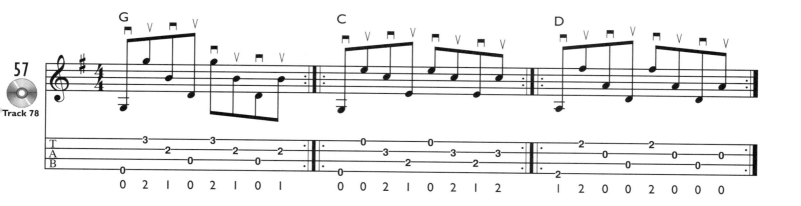

Here are the two tunes from page 76 using arpeggio patterns.

THE LONG FORGOTTEN DAZE OF MY YOUTH (ARPEGGIO CHORDS)

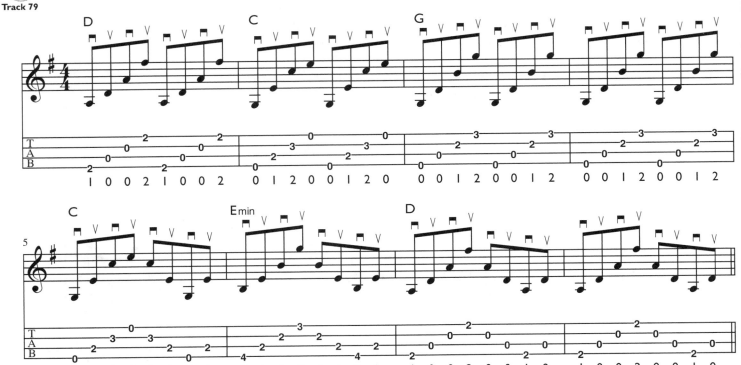

THE BATTLE OF THE ELVES, DRAGONS AND ROCK VOCALISTS (ARPEGGIO CHORDS)

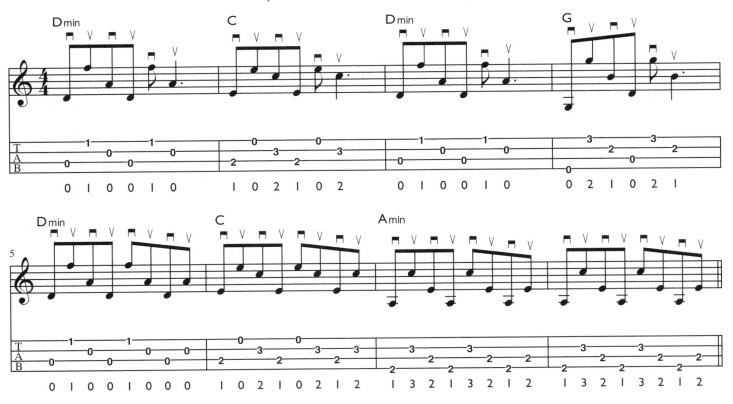

Playing solos on rock songs is not all that different from the other styles you've been working on. You can use influences and licks from blues, fiddle tunes, bluegrass and any thing else that strikes you.

Here's a solo for "The Long Forgotten Daze of My Youth" that incorporates *double stops* (two-note chords), drone notes, hammer-ons, slides and passing tones. This solo is organized around the chords of the tune, and creates a simple, strumming sound. For examples of this sound, check out Rod Stewart's "Maggie May" or "Losing My Religion" by R.E.M.

To make up your own solo, use the G Major Scale (page 47) or the G Blues Scale (page 59). On the CD for this book, this tune is played twice: once with the solo shown below and once without, so you can solo over the accompaniment.

 THE LONG FORGOTTEN DAZE OF MY YOUTH (SOLO)

Track 81

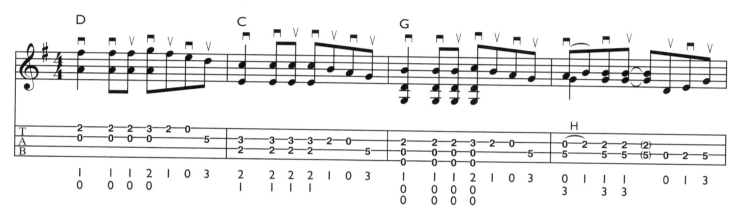

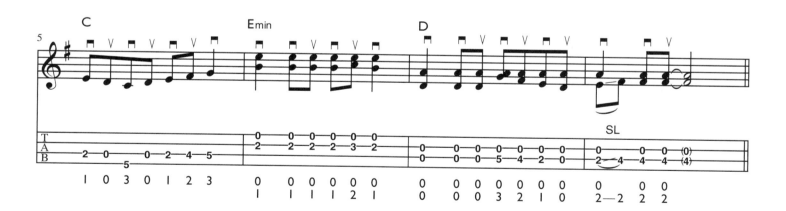

Now here's a solo for "The Battle of the Elves, Dragons and Rock Vocalists." This one also uses some double stops and drone notes, but they are played separately. This allows the melody to alternate with the drone note, increasing the "chimey" sound of the mandolin. Note that an arpeggio sneaks in on the G chord! You can hear examples of this style on Led Zeppelin's "Going to California" and "The Battle of Evermore." On the recording for this book, this tune is played twice: once with the solo shown below and once without, so you can solo over the accompaniment.

THE BATTLE OF THE ELVES, DRAGONS AND ROCK VOCALISTS (SOLO)

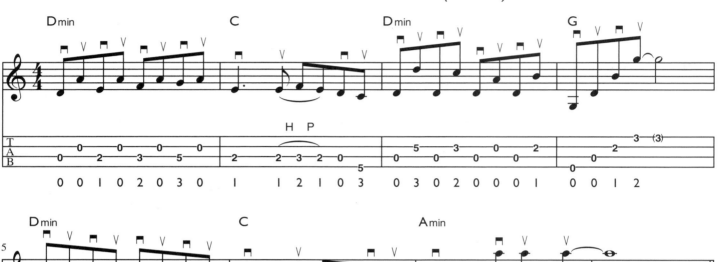

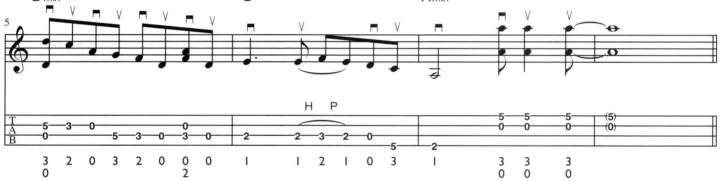

To make up your own solo for this tune, use the D Minor scale shown below.

D NATURAL MINOR SCALE

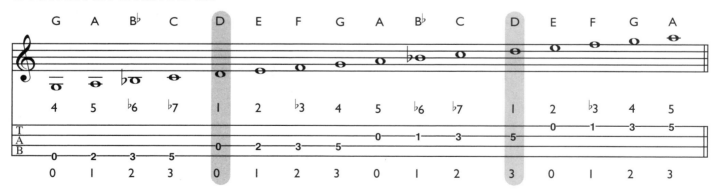

Congratulations, you have finished the *Beginning* section! It is very important, however, that you know the material in all three of the appendices that follow before going on to the *Intermediate* section. They contain the theory, technical and chord information you will need to continue your musical growth and development as a mandolinist. See you in the next section!

APPENDIX 1

The Elements of Music

This section is designed to put the basic theory used in this book all together in one place. You can work through this material all at once and/or use it as a reference for other parts of the book.

LESSON 1: THE MAJOR SCALE

DOE, A DEER...

A *scale* is an arrangement of notes in a specific order of whole steps and half steps (see page 11). Of all the dozens of scales used in music, the *major scale* has the most instantly recognizable sound. It is the "standard of measurement" that musicians use in order to differentiate between all the other scales. In other words, we define all other scales by noting exactly how they are different from the major scale.

The sound of the major scale is that of the traditional "Do–Re–Mi–Fa–Sol–La–Ti–Do" melody (made famous in the song "Do, Re, Mi" from the musical, *The Sound of Music*). It has seven different notes, and uses each letter name from the musical alphabet (page 11) once—though some may be sharped or flatted. The first note, called the *tonic* (or sometimes *key note*) is repeated at the end, for a total of eight notes. The easiest major scale to learn is the C Major scale, which uses no sharps or flats. Notice that the notes are numbered. These numbers are called *scale degrees*.

THE C MAJOR SCALE

	C	D	E	F	G	A	B	C
Scale degree:	1	2	3	4	5	6	7	8(1)

```
T
A
B
              0        2        3
        5
        3    0    1    2    3    0    1    2
```

THE SECRET FORMULA

If you look at the C Major scale as a series of whole steps and half steps, you will learn the "formula" for all major scales. Say it over and over to yourself and memorize it like you would your own phone number: whole–whole–half–whole–whole–whole–half.

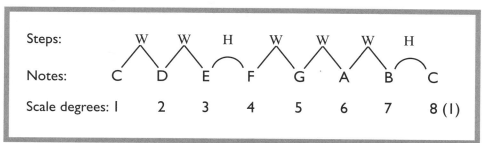

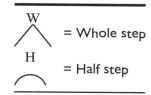

W = Whole step

H = Half step

IMPORTANT NOTE:

The notes of a major scale comprise the notes of a major *key*. For example, the notes of the C Major scale comprise the *key of C Major*.

"SPELLING" THE MAJOR SCALE IN ANY KEY—POP QUIZ

With careful use of the formula, you can *spell* (apply the formula of whole steps and half steps) the major scale starting on any note. Just start with the tonic and then follow the formula, using each letter only once. The D Major scale is shown below. Notice that to make E to F a whole step, as the formula requires, we must raise the F a half step to F♯. Try spelling the A and B♭ Major scales (the correct answers are at the bottom of the page).

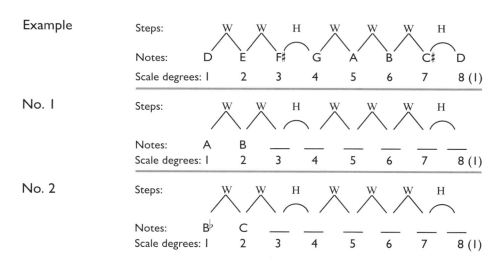

Example

Steps:	W	W	H	W	W	W	H	
Notes:	D	E	F♯	G	A	B	C♯	D
Scale degrees:	1	2	3	4	5	6	7	8 (1)

No. 1

Steps:	W	W	H	W	W	W	H	
Notes:	A	B	—	—	—	—	—	—
Scale degrees:	1	2	3	4	5	6	7	8 (1)

No. 2

Steps:	W	W	H	W	W	W	H	
Notes:	B♭	C	—	—	—	—	—	—
Scale degrees:	1	2	3	4	5	6	7	8 (1)

HOT TIPS:
1. Use every letter in the musical alphabet *once*, in alphabetical order.
2. The last note is the same as the first.
3. You will need to use either sharps or flats (never both) to make the notes fit the formula.

Try playing the D Major scale by ascending the 3rd string. Playing the scale on a single string makes it easy to see the whole steps and half steps. The half steps are adjacent frets; for the whole steps, skip a fret. When you become comfortable with it, try it backwards!

LESSON 2: THE CIRCLE OF 5THS

The *circle of 5ths* is like the "secret agent decoder ring" of music theory (and you don't have to send in any cereal box tops to get it!). A 5th is the distance between the 1st and 5th degrees of a scale. To make a circle of 5ths, just take the keys and arrange them in a circle so that the next note (going clockwise) is the 5th degree of the last scale. For example, the 5th degree of a C Major scale is G, so the next key in the circle after C is G.

The circle of 5ths makes it easy to learn the key signatures (page 31) for each key. The sharp keys (clockwise on the circle) add one sharp for each new key. The new sharp is always the 7th scale degree of that key. The flat keys (counterclockwise) add one new flat for each key. That flat is always the 4th scale degree of the key.

Notice that the keys of G♭ and F♯ are in the same position in the circle. The two scales are played on exactly the same strings and frets and sound exactly the same. When two notes have the same sound but different names, they are *enharmonic equivalents*.

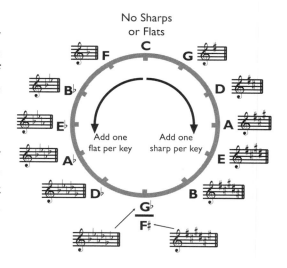

LESSON 3: INTERVALS

An *interval* is the distance between two pitches. You already know three intervals: the whole step (which in interval lingo is a *major 2nd*), the half step (*minor 2nd*) and the 5th (seven half steps). Intervals are best understood relative to a scale. For example, the distance from the 1st degree to the 2nd degree of a scale is an interval of a 2nd; from the 1st degree to the 3rd degree of a scale is an interval of a 3rd, and so on.

INTERVAL QUALITY

Every interval has a *quality*. The quality is the type of sound it makes, such as major or minor. Don't panic! The qualities will be disussed in greater detail in Lesson 4. The major scale generates only major and perfect intervals when measuring up from the tonic:

INTERVALS IN THE MAJOR SCALE

From the Tonic to the:	Interval	Abbreviation
1st Degree	Perfect Unison	PU
2nd Degree	Major 2nd	M2
3rd Degree	Major 3rd	M3
4th Degree	Perfect 4th	P4
5th Degree	Perfect 5th	P5
6th Degree	Major 6th	M6
7th Degree	Major 7th	M7
8th Degree	Perfect Octave	P8

Here are the intervals from the major scale in standard notation:

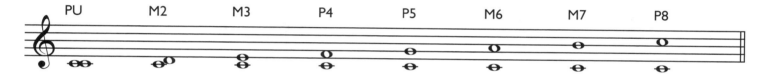

Each interval quality can be measured in half steps. For example, a major 2nd (whole step) equals two half steps. A major 3rd equals four half steps. There are also other kinds of intervals besides major or perfect. If you make a major interval smaller by one half step, it becomes *minor*. For example, C to E is a major 3rd (four half steps), but C to E♭ is a *minor 3rd* (three half steps). If you make a perfect interval smaller, it becomes *diminished*; if you make it bigger, it becomes *augmented*. Here is a chart showing all the intervals and their measurements in half steps, plus examples measured up from C and up from A.

INTERVALS FROM THE UNISON TO THE OCTAVE

Interval	Abbreviation	Half Steps	From C	From A
Perfect Unison	PU	0	C	A
Minor 2nd	m2	1	D♭	B♭
Major 2nd	M2	2	D	B
Minor 3rd	m3	3	E♭	C
Major 3rd	M3	4	E	C♯
Perfect 4th	P4	5	F	D
Augmented 4th or *Tritone*	Aug4 or TT	6	F♯	D♯
Diminished 5th or *Tritone*	dim5 or TT	6	G♭	E♭
Perfect 5th	P5	7	G	E
Minor 6th	m6	8	A♭	F
Major 6th	M6	9	A	F♯
Minor 7th	m7	10	B♭	G
Major 7th	M7	11	B	G♯
Perfect Octave	P8	12	C	A

Here are the intervals from the unison to the octave, measured up from C, in standard notation:

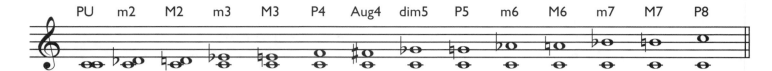

Here are the intervals from the unison to the octave, measured up from A, in standard notation:

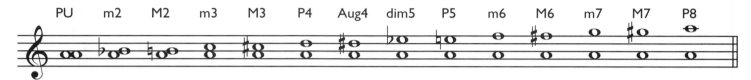

Don't Panic! Lesson 4 will allow you to play, hear and understand the intervals in easy doses.

INTERVAL INVERSION

Each interval can be *inverted*. To invert an interval, we simply take the bottom note and put it on top (or vice versa). For example, if we take C up to E (a major 3rd) and put the C on top so that it is now E up to C (a minor 6th), we have inverted the interval. The numbers of an inverted interval always add up to 9 (a 3rd inverts to a 6th; 3 + 6 = 9). Also, when inverted, major intervals become minor and minor intervals become major; diminished intervals become augmented and vice versa. Perfect intervals remain perfect (that's what's perfect about 'em). The table at the right can be read right-to-left and left-to-right.

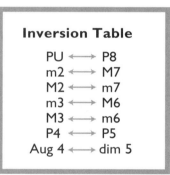

Inversion Table

PU ⟷ P8
m2 ⟷ M7
M2 ⟷ m7
m3 ⟷ M6
M3 ⟷ m6
P4 ⟷ P5
Aug 4 ⟷ dim 5

Here are the interval inversions, all beginning with an interval built on C, in standard notation:

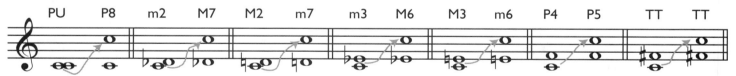

CONSONANCE AND DISSONANCE

Intervals are often described by the qualities of their sound. A *consonant* interval has a harmonious sound that produces a feeling of rest or *resolution*. There is no feeling that further musical movement is required. Consonant intervals include PU, P8, m3, M3, m6, M6 and P5. A *dissonant* interval has a clashing sound that produces an unresolved feeling often called *tension*. Dissonance asks for musical movement to a point of *resolution*. Dissonant intervals include m2, M2, TT, m7 and M7. A P4 can be considered either a consonance or dissonance, depending on the context.

It is the fluctuation between tension and resolution that gives music a sense of motion, direction and emotional effect.

LESSON 4: FINGERINGS FOR INTERVALS

Learning intervals on the fretboard can take a little work but it will help you thoroughly master the instrument. It is easy if you concentrate on one or two interval types at a time.

To make things consistent in this lesson, each interval fingering is indicated for the same set of pitches (for example, all of the perfect octave fingerings are for A to A). You will be able to hear that each fingering generates the same pitches. Play the notes shown in the fingerings one after another (*melodically*) and simultaneously (*harmonically*), and get used to the sounds of the different intervals.

PERFECT OCTAVE = 12 HALF STEPS

Below are the fingerings for a perfect octave. The frets indicated will sound the notes C and C.

Octaves are one of the best interval shapes to memorize. When the two notes are played simultaneously, the octave shape can be moved up or down the neck to create melodies. We call these *parallel octaves*. An octave corresponds to the first two notes of the "Somewhere Over the Rainbow" from *The Wizard of Oz*. Octaves can help you learn the notes on the fretboard much faster. Every time you learn a note, use the octave shapes to find other locations of the same pitch on the fretboard.

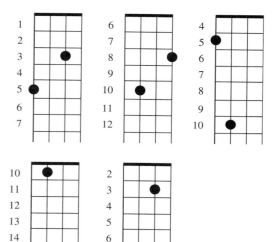

PERFECT 4TH = 5 HALF STEPS

At the right are the fingerings for the interval of a perfect 4th. The frets indicated will sound the notes C and F.

Perfect intervals have a resonant, "in tune" sound. The perfect 4th interval corresponds to the first two notes of the melody to "Here Comes the Bride" ("The Wedding March" by Felix Mendelssohn, 1809–1847). It can be inverted to form a perfect 5th.

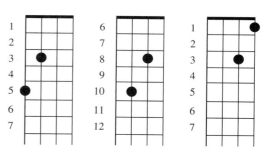

PERFECT 5TH = 7 HALF STEPS

At the right are the fingerings for the interval of a perfect 5th. The frets indicated will sound the notes D and A.

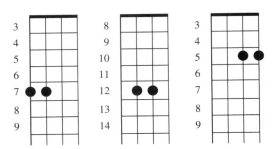

The perfect 5th is also known to rock musicians as the *power chord*. Power chords are named after the lower note. For example, a perfect 5th with D as the low note is known as a *D Power Chord* or *D5*. The perfect 5th corresponds to the first two notes of the famous theme from "Also Sprach Zarathustra" by Richard Strauss (1864–1949) which was used in the movie, *2001: A Space Odyssey*. The perfect 5th can be inverted to form a perfect 4th.

TRITONE = 6 HALF STEPS

Here are the fingerings for the interval of a tritone. The frets indicated sound the notes C to F♯.

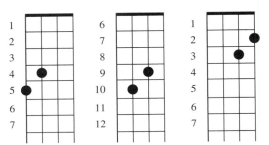

The tritone is a very special interval. It divides the octave equally in half. In other words, the distance from C to F♯ is the same as the distance from F♯ to C (six half steps—three whole steps, hence the name). This means that a tritone inverted is still a tritone.

The tritone is the most unstable-sounding interval, even though it is not necessarily the most dissonant. The tritone carries a lot of tension. Try playing a tritone and then moving each pitch by one half step in opposite directions. Hear the tension resolve!

The tritone is halfway between the perfect 4th and perfect 5th. Therefore, it is also known as an augmented 4th (one half step larger than a perfect 4th) or a diminished 5th (one half step smaller than a perfect 5th), depending on whether the note is sharp or flat.

The first two notes of the melody to "Maria" from the musical play *West Side Story* by Leonard Bernstein are a tritone. The two pitches of the tritone can be alternated to imitate the characteristic sound of European ambulance sirens in World War II movies.

MINOR 2ND = 1 HALF STEP

Below are the fingerings for the interval of a minor 2nd or half step. The frets indicated sound the notes E to F.

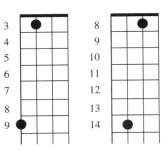

Minor and major 2nds are the building blocks of scales and melodies. Minor 2nds, when played harmonically, are among the most dissonant of intervals. Try moving a minor 2nd shape up and down the neck, playing a melody in parallel minor 2nds. Unless the sound of fingernails on a blackboard bothers you, this can be a cool effect. The minor 2nd corresponds to the first two notes of the theme to the movie *Jaws* by John Williams. The minor 2nd can be inverted to form the major 7th.

MAJOR 7TH = 11 HALF STEPS

Below are the fingerings for the interval of a major 7th. The frets indicated will sound the notes F to E.

The major 7th is the inversion of the minor 2nd. A major 7th sounds the interval between the first and third note of "Bali-Ha'i" from the musical *South Pacific* by Rodgers and Hammerstein. A major 7th can also be thought of as one half step below an octave. To try this, make an octave shape and move the higher note down one half step. Whammo—major 7th!

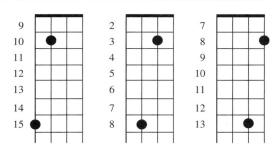

MAJOR 2ND = 2 HALF STEPS

Here are the fingerings for the major 2nd (whole step). The frets indicated will sound the notes B♭ to C.

The major 2nd, as mentioned above, figures heavily in constructing scales and melodies. The major 2nd corresponds to the first two notes of "Do-Re-Mi" from *The Sound of Music*. The major 2nd can be inverted to form the minor 7th.

MINOR 7TH = 10 HALF STEPS

Here are the fingerings for the interval of a minor 7th. The frets indicated will sound the pitches C to B♭.

7ths are important intervals in coloring blues and jazz chords and melodies. The minor 7th can also be thought of as one whole step below the octave. Try making an octave shape and move the higher note down one whole step. The minor 7th corresponds to the first two notes of the song "Somewhere" from Leonard Bernstein's *West Side Story*. The minor 7th can be inverted to form the major 2nd.

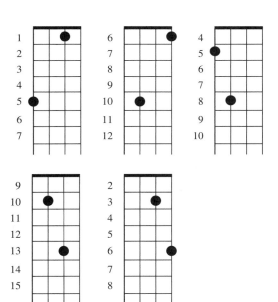

MINOR 3RD = 3 HALF STEPS

Here are the fingerings for the interval of a minor 3rd. The frets indicated will sound the notes D and F.

Minor and major 3rds are the building blocks of chords, including all of the chords you now play. The minor 3rd corresponds the interval between the first two notes of the melody to the famous lullaby by Johannes Brahms (1833–1897), now called "Brahms' Lullaby" ("go to sleeeeeeep, go to sleeeeeeep...."). The minor 3rd can be inverted to form the major 6th.

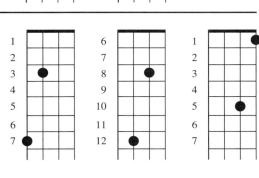

MAJOR 6TH = 9 HALF STEPS

At the right are the fingerings for the interval of a major 6th. The frets indicated will sound the notes F and D.

Both 3rds and 6ths are used to create harmonies for melodies. The major 6th corresponds to the first two notes of the melody to "My Bonnie Lies Over the Ocean." The major 6th can be inverted to form the minor 3rd.

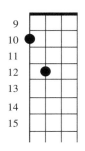 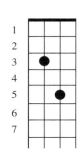 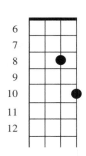

MAJOR 3RD = 4 HALF STEPS

Here are the fingerings for the interval of a major 3rd. The frets indicated will sound the notes D and F#.

The major 3rd, with the minor 3rd (and their inversions, the 6ths) are crucial to building chords and harmonies. The major 3rd corresponds to the first two notes of the chorus of "Ob-la-di, Ob-la-da" by the Beatles and the guitar riff to "Stir It Up" by Bob Marley. Another example is the the beginning of the last line of the Stanley Brothers' classic "Rank Stranger;" the major 3rd corresponds to the words "I found." The major 3rd can be inverted to form the minor 6th.

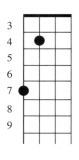 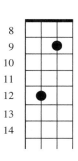 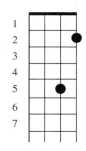

MINOR 6TH = 8 HALF STEPS

Here are the fingerings for the interval of a minor 6th. The frets indicated sound the notes F# and D.

The minor 6th interval, when played melodically (one note at a time), has an unresolved quality that makes it easy to confuse with the tritone. But when the notes are played harmonically (simultaneously), a very consonant sound emerges. The minor 6th can be inverted to form the major 3rd. The minor 6th corresponds to the first two notes of "Where Do I Begin" by Francis Lai from the movie *Love Story*.

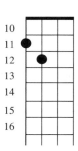 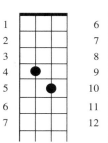 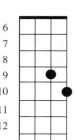

LESSON 5: HARMONY AND CHORDS

As you know, a *chord* is any three or more notes played together. The subject of chords and how they behave is called *harmony*. The most basic kind of chord is called a *triad*. A triad is a three-note chord, generally made by stacking one interval of a 3rd on top of another. All of the chords (except the dominant-7th chords) you have learned in this book are triads. Even though you may play up to four strings, there are only three possible notes; some may be repeated.

Below is a C Major scale that has been *harmonized*. This means that 3rds have been stacked above each note of the scale to form triads. The harmony notes are all within the scale— no sharps or flats have been added or changed. This is called *diatonic harmony*, or harmony within the key. These triads are shown in closed position. This means the notes are as close together as possible. The mandolin cannot comfortably accomodate many closed position triads, but the fingerings shown will help you hear the chords. You will find three types of triads—major, minor and diminished, which are all explained below.

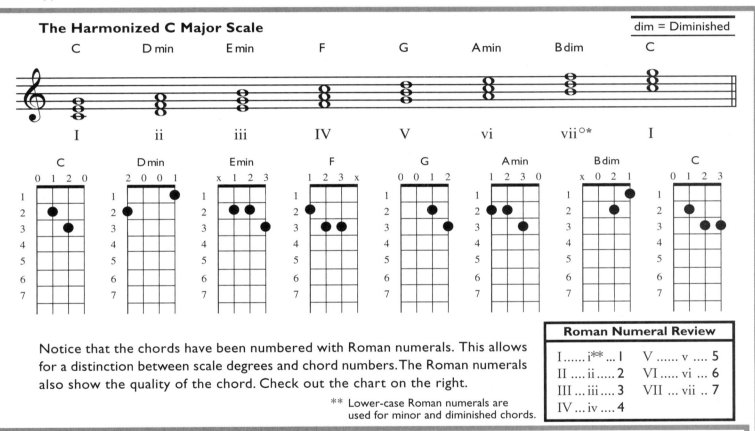

The Harmonized C Major Scale

dim = Diminished

Notice that the chords have been numbered with Roman numerals. This allows for a distinction between scale degrees and chord numbers. The Roman numerals also show the quality of the chord. Check out the chart on the right.

** Lower-case Roman numerals are used for minor and diminished chords.

Roman Numeral Review

I......i** ... I	V ...... v 5
II ....ii.....2	VI ..... vi ... 6
III ...iii....3	VII ... vii .. 7
IV ...iv 4	

THREE KINDS OF TRIADS

The three types of triads that result from harmonizing the major scale are all made with different combinations of major and minor 3rds.

- A major triad is a major 3rd with a minor 3rd on top.
- A minor triad is a minor 3rd with a major 3rd on top.
- A diminished triad is a minor 3rd with another minor 3rd on top.

The bottom note of the triad is called the *root*. The middle note, which is a 3rd above the root, is called the *3rd*. The top note, which is a 3rd above the 3rd and a 5th above the root, is called the *5th*.

5th
3rd
Root

For easy comparison, the example below shows all three triad types built on a C root.

C Major Triad   C Minor Triad   C Diminished Triad

THREE PRIMARY CHORDS

The primary chords in every major key are the I, IV and V (one, four and five) chords.

Here are the note names from the D Major scale with the roots of the I, IV and V chords circled.

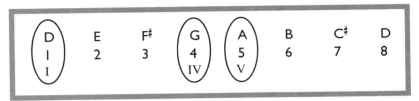

Here is a chord *progression* (series of chords) using I, IV and V. The key of D Major is indicated. Also try it in G and A Major. Use any chord fingerings or strum patterns you like.

Key of D Major

Key of G Major
Fill in the blanks. The answers are at the bottom of the page.

Key of A Major
Fill in the blanks. The answers are at the bottom of the page.

THE TRIUMPHANT RETURN OF THE CIRCLE OF 5THS

The Circle of 5ths can be used to show basic harmonic movement. Instead of keys, these are major chords. Box or circle any three adjacent chords. The one in the middle is I. The one going clockwise is V. The one going counter-clockwise is IV.

Now that you have experimented a bit with intervals, the major scale and chords, it's time to make the magic happen!

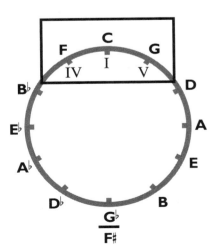

LESSON 6: MUSICAL EXPRESSION

EXPRESSION

Music is not just about keeping time and playing the right notes or chords. In order for music to have an emotional effect, it needs a sense of *expression*. Two very important elements of musical expression are *phrasing* and *dynamics*.

PHRASING

Phrasing is the way that touch, volume and tempo are used to imply a sense of direction, movement and rest in a piece of music. If notes are like words, then phrasing is the way that the words are made to sound like sentences, or complete thoughts.

Phrase markings

Written music uses a number of markings and terms to communicate phrasing and expression to the performer. Many of these terms are Italian. A quick tour of a few commonly used terms should give you some ideas for your own music. First, the *phrase mark* is a curved line that loosely connects a passage of music. It can be confused with a slur or a tie, but the phrase mark is usually shown above the staff and may have slurs or ties beneath it.

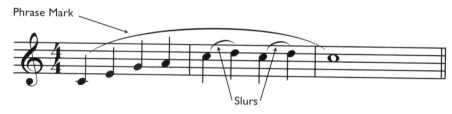

OTHER PHRASING AND EXPRESSION TERMS		
TERM	DEFINITION	MARKING
Legato	Notes are to be played in a smooth, connected fashion.	The word "*Legato*" marked above the music.
Staccato	Short, detached, unconnected notes.	The word "*Staccato*" marked above the music, or small dots above or below individual note heads.
Accent	A note played louder than the surrounding notes.	This sign ＞ above or below the note heads.

DYNAMICS

Dynamics define how loud or soft the notes or passages of music will sound. Dynamic expression and contrast is very important to imparting a sense of emotion in a piece of music.

LOUD			SOFT		
Mark	**Term**	**Definition**	**Mark**	**Term**	**Definition**
mf	Mezzo Forte	Medium Loud	*mp*	Mezzo Piano	Medium soft
f	Forte	Loud	*p*	Piano	Soft
ff	Fortissimo	Very Loud	*pp*	Pianissimo	Very soft
fff	Fortississimo	Very, very loud	*ppp*	Pianississimo	Very, very soft
—	Crescendo	Gradually becoming louder	—	Decrescendo	Gradually becoming softer

THE DYNAMIC SCALE

Arranged from softest to loudest, the dynamic markings look like this:

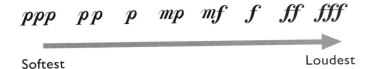

ppp   *pp*   *p*   *mp*   *mf*   *f*   *ff*   *fff*

Softest   Loudest

THE "ARCH"

Many times a phrase or an entire piece of music will lend itself to a dynamic "arch" that begins at a softer dynamic, climaxes at a louder dynamic, then returns to a softer level. This is especially true if the melody moves from low notes up to high notes, then back down. Look for opportunities to place this kind of expression in your music. Also look for spots where a "reverse arch" (loud to soft to loud) might work.

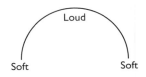

TIPS FOR EXPRESSIVE TECHNIQUE

It takes good control of the pick to bring out dynamics and phrasing with your right hand. Here are a few tips:

To play louder
Slightly tighten the grip on your pick. Do not pick "deeper" into the strings, or try to use more muscle force. This makes a harsh tone.

To play softer
Slightly loosen the grip on your pick (but don't drop it!).

To play legato
Try to pick notes at the same time you fret them. Make sure your pick doesn't touch a vibrating string before it's time to pluck again, cutting off the previous note.

To play staccato
You can use your pick to cut off the note by placing it back on the string, or use your left hand to cut off the note by lifting your finger(s) slightly from the fret(s).

APPENDIX 2

Guide Fingers

As you begin to move up the neck using moveable chords and scales (and as you move into the intermediate level of this series), it helps to apply a bit of mindfulness to your left-hand posture. First, review the "Fingering Alert" on page 25.

In many major scales, the 1st and 3rd finger maintain the interval of a minor 3rd (three frets). Try the G Major scale below. Notice that the 1st and 3rd finger are always on the 2nd and 5th frets respectively. While this proximity sometimes changes (as when your 1st finger scoots back to play the 1st fret in other scales), you can still train your hand to hold your 1st and 3rd fingers over a three-fret span as a "home base" or "guide position."

Play the scale again and pay close attention to your 1st and 3rd fingers. Keep them close to the 2nd and 5th fret respectively. Notice that your 2nd finger now will touch the side of your 1st finger when it plays the 3rd fret, and it will touch the side of your 3rd finger when it plays the 4th fret. (Read this last sentence aloud to yourself slowly as you play and watch your hand, it's not as confusing as it sounds.) Your 1st and 3rd fingers are "guiding" the placement of your 2nd finger.

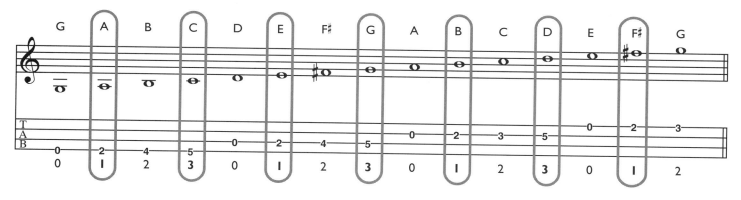

Try this blues lick in G. Then try it in A (up one whole step). As you move up the neck, keep your 1st and 3rd fingers in the guide position: spread apart by three frets and staying close to the strings. Then try it up in D (up another five frets).

APPENDIX 3

Chord Forms

This page brings together many chord forms you have learned, plus a few new variations. Below each diagrams, the chord tones are listed ("R" for root, "3" for 3rd, "5" for 5th, "7" for 7th). Note that minor chords have a ♭3 and dominant 7ths have a ♭7. While not every chord in every key is shown, you can use the moveable forms to make any major, minor, or dominant 7th chord you need. Just locate the root (R) of the form on the right fret for the chord you want, and build the rest around it. Happy hunting!

OPEN CHORDS

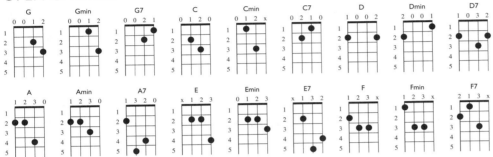

MOVEABLE FINGERING NO. 1
(Root on 3rd/1st string)

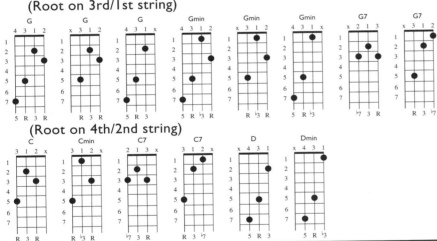

(Root on 4th/2nd string)

MOVEABLE FINGERING NO. 2
(Root on 3rd string)

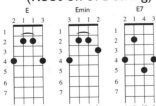

MOVEABLE FINGERING NO. 3
(Root on 4th/1st string)

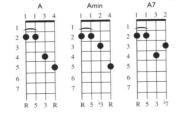

(Root on the 2nd string)

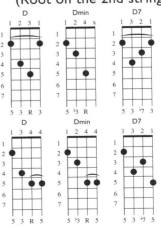

How to Practice

"HOME BASE" TECHNIQUE; WHEN AND WHAT

It is important from the beginning to play with the best, most relaxed technique you can. Though you will see and learn many variations of technique, this will become the "home base" to which your body will always return. Building these good habits requires two elements:

1. **Technique Exercises**
    These allow you to concentrate on technique without worrying about keeping your place in the music.

2. **Mental Focus**
    When you work on new songs or skills, be aware of your hand positions, body posture, rhythm and touch.

WHEN TO PRACTICE

When you are first beginning, or when you are learning new skills, it is best to practice often. Five to ten minutes here and there on a new skill will work much better than an hour every three or four days. If you're lucky enough to be able to practice at the same time every day, you will see great improvement. You will also notice that you develop a better ability to focus on mandolin playing at that time. If it's not possible to practice at the same time every day, at least try to pick up the instrument for a few minutes every day, and then reinforce with longer sessions every couple of days.

WHAT TO PRACTICE

It is a great idea to have a small number of different "projects" going on in your practice sessions. This keeps you from feeling bored or bogged down, and it helps you improve several skills at once. Pick two or three things to work on every day for a week, then adjust your plan for the next week. Some of these projects might include reading music, learning to improvise, playing a new melody or learning a new chord progression. Be sure to spend time on each project every time you play.

ORGANIZING A PRACTICE SESSION

Here's a sample 30-minute practice session you may want to try for a few weeks. If you have more or less time, adjust the time on each item.

1. **Technical Exercises** *5 minutes*
    These include finger exercises, counting and foot-tapping practice, warm-ups and scales.

2. **Reading Music/Melody** *10 minutes*
    Try reading lots of new material in order to keep your reading skills in shape. If you are not working on reading music, work on melody playing and improvising.

3. **Playing Melodies/Chords** *10 minutes*
    Spend some time every day working on melodies and chords. Learn fiddle tunes, new bluegrass, rock, blues or jazz songs.

4. **Reviewing Old Material** *5 minutes*
    Always save a little time to go back and play songs you are already good at. This keeps them "tuned up" and ready to go for times when you want to play with relaxation or for other people.

A *metronome* is an adjustable device (either wind-up or battery-powered) that generates a beat pulse for you to play along with. You can adjust the pulse from very slow to very fast. The speed is marked in beats-per-minute. A metronome speed of 60 is the same as one beat per second. The simplest metronomes make a ticking sound, while the more involved ones will make drum sounds and even mark measures for you.

When used regularly (and with a Zen-like patience), the metronome will help you learn to play with a steady rhythm. The only practice technique that is as valuable is to play with another person who has good rhythm—this can be difficult to do on a daily basis.

Don't let the metronome drive you crazy! At first, it may seem to be speeding up and slowing down while you play. Listen carefully—it's probably you. Pick a consistent, slow tempo to work with for the first few days and try the metronome with one favorite song. See how many measures you can play before you and the metronome have a parting of the ways. Gradually increase your endurance before you increase the speed.

INSPIRATIONAL LISTENING
Here are some players and bands to check out:

OLD-TIME
Norman Blake
Fuzzy Mountain String Band
Hollow Rock String Band

BLUES
Howard Armstrong
Steve James
Memphis Jug Band
Yank Rachell

BLUEGRASS
Sam Bush
Kentucky Colonels
Bill Monroe
Osborne Brothers
Chris Thile/Nickel Creek
Rhonda Vincent

ROCK/JAZZ/WORLD MUSIC
Dave Apollon
Jacob do Bandolim
David Grisman
Led Zeppelin
Mike Marshall
R.E.M.

INTERMEDIATE MANDOLIN

GREG HORNE

This book was acquired, edited, and produced
by Workshop Arts, Inc., the publishing arm of
the National Guitar Workshop.
Nathaniel Gunod, editor
Nathaniel Gunod, acquisitions, managing editor
Ante Gelo, music typesetter
Timothy Phelps, interior design
Audio tracks recorded at Grinning Deer Studios, Knoxville, TN

CONTENTS

MP3 CD

00
Track 1

An MP3 CD is included with this book to make learning easier and more enjoyable. The symbol shown at bottom left appears next to every example in the book that features an MP3 track. Use the MP3s to ensure you're capturing the feel of the examples and interpreting the rhythms correctly. The track number below the symbol corresponds directly to the example you want to hear (example numbers are above the icon). All the track numbers are unique to each "book" within this volume, meaning every book has its own Track 1, Track 2, and so on. (For example, *Beginning Mandolin* starts with Track 1, as does *Intermediate Mandolin* and *Mastering Mandolin*.) Track 1 will help you tune to this CD.

The disc is playable on any CD player equipped to play MP3 CDs. To access the MP3s on your computer, place the CD in your CD-ROM drive. In Windows, double-click on My Computer, then right-click on the CD icon labeled "MP3 Files" and select Explore to view the files and copy them to your hard drive. For Mac, double-click on the CD icon on your desktop labeled "MP3 Files" to view the files and copy them to your hard drive.

ABOUT THE AUTHOR

PHOTO • JOHN BLACK

Greg Horne is a performer, writer, producer and teacher. He holds a Bachelor of Arts in Music from the College of Wooster, and pursued graduate studies at the University of Mississippi's Center for the Study of Southern Culture. Greg has been an instructor at the National Guitar Workshop's summer campuses since 1990, specializing in songwriting and acoustic courses. He is the author of *The Complete Acoustic Guitar Method*, and co-author of *The Multi-Instrumental Guitarist*, also published by the National Guitar Workshop and Alfred. Greg has produced several albums of his own songs, as well as producing and performing on projects for other artists. He lives in Knoxville, Tennessee. For more information or to contact Greg, visit www.greghornemusic.com.

Greg Horne plays Weber Mandolins made by Sound to Earth, Ltd in Montana (www.soundtoearth.com). They are heard on the CD that accompanies this book.

Greg Horne sends his special thanks to Paula Jean Lewis and Bruce Weber of Sound to Earth, David Lovett, Tim Worman, Pick'n'Grin (www.pickngrin.com), Nat Gunod, Wayne Fugate and his students.

INTRODUCTION

Welcome to the *Intermediate* section, which picks up directly from the skills and tunes you learned in the first section. Here you will expand those skills, build your repertoire and solidify your foundation in music theory and improvisation.

WHO THIS SECTION IS INTENDED FOR

While this section can benefit players at all stages, it assumes that you know some of the basics covered in the *Beginning* section. In order to get the most out of this section, you should be comfortable with the following techniques and skills:

- The names of the open strings and the structure of the music alphabet (also called the chromatic scale)
- Alternate (or "down-up") picking
- The basic structure and fingering of a major scale
- Strumming a steady beat using open chords
- Moveable chords (chords with no open strings) and finding new chords on the neck using moveable shapes
- Playing chords and improvising a simple lead on a 12-bar blues

DO I HAVE TO READ MUSIC/WILL I LEARN TO READ MUSIC?

You do not have to read music to use this book, all examples include TAB or chord graphs. However, a basic knowledge of pitch and rhythm notation (see pages 102–103) will help you learn the examples more accurately. This book does not teach you to read music without TAB. The *Beginning* section covers this in a clear, step-by-step chapter.

WHAT'S IN THIS SECTION?

- Technique and skill development for more fluid picking and fingering
- Repertoire building using fiddle tunes, bluegrass standards and the blues
- Extensive improvisation and soloing using scales, chords, theory and practical applications
- New styles and techniques from jazz, Celtic, funk and Brazilian music
- Theory and knowledge of the fretboard covering the major scale, natural minor scale, pentatonic scales, triad chords, 7th chords, arpeggios and blues scales

HOW TO USE THIS SECTION

This section is arranged in individual lessons grouped into chapters by topic. You can work from the beginning to the end, or skip around and work on a couple of chapters at a time. Each chapter is progressive, meaning each lesson within a chapter builds on the previous lesson.

WHERE DO I GO FROM HERE?

The *Intermediate* section is designed to give you the basic foundation you need to go to jams and festivals, play in groups, and most of all to play for your own enjoyment. This section progresses directly to *Mastering Mandolin*, the third section of this book, where you will further refine your skills and deepen your knowledge.

CHAPTER 1

Review: Reading Music

LESSON 1: PITCH

This book assumes that you have either completed the *Beginning* section, or you consider yourself an intermediate player because of what you have learned from a teacher or on your own. While you don't have to read music to use this book, it will definitely help if you can. This section is included as a quick review or introduction to reading standard music notation and tablature (TAB). For a more thorough treatment of the subject, check out pages 19–34.

STAFF

Music is written on a *staff* containing five lines and four spaces. *Notes* are written on the lines and spaces, which are assigned letter names from the musical alphabet: A-B-C-D-E-F-G-A-B-C, etc.

CLEF

The *clef* indicates which note names coincide with a particular line or space. Different clefs are used for different instruments. Mandolin music is written in *G clef*. The inside curl of the G clef encircles the line which is called "G." When the G clef is placed on the second line, as in mandolin music, it is called the *treble clef*.

G clef

Using the G clef, the notes on the staff are as follows:

E   G   B   D   F   F   A   C   E

LEDGER LINES

Ledger lines are used to indicate pitches above and below the staff.

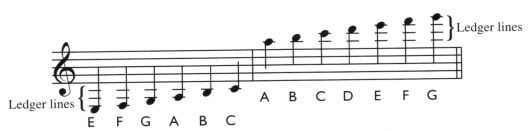

LESSON 2: TIME

The staff is divided by vertical lines called *bar lines*. The space between two bar lines is a *measure*. Each measure (or *bar*) is an equal unit of time. *Double bar lines* mark the end of a section or example.

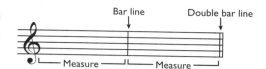

TIME SIGNATURE

Every piece of music has numbers at the beginning that tell you how to count the time.

Examples: $\frac{4}{4}$ $\frac{3}{4}$ $\frac{6}{8}$

The top number represents the number of beats, or counts, per measure.
The bottom number represents the type of note receiving one count.
   For example:

When the bottom number is 4, the quarter note (see below) gets one count.
When the bottom number is 8, the eighth note (see below) gets one count.

Sometimes a **C** is written in place of $\frac{4}{4}$ time. This is called *common time*.

NOTE AND REST VALUES IN $\frac{4}{4}$ TIME

These symbols indicate rhythm:

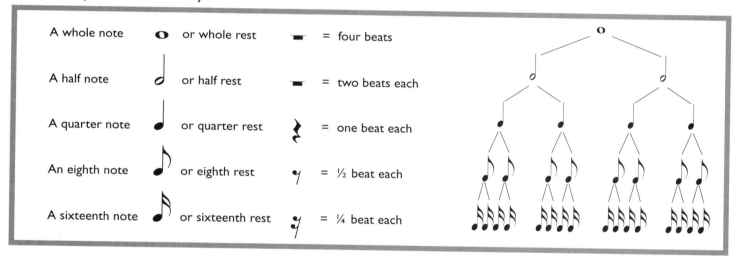

A whole note	**o** or whole rest ▬	= four beats
A half note	♩ or half rest ▬	= two beats each
A quarter note	♩ or quarter rest 𝄽	= one beat each
An eighth note	♪ or eighth rest	= ½ beat each
A sixteenth note	♬ or sixteenth rest	= ¼ beat each

Notes shorter than a quarter note are usually beamed together in groups:

LESSON 3: TABLATURE

Tablature (TAB) is a graphic representation of the strings of the mandolin. The top horizontal line represents the 1st string; the bottom line represents the 4th string. The numbers on the lines indicate which frets to play. The numbers below indicate left hand fingers.

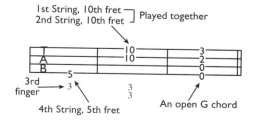

CHAPTER 2

Review: Scales and Chords

LESSON 1: MAJOR SCALES

In the *Beginning* section, you learned to play the major scale in the keys of C, G, D and A. This section uses these keys extensively, especially in Chapter 4 (page 118). To review, remember that the major scale makes the familiar sound of "Do, Re, Mi, Fa, Sol, La, Ti, Do" (made famous in the movie *The Sound of Music*). The major scale is always constructed using the same formula of whole steps and half steps.

W = Whole step

H = Half step

THE MAJOR SCALE FORMULA

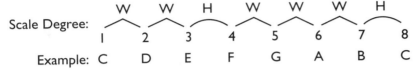

Here are fingerings for the major scale in the keys of C, G, D and A in the open position of the mandolin. The *tonic* notes (scale degree number 1, the note the key is named for) have been highlighted.

C MAJOR SCALE

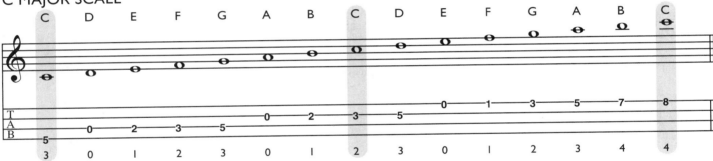

G MAJOR SCALE

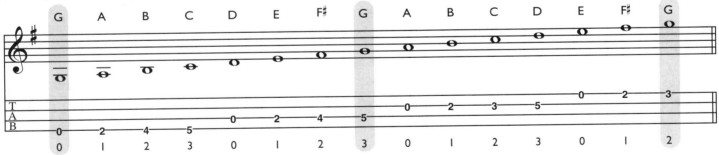

D MAJOR SCALE

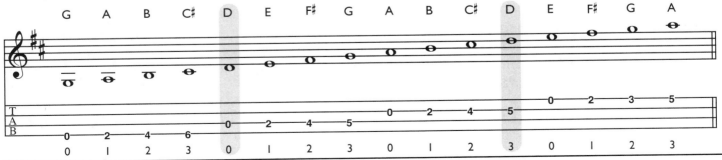

A MAJOR SCALE

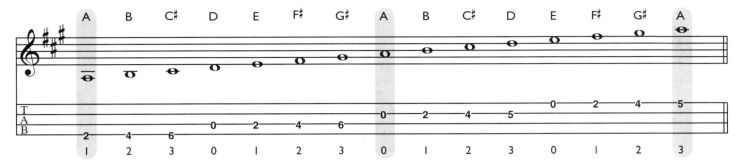

LESSON 2: CHORDS

Below are many of the chord shapes you learned in the *Beginning* section. These will be used throughout this section. Use this page as a reference for how to play these common chords. Some chords have many fingering possibilities. Unless the lesson gives you a specific fingering, you are free to experiment. New chords will also be introduced in later lessons.

Chords marked with an asterisk (*) are considered *moveable*. They can be moved up and down the neck to form chords in keys not shown here. For example, B7 can be moved one half step lower to form B♭7. All chords have the chord tones shown under the diagram (R=root, 3=3rd, 5=5th, 7=7th).

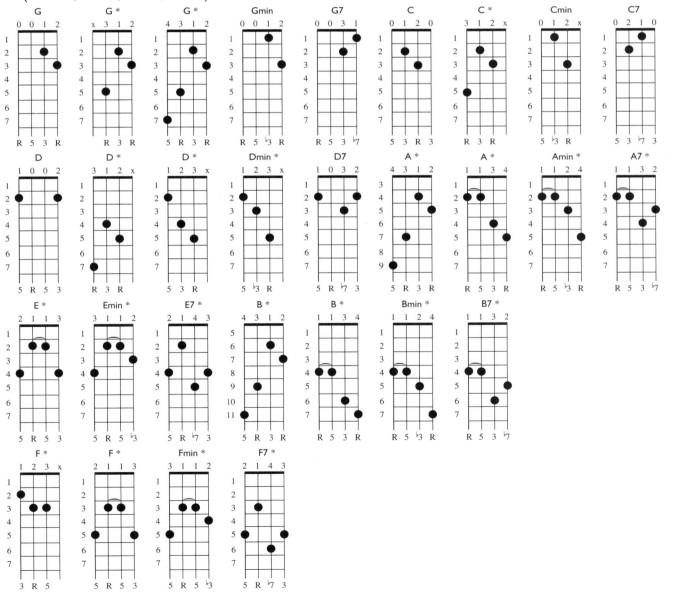

CHAPTER 3

Developing Technique

LESSON 1: BUILDING SPEED AND AGILITY

ACCURACY AND ECONOMY

Accuracy and economy of motion are the keys to building speed and agility in your playing. Try to identify the specific muscle movements required to play specific passages on the mandolin, and then eliminate any extra motion that detracts from your efficiency. Here are three crucial elements to improving your technique:

1. Be observant of your playing technique. Pay attention to how you hold the mandolin, your hand positions, your finger movements and your breathing.

2. Strive for economy of motion in your playing. Play with as little movement as possible and try to avoid tension. Stay loose and relaxed.

3. Practice exercises that address specific movements or techniques, and concentrate on the effects that the exercises were designed to achieve. Exercises have little effect if you simply try to play them as fast as possible.

Below are some exercises you can use to warm up your fingers and to build speed and accuracy. To get the maximum effect of these exercises, follow these pointers:

1. Concentrate on the motion of your fingers. Keep them "floating" close to the frets. Move them up and down like pistons in a car engine. *Don't play too fast!* It is better to play slowly and to focus on technical improvement than it is to concern yourself with simply being able to play fast.

2. Concentrate on synchronizing your picking hand with your fretting fingers. Feel the simultaneous forearm "twitch" that makes each note.

3. Practice these exercises for a few minutes at the beginning of each practice session. This will allow you to start off with the best technique possible. Soon the technique you develop in the exercises will start to show up in your regular playing.

The following exercises are shown on the 2nd string, but practice them on each string (using the same frets).

These exercises are written in $\frac{9}{8}$ and $\frac{6}{8}$. In $\frac{9}{8}$, there are nine eighth notes per bar, grouped in threes. This is called a *compound meter*, meaning that each beat is subdivided into three parts, resulting in a feeling of three beats per bar. $\frac{6}{8}$ feels like two beats per bar. This grouping is good for these exercises because it challenges you to keep track of your alternate picking, which must remain strict throughout! For more on compound meters and other picking patterns, see page 134. This issue is addressed again in the *Mastering* section.

This one uses a major scale pattern that allows you to practice different finger spacings as you work up the neck. Try to play this with a *legato* touch, meaning the notes should be smoothly connected.

PISTON EXERCISE A: ASCENDING

Track 2

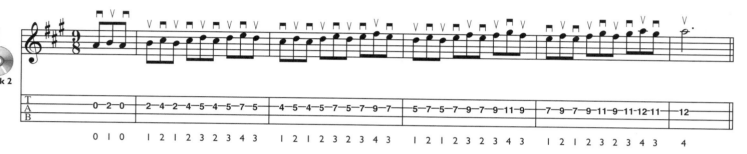

Here's the same pattern coming down from the 12th fret. Try it on each string.

PISTON EXERCISE A: DESCENDING

Track 3

Here's another one with notes grouped in threes to challenge your picking and give your 4th finger a workout.

PISTON EXERCISE B

Track 4

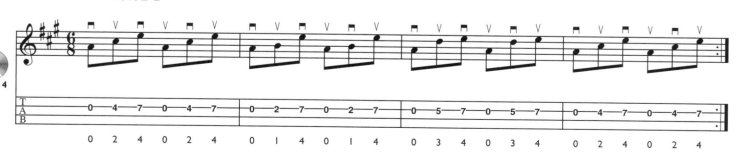

On pages 47–48, you learned the techniques of hammer-ons and pull-offs. To review, hammer-ons and pull-offs are the mandolinist's way of executing a *slur*. A slur is not what you do to your words after you've been to the dentist, but a term of musical expression. A slur connects two or more notes of different pitches so that the first one is articulated (played with the pick) and the others follow along without being picked.

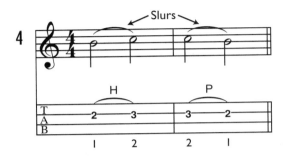

H = Hammer-on
P = Pull-off

It takes a bit of strength and a lot of accuracy to execute good hammer-ons and pull-offs on the mandolin. Here are a couple of tips:

HAMMER-ONS: Lift your finger directly over the note, then bring it down as if it was spring-loaded. Imagine that your finger is going to keep going on past the note and right through the neck. This is not so that you use more *force*, but so that you *follow through*. This will keep your finger from momentarily stopping at the string before it attempts to push the string to the fret.

PULL-OFFS: Remember to have both notes of the pull-off group pressed down before plucking. When pulling off, don't lift straight up. Instead, give a little sideways *snap* to the note. Some people snap their finger in toward the hand (a pulling motion), others push off of the note, away from the hand. Either way, this snapping motion will cause the note to sound much more clearly.

Try this exercise. It doesn't use every possible hammer-on or pull-off, but it gets most of them in there. Although there is no key signature, this exercise is written in A Major on the 2nd string. You could change it to A Minor by moving the 4th fret note (C#) to the 3rd fret (C♮). Also try the same frets on other strings.

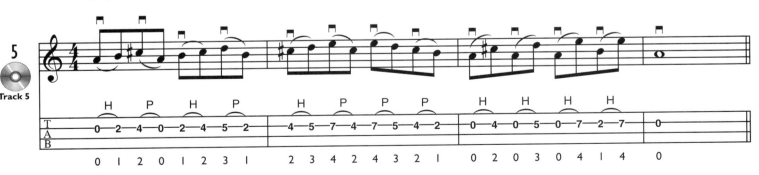

Track 5

This exercise requires you to combine hammer-ons and pull-offs into triplets. It is shown in A Minor on the 2nd string, and D Major on the 3rd string. Practice both versions on every string.

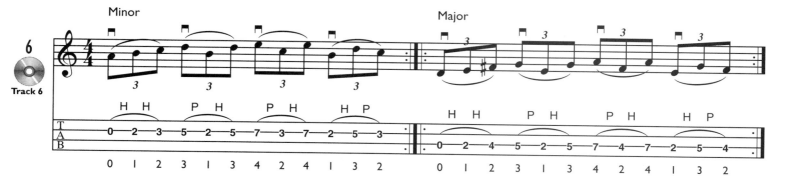

This one is a cool tag lick that could be used at the end of a solo. Try to pick each string only once!

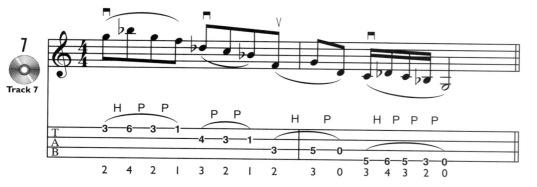

LESSON 3: IMPROVING TREMOLO

Tremolo (achieving sustain by rapidly repeating a note) is one of the most expressive characteristic sounds of the mandolin. It is also one of the most challenging. If you have worked through the *Beginning* section, you have already experimented with tremolo.

TO MEASURE OR NOT TO MEASURE

In the *Beginning* section, you learned about *unmeasured tremolo*. This means moving the pick down and up as rapidly as you can (or want to). Unmeasured tremolo allows you to change the speed and intensity of the effect at will. It is indicated in music by placing three slashes above or below the note head. Another kind of tremolo is *measured tremolo*. This means moving the pick to a specific division of the beat, often sixteenth notes. Sixteenth note measured tremolo is indicated with two slashes above or below the notehead.

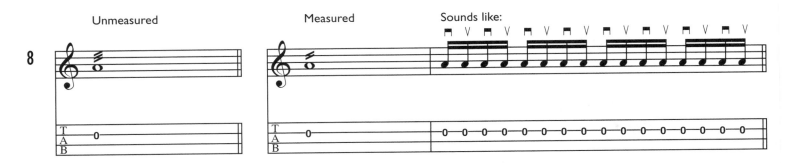

You can use measured tremolo to build and refine your technique. Try example 9, following these tips:

- Hold your arm and pick in a firm but relaxed grip, not the death grip used by the ancient warriors of the planet Voltron.

- Allow only the very point or tip of the pick to travel across the string.

- As you speed up, you will tighten up your muscles. This is natural. Stop often and relax. A little at a time, build up the length of time you can tremolo *and still stay relaxed*!

Track 8

TO PUNCTUATE OR NOT TO PUNCTUATE

Another aspect of fine-tuning your tremolo is punctuating the end of the note. Sometimes you will want to tremolo the entire duration of the note. Other times, you may want to stop the tremolo before the end of the note, allowing the note to decay naturally a bit before the next note. This punctuation generally occurs on a specific beat. The funny thing about punctuating tremolo is that it is very rarely notated in the music. It is generally left to the taste of the performer (that's you!)

One way to indicate the punctuation in music is to tie the tremoloed note to an untremoloed note, indicating where the tremolo should stop. The following tune incorporates this technique in a few spots, particularly the end of each repeated section.

This tune has a classical sound and challenges you to try tremolo with one string, two strings and four-string chords. Watch out for untremoloed notes and measured tremolos (only two slashes, indicating a sixteenth-note tremolo).

AIR ON THE SIDE OF CAUTION
Track 9

The mandolin's sound as a lead instrument in old-time and bluegrass music is heavily influenced by the fiddle. Mandolinists use *slides* as a way to imitate the more slippery, fretless sound of the fiddle. A slide is accomplished by gliding a finger along a string from one fret to another to create a smooth, sliding connection between the notes. Like hammer-ons and pull-offs, slides take a bit of practice. Spend some time working on slides with each finger on each string, ascending and descending. Keep in mind the following tips:

- As you slide, keep up the pressure on the string, so the sound continues.

- If the slide is only a distance of one fret (one half step), you can probably move just your finger without moving your whole hand position.

- If the slide is a distance of two frets (one whole step) or more, you should move your hand position with the slide. This will allow you to focus your strength on keeping the sliding finger in a good, firm fretting position while your hand and arm actually execute the slide.

Here's a cool blues lick that uses a slide for every finger.

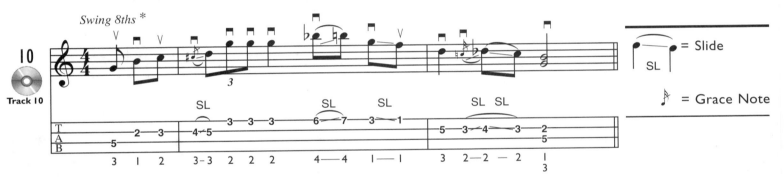

Note that slides may be articulated many ways. Here's a play-by-play of the lick in example 10.

1. The first slide in this lick is written with a *grace note* (a small note with a slash through it, played quickly, directly before the main note) connected with a dash (indicating the slide) and a slur. This means the slide will sound like a swoop up to the main note (D at the 5th fret of the 2nd string).

2. The second slide in this lick requires you to play an eighth note on B♭ (6th fret, 1st string), then slide it to B♮ (7th fret) without picking it (because of the slur marking). You should hear both notes distinctly and in rhythm.

3. The third slide connects a G (3rd fret) and an F (1st fret) on the 1st string, without a slur. You pick the G, slide down, and pick the F when you get there (no slur).

4. The fourth slide requires you to slide your 2nd finger from the 3rd fret (C) to the 4th (D♭) and back.

* Swing 8ths are discussed on pages 55 and 132.

UNISON SLIDES, DOUBLE-STOP SLIDES AND BEYOND

On page 43, you learned how *unison doubles* can add a fuller sound to notes played on the open E, A and D strings. For example, you can double an open E-note on the 1st string with the 7th fret of the 2nd string. To add even more zing to this effect, *slide into the fretted note* while picking the open note. Since you are sliding from the 5th fret to the 7th fret, you could use either your 4th finger or your 3rd finger. You will find situations that favor each one, so try it both ways!

You can also slide *double stops* (two notes played at once). Just keep the pressure on, and keep your fingers firmly planted, allowing your hand and arm to do the work. Some players even like to slide three or four-note chords! This can be particularly cool (or sickly melodramatic, depending on your taste) when combined with tremolo.

Here's a little piece to try that incorporates all of the sliding techniques. Note that double-stop slides sometimes require you to end up in a slightly different finger placement from where you started! This happens in the slides in the last four bars.

SIGN SAYS "GONE NOODLING"

Track 11

LESSON 5: CROSSPICKING

Crosspicking is a technique used by mandolinists, guitarists and banjo players to create a sustaining, harp-like effect with melodies. In crosspicking, the individual notes of a melody are played on separate strings, allowing the decay of one note to overlap the start of the next. Crosspicking is also called *cross-string picking*.

Crosspicking was brought to the mandolin most dramatically by Jesse McReynolds of the famed bluegrass-brother duo, Jim and Jesse. Jesse wanted to imitate the three-finger banjo rolls he heard from players like Earl Scruggs. McReynolds' crosspicking style combines chords and rolls, scale runs and a peculiar picking pattern that makes an instantly recognizable, nearly unduplicatable sound.

You can develop your own style of crosspicking by finding ways to play melodies where the notes are played on separate strings. This takes some creative thinking, because often you have to use an open string or play a *lower* pitch on a *higher* string. To see how it works, here is a descending G *Major Pentatonic* scale (a five-note scale including the 1st, 2nd, 3rd, 5th and 6th degrees of the major scale, in this case, G, A, B, D and E) played first in open position, then using crosspicking.

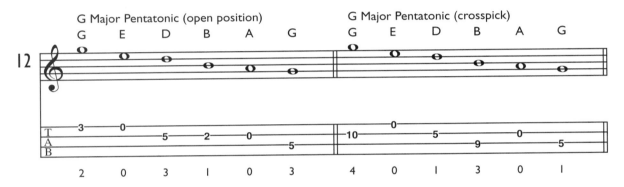

FINDING THE NOTES UP THE NECK

As you can see, crosspicking depends on an awareness of different spots on the neck to play the same note, so that you have choices for placement. There is a trick to it, though. Remember that each string tunes to the next lower adjacent string at the 7th fret. Therefore, the notes on the 2nd string, for example, from the 7th fret on, are the same as the notes on the 1st string, from the open string on. Chords also repeat up the neck in this way.

Here is an A Major scale in the first five frets, then starting on the 7th fret. Imagine that the 7th fret is a dividing line at which all open position scales and chords move one string lower. While these are not crosspicking fingerings, they illustrate how you can find new locations for notes and scales you already know.

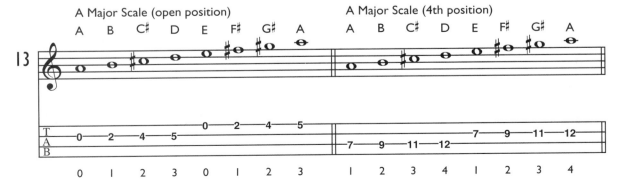

Here is the traditional fiddle tune "Turkey in the Straw" set in the key of G for crosspicking. In this tune, use alternate picking and watch all the fingerings very carefully! You may want to review the G Major scale (page 104). Chords are indicated above the music so that you use this opportunity to practice playing chords too. Chord fingerings may be found on page 105.

TURKEY IN THE STRAW (CROSSPICKING)
Track 12

LESSON 6: MCREYNOLDS-STYLE ROLLS AND PICKING PATTERNS

A major feature of the Jesse McReynolds style is picking arpeggios (broken chords) in a *banjo-roll* style. Banjo rolls tend to group notes in threes. You can use two ways of picking to accomplish these rolls.

Strict Alternate Picking (Down-Up): Pick in the same strict down-up pattern you always use for eighth notes. This may cause you to make some interesting jumps from string to string with your pick, but it will keep your rhythm solid and will require less relearning for your hand.

Jesse McReynolds Roll Picking (Down-Up-Up): McReynolds uses a pattern in which he picks down on the lower string of a two- or three-string group, then up on the highest string, and up again on the adjacent lower string. While this can be very awkward at first, it can turn into a fluid motion that moves your hand in tiny circles, allowing you to build speed. This pattern is limited in its agility, however, and will often require you to break the pattern or turn it around backwards to get to the notes you want.

Here are two A chord rolls shown with both picking patterns.

A-Chord Roll No. 1

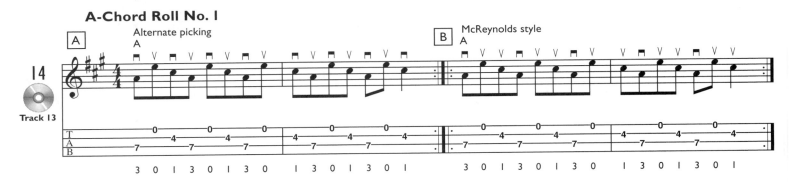

A-Chord Roll No. 2

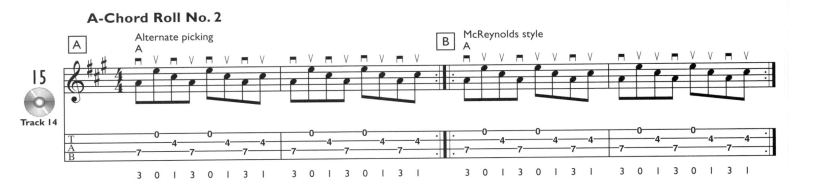

Here is a crosspicking tune based on the bluegrass standard "Lonesome Road Blues," also known as "Goin' Down the Road Feelin' Bad." This version is set in the key of A Major, and uses many chord shapes up the neck. Watch the fingerings carefully! The picking patterns are shown in the McReynolds style, but you should also try strict alternate picking to see which works better for you. It is a good idea to review the A Major scale on page 105. Chords are indicated above the music. Chord fingerings may also be found on page 105.

🎵 LONG LONESOME ROAD (CROSSPICKING)
Track 15

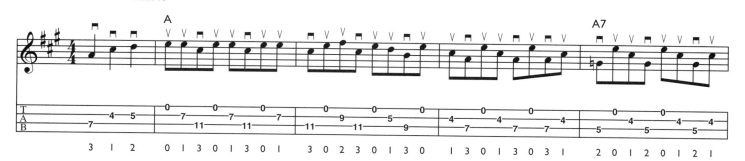

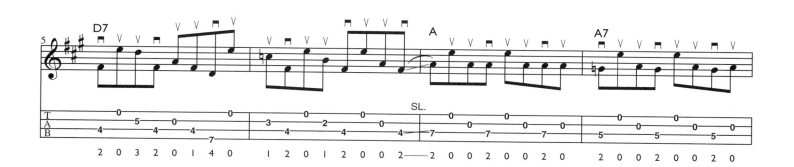

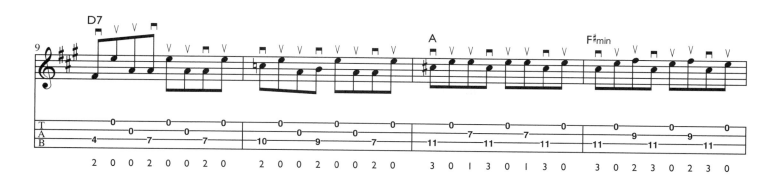

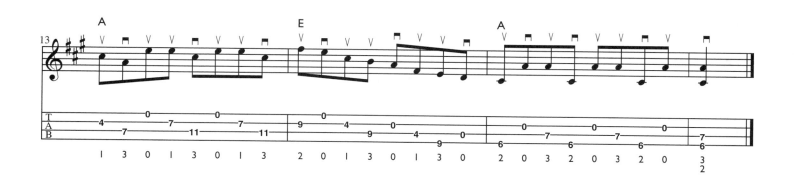

CHAPTER 4

Better Picking Through Fiddle Tunes

This chapter picks up from the fiddle tune techniques and tunes you learned in *Beginning Mandolin*. Because the mandolin's left-hand fingering is so similar to the fiddle, many of the moves and combinations heard in mandolin playing can be found in fiddle tunes. Learning fiddle tunes also builds a repertoire of music you can play at jams, parties, contests and gigs. The more tunes you learn, the faster you will be able to pick up new tunes on the fly.

The tunes in this chapter were chosen to illustrate moves and licks that come up in many tunes and solos. These licks are like *modules* that turn up in tune after tune. While there are hundreds of these modules in the tunes of the old-time, bluegrass and Celtic (British Isles) traditions, this chapter will introduce you to a very useful "starter set." These tunes are mostly from the Appalachian old-time tradition, but some come from the Celtic repertoire, and most cross over into bluegrass.

LESSON 1: HOW TO LEARN FOLK MUSIC

The music in this chapter is based on several folk music traditions. Folk music is considered an "oral tradition." This means that the method of learning was traditionally from the mouth of one person to the ears of another. With musical instruments, a better term might be an "aural tradition." In the days before mass media (most of the days of human history, in fact) an aspiring musician would sit at the feet of an elder player, watching and listening with the focus of a dog on a tennis ball, then run home and try to do the same thing.

Even now, there is no teacher of folk music like observing and playing music with other people who have mastered an instrument or style. There are nuances of sound and touch that are different from region to region, county to county and person to person. You will add your own stamp to the tradition when you play music with others.

HOW TO LEARN TUNES THE WRONG WAY

When you read music in a book, your instinct will be to try to play the whole tune, to "find out what happens next." As you reach a certain level of proficiency, you can indeed do this.

However, beginners often find that after they work on a tune long enough to figure it out, they are then "stuck" to the book. In other words, they have become proficient at reading the tune from the book, instead of playing the tune. When they encounter variations on the tune from other players, it can be confusing and frustrating. Remember, folk music and improvisational music like blues and jazz are fluid, living traditions. Everybody has a different version of a tune, but most of them will fit together one way or another!

HOW TO LEARN TUNES THE RIGHT WAY

Think about the goal of learning a tune: It may be to play with others, or just to have a new tune to play yourself. The important thing is to memorize the tune. You don't want to be dependent on your music books in a jam session. Folk music requires you to be flexible, quick to adapt and above all to have fun! If you know one or two tunes really well, you will have more fun than halfway knowing 20. As you go along, you may be able to pick up new songs by just hearing them. This is because you can hear the similarities and differences between the new tunes and those you already know.

Learn in Small Blocks and Get Away from the Written Music as Soon as Possible!
To take full advantage of the limited time you have to practice, try this technique when learning folk music:

1. **Get a general picture of the tune.** Look through the music to get an idea of the basic "shape" of the melody, as well as the structure of the tune. If you can, listen to the tune several times, both while looking at the music and without the music. Try to hum or sing along. The more the melody gets in your ear through singing, the easier it will be to know if you are playing it right. Old-timers call this process "setting the tune in your head."

2. **Work on just a small block of information at a time.** This may be as small as one move or one beat, or as much as a bar or phrase. Most folk music is made up of tiny melodic ideas and moves. Many of these little blocks or modules occur over and over again as you learn new songs. They just combine and recombine in different ways like atoms and molecules. Be aware that as you learn one tune, some of the same moves may appear in many other tunes. The hard work you do now will pay off tenfold!

3. **Start memorizing right away.** Play your tiny block over and over (and over and over) without looking at the music. Check back occasionally to make sure you've got it right, but then go back to playing it from memory.

4. **Work on the next block.** When you have it down, go back and attach it to the first block to make a bigger block. Think of those little plastic blocks kids play with: two small blocks stick together to make one big one. Pretty soon the kid's built a space city with a working monorail and sustainable power grid. And all you want to do is to play a 16-bar fiddle tune!

5. **Go back and play your old tunes often!** This is called *repertoire building*. You need to build your collection of tunes, then make sure they stay dusted off and road-worthy. You never know when you might need to jam "Cripple Creek" one more time.

This process may seem slow, but actually it is the fastest way to learn a tune. If you learn just one or two bars of music a day, you can learn a new tune every week. One year and you've got fifty tunes by heart (or five tunes on ten instruments, you pickin' fool, you), with two weeks off for summer bluegrass festivals.

GET OUT AND PLAY

Folk music is meant to be shared, like conversation, food and love. Don't be afraid to get out and play. Just pay attention to what other people are doing and try to match them, even if it's only for one session. Every tradition deserves respect. Good luck and remember to have fun!

LESSON 2: CUT TIME

In *Beginning Mandolin*, the fiddle tunes and bluegrass songs were written in $\frac{4}{4}$ time, counting four quarter notes to every measure. This is a good way to count when you are practicing slowly to learn a tune. When you get the tune up to speed, however, you may find that counting every beat will just wear out your foot from tapping, and may even slow you down.

Most old-time, Celtic, and bluegrass music is actually set in *cut time*. Cut time looks just like $\frac{4}{4}$ on the page except for the inclusion of the symbol for cut time (¢), but instead of tapping and counting all four beats, you tap on the half notes (every two beats). In other words, you have "cut" $\frac{4}{4}$ into $\frac{2}{2}$ (two half notes per measure). Here's what it looks like to your foot:

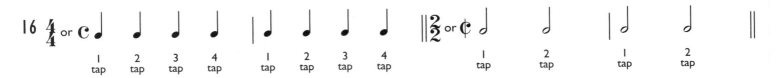

The fiddle tunes in this book will be shown in cut time. As you start learning them, you may want to count and tap all four beats at a slow speed. Then, as you speed up, just cut your number of foot taps in half.

MODULE NO. 1: THE "FIRE ON THE MOUNTAIN" LICK

This chapter will introduce you to many moves that are used to make up fiddle tunes and improvise *breaks* (solos). These moves do not actually have names or numbers, nor do they originate with any particular tune. The names and numbers given are just to help you as memory aids.

Here is a move that shows up in dozens of tunes, and gets a real workout in "Fire on the Mountain." This tune uses the lick in two keys, A Major and D Major. You may want to review these scales on pages 104 and 105. Try each of these variations on the move.

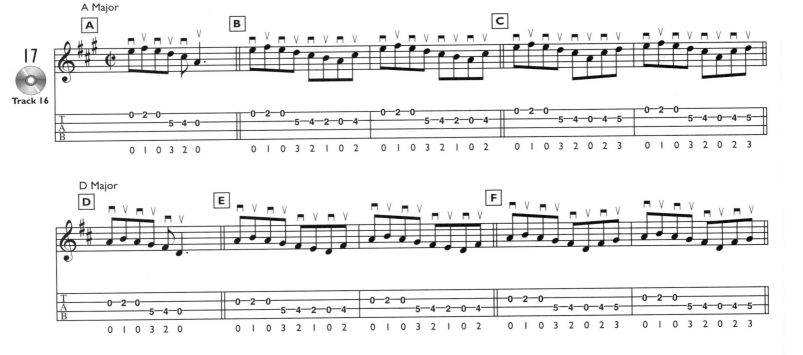

Now try the whole tune. Chords are indicated above the music, and fingerings may be found on page 105. You can find great versions of this tune from many bands, including Bill Monroe, the Stanley Brothers, the Highwoods String Band and others. The title is very common, however, and sometimes refers to other tunes or variants. Tracking down tunes is part of the fun of being a musician!

Many tunes you will learn have an A part and a B part that are equal in length, with each part repeated before moving on. This tune has a little extra part that extends the end of the B part (shown as the 2nd ending of the B part). Old-timers call tunes that have unequal A and B parts, extra beats, or unusual phrasing "crooked" or "uneven."

FIRE ON THE MOUNTAIN

Track 17

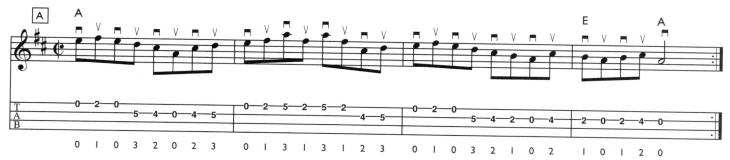

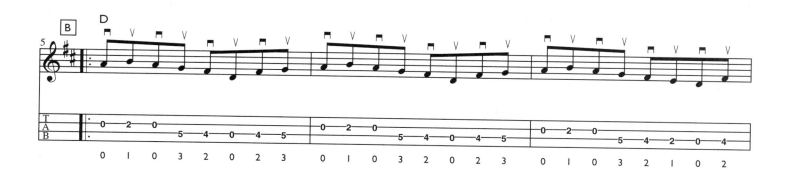

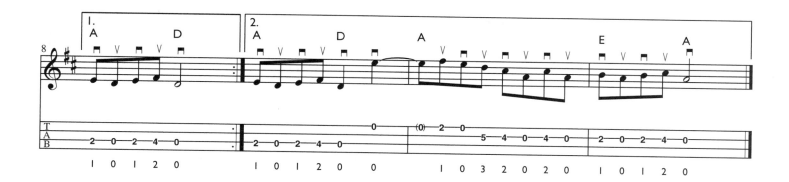

Sally Goodin was one of the first "hillbilly" songs recorded in the early 20th century. The performer was fiddler "Eck" Robertson, and his version represented what is known as *contest style*. In the contest style, a musician takes a traditional tune, often a hoedown or square dance tune, and creates many variations on the basic melody to demonstrate skill and virtuosity. Robertson's 1922 recording was so influential that musicians have been basing their versions on his variations ever since.

Part of the character of this tune is the way a few notes of the A Major scale (page 105) are used on the 2nd string at the start of the tune. In this version, based on "Eck" Robertson's, you get to combine and recombine ways of playing the A, B and C♯ notes in the open position of the 2nd string. You should work these out four notes (one big beat) at a time, then begin to string them together.

Here's "Sally Goodin" in a standard, two-part form. This is the basic tune upon which variations are built. Notice that in the 2nd and 3rd bar of the B part, the "Fire on the Mountain" lick from Lesson 2 makes an appearance. Chords are indicated above the music and fingerings may be found on page 105.

SALLY GOODIN (STANDARD TWO-PART VERSION)
Track 18

On the next page are four variations that are used in contest versions of the tune. They sound good played in this order, but they can be shuffled around or recombined with the original A and B part of the tune. These variations are adapted from the fiddling of "Eck" Robertson, Kenny Baker, Ricky Skaggs and the mandolin of Bill Monroe.

Note that each variation should be repeated, and Variation No. 4 is twice as long as the others. Take it slow and steady. You'll be able to use the moves from this tune in lots of other solos and tunes soon!

SALLY GOODIN VARIATION NO. 1

Track 19

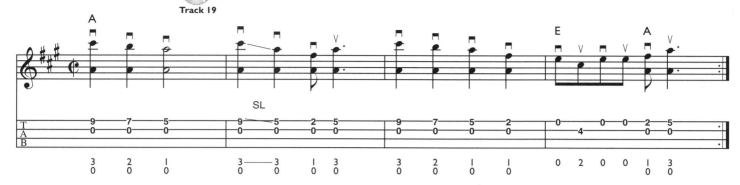

SALLY GOODIN VARIATION NO. 2

Track 20

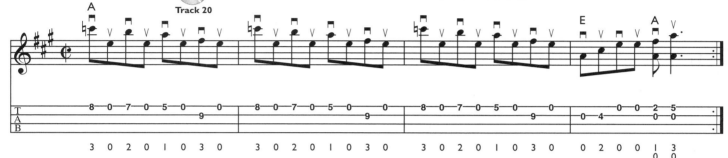

SALLY GOODIN VARIATION NO. 3

Track 21

SALLY GOODIN VARIATION NO. 4

Track 22

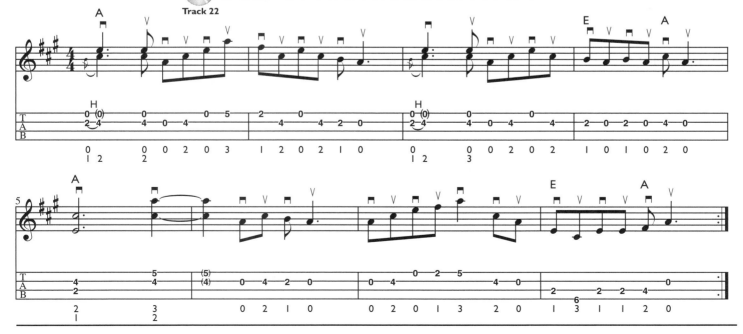

The last two lessons have mostly been in the key of A Major. "Kitchen Gal" on page 125 falls into the category of *modal tunes*, which are tunes that incorporate scales other than the major scale, often with a minor sound. Modal tunes generally have in common the lowered 3rd ($\flat$3) and lowered 7th ($\flat$7) scale degrees, but may have other variations to the scale as well.

"Kitchen Gal" uses two scales to make up its modal sound:

> A *Mixolydian mode*—Major scale with a $\flat$7, or G$\natural$ instead of G$\sharp$ in the key of A.
>
> A *Dorian mode*—Very much like a natural minor scale ($\flat$3, $\flat$6, $\flat$7, see page 71) except 6 is not lowered, leaving a $\flat$**3 and** $\flat$**7**, or C and G in the key of A. Here are the two scales.

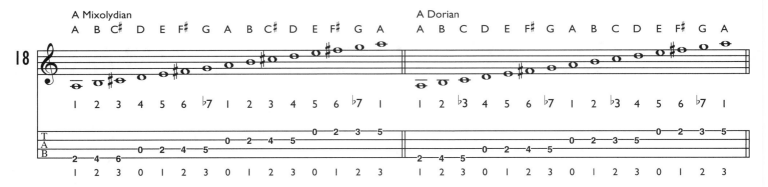

MODULE NO. 2 —THE SYNCOPATED FIDDLE SHUFFLE RHYTHM

On page 41, you learned a basic picking rhythm based on the *shuffle* bowing pattern used by fiddlers. Here is that rhythm shown on an open E-note, followed by a new syncopated (emphasis shifted to the offbeats) variation you can use to jazz up your picking.

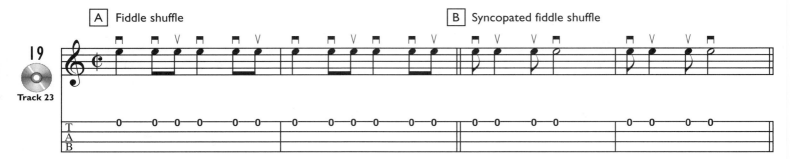

MODULE NO. 3 — THE "KITCHEN GAL" ENDING LICK

At the end of the B part of "Kitchen Gal," there is a small lick using part of the A Dorian scale. This lick turns up in variations in many modal, minor and Irish tunes. You will even see it later in this chapter in the key of G Major!

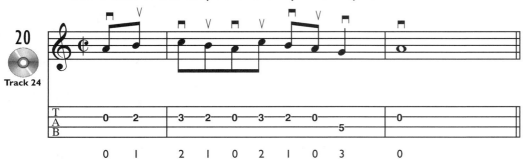

Now try "Kitchen Gal." Chords are indicated above the music and fingerings may be found on page 105. You will see several variants of the "Fire on the Mountain" lick, a syncopated fiddle shuffle and the A Dorian lick you just learned. Note that the A part is in A Mixolydian (using major A, G and E chords), while the B part is in A Dorian (using A Minor, G Major and E minor chords). This version is inspired by the fiddle of Alan Jabbour and the mandolin of Bertram Levy, both of the Hollow Rock String Band.

KITCHEN GAL

Track 25

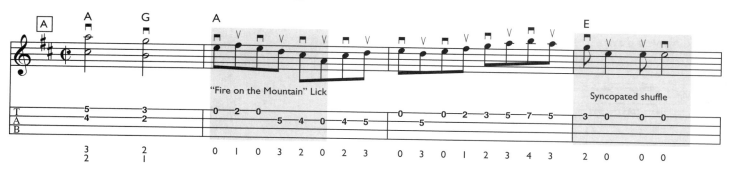

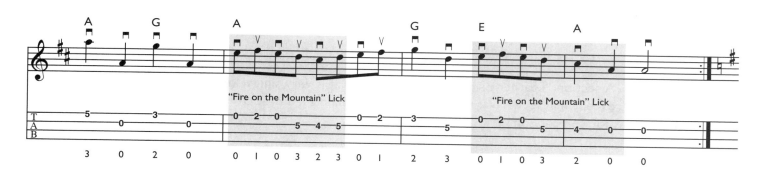

"Leather Britches" is another hoedown/square-dance/contest tune that has a minimalism and drive reminiscent of "Sally Goodin." It is in the key of G Major (page 104), allowing you to adapt some of what you have learned in A Major to this key. "Leather Britches" is thought to have descended from a Celtic tune called "Lord MacDonald's Reel," which does share many melodic passages in common with this tune.

"Leather Britches" has buried within it a couple of the moves you have already learned. For example, at the end of the first line, you will see a version of the "Fire on the Mountain" lick, moved down to the 3rd and 4th strings for the key of G.

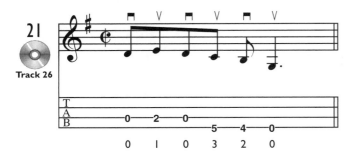

At the end of the A section, "Leather Britches" uses a move that is very similar to the end of "Kitchen Gal," except that it resolves to the key of G Major instead of A Dorian. Here are both passages for comparison.

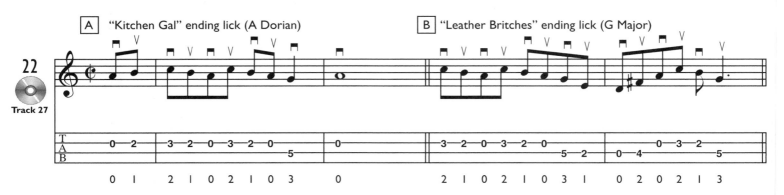

Now try the full "Leather Britches" on page 127. Chords are indicated above the music and fingerings may be found on page 105. Note that the B part is only half as long as the A part. Also included is a variation on the A part in a higher octave. If you use this variation, you should still follow it with the regular B part. This is indicated in the music with *D.S. al Fine* (*Del Segno al Fine*), which means "return to the sign 𝄋 and play until the *Fine*." Ordinarily, we would ignore repeat signs after having returned to the 𝄋 sign, but in this case one *should* take all of the repeats.

This version of "Leather Britches" is influenced by the fiddling of Vassar Clements.

LEATHER BRITCHES

Track 28

Here's another tune in the key of G Major that will give you a break from the steady eighth notes you've been picking. "Seneca Square Dance" is another tune with many possible titles and relatives, including "Waiting on the Federals," "Georgia Boys," "Shoot That Turkey Buzzard" and "Davy Dugger," to name a few!

MODULE NO. 4 — THE SENECA SQUARE-DANCE-ENDING LICK

This lick appears at the end of both parts of this version of the tune. It also appears (moved one string higher) in many D Major tunes, including Lesson 7's "Johnny Don't Get Drunk." It provides a nice way to wrap up a phrase in a major key.

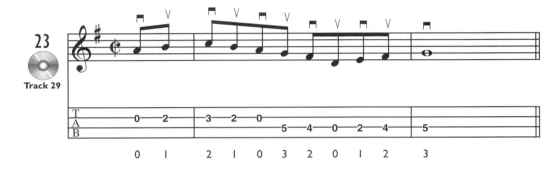

23

Track 29

PHOTO•MARK CARBONELL/COURTESY OF SCOTT O'MALLEY & ASSOCIATES

Norman Blake *is famous for his proficiency on a variety of stringed instruments, including mandolin and acoustic guitar. He was one of the major bluegrass musicians of the 1970s, coming into prominence in the late 1960s, when he began appearing as a sideman with artists as diverse as June Carter and Bob Dylan. During the 1970s, he began a solo career that quickly became one of the most important and musically adventurous in the bluegrass style.*

Now try the whole tune. Chords are indicated above the music and fingerings may be found on page 105. You will get a chance to use the ending lick from page 128 and the syncopated fiddle shuffle rhythm (page 124) a couple of times in the B part. This tune has a march-like sound that doesn't need to go too fast. This version is inspired by the 1927 recording by Fiddlin' Dave Neal, as well as John Hartford and Knoxville, Tennessee fiddler Tim Worman.

SENECA SQUARE DANCE

Track 30

LESSON 7: "JOHNNY DON'T GET DRUNK"

This tune is in the key of D Major (page 104) but uses some moves from other tunes. The first one is Module No. 4 from "Seneca Square Dance." In "Johnny Don't Get Drunk," the lick is moved up one string for the key of D Major. Here are both versions.

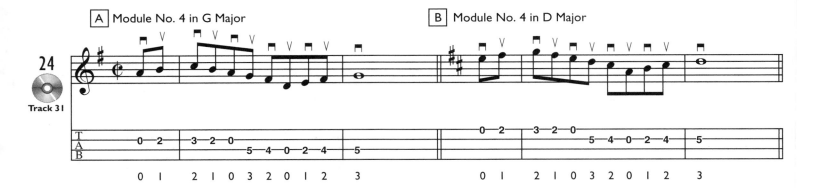

MODULE NO. 5 — THE I-V-I CADENCE LICK

A cadence is a melodic or harmonic statement at the end of a musical phrase which helps state the key of the tune. This little move first outlines the I chord of D Major (D), then the V chord (A) and then returns to I. The movement happens so quickly that it is often only heard in the melody and not in the accompanying chords. This is a good finger combination to work on for your fretting hand, and will also challenge your picking hand to move between strings on alternate strokes. If you look closely back at "Turkey in the Straw" on page 115, you will see this move transposed to G at the end of the A and B parts.

Here's the lick shown in D Major in both the high and low octaves.

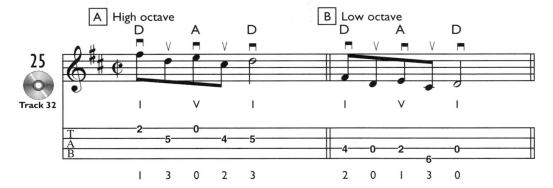

Now try the whole tune. Watch for syncopated rhythms and observe the picking indications. Chords are indicated above the music and chord fingerings may be found on page 105.

Track 33

JOHNNY DON'T GET DRUNK

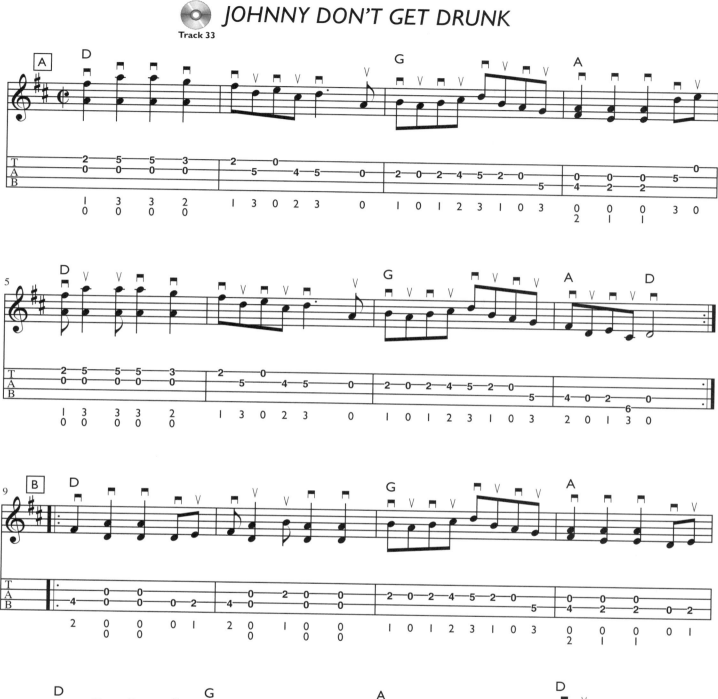

Ragtime tunes (called *rags*) are extremely fun to play on the mandolin. The classic ragtime instrument in the late 19th and early 20th century was the piano. Many piano tunes were adapted to string instruments, and new tunes were also composed by string players. Rags are characterized by very syncopated phrasing, more sophisticated harmony and multiple sections. The sharp attack of the mandolin string recalls the percussive sound of the piano, and makes the mandolin a perfect instrument for this music.

To get ready for this tune, review the C Major scale on page 104.

SWING 8THS—REVIEW

You learned about *Swing 8ths* on page 55. Many rags use the swing feel. To review, the underlying pulse of swing is a triplet feel. To get the feel of triplets, say this aloud to a steady beat: "trip-pul-let, trip-pul-let."

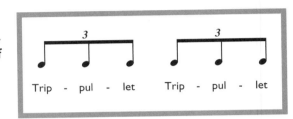

The *Swing 8ths* feel can be illustrated as a triplet with the first two notes tied together. In *Swing 8ths*, "1" is the first note of the triplet and the "&" is the last. In example 26, the *Swing 8ths* feel is shown in triplets and in regular eighth notes with the designation "*Swing 8ths.*" These two notations produce an identical rhythm.

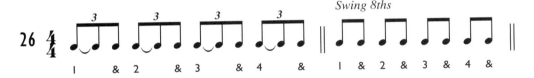

MODULE NO. 6 — PICKING IN GROUPS OF THREE

The highly syncopated sound of ragtime is often a result of the grouping of notes in threes. These are not triplets, but instead normal eighth notes that are phrased in groups of threes. These phrases will challenge you to watch your alternate picking, as one group begins "down-up-down" and the next begins "up-down-up." Try the licks in example 27. They will reappear with harmony notes in the following tune.

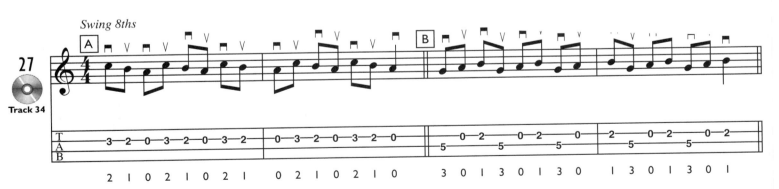

Track 34

Here's a new tune written in the ragtime style. It pays tribute to the two most important influences on the construction of the modern American mandolin, Orville Gibson and Lloyd Loar. Most rags have three or more parts. This one is in two parts, but it includes a repeat of the A part at the end. This is designated by the marking *D.C. al Fine* (Da Capo al Fine), which means to repeat from the top until you reach the point marked *Fine* (Italian for "song's over, clap now"). Chords are indicated above the music and chord fingerings may be found on page 105.

ORVILLE AND LLOYD'S RAG

Track 35

Swing 8ths

WORKING IN A COMPOUND METER

In this lesson you will cross the ocean to Ireland (unless you are already there) to explore the playing of *jigs*. A jig is a lively dance often based on a *compound meter*. The other tunes you have learned so far (except for a couple of short exercises on page 107) are in simple meters, where each beat is divided into two equal eighth notes. In a compound meter, the beat is divided into three equal eighth notes. The time signatures for compound meters usually have an 8 on the bottom. The top number, usually either a 6, 9 or 12, can be divided by 3 to produce the number of pulses (foot taps) in the measure.

The most common time signature for jigs is ⁶⁄₈. This time signature tells us that there are six eighth notes in every bar. Six divided by three gives us two big beats in each measure, with the dotted quarter note equaling one beat. In other words, ⁶⁄₈ is actually felt as two groups of three. You can count it either as "1–2–3–4–5–6," or more accurately, "1–&–ah, 2–&–ah." Try this counting and tapping exercise to get the idea. Stomp your foot loudly to make sure you get the feel of the two big beats that divide up the six small beats.

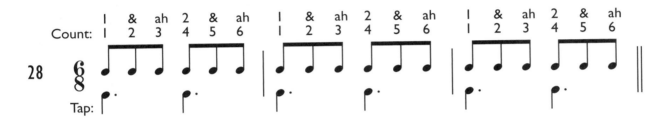

You may have realized by now that your pick can only move two directions (down and up, that is) and your beat now has three parts. How will you resolve this perplexing conundrum? Well, you could venture high into the Himalayas to seek the advice of a charming-yet-weatherbeaten guru, or you could try one of the following solutions.

⁶⁄₈ PICKING SOLUTION NO. 1 (DOWN-UP-DOWN, DOWN-UP-DOWN)

This pattern is favored by the largest number of picked instrument players who play Celtic music. It allows you to feel the accent pattern of the two big beats, and brings that *accent* (louder note) pattern out in your tone naturally. It also makes it easy to transfer the technique to *slip jigs* in ⁹⁄₈. It takes a bit of practice to get the move going and keep the tempo even, so work slowly and be patient. Try this exercise on any open string.

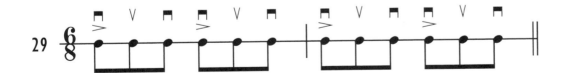

> = *Accent (Play louder)*

⁶⁄₈ PICKING SOLUTION NO. 2 (STRICT ALTERNATE PICKING)

This option adapts strict alternate picking (down-up-down-up-down-up) to the accent pattern felt in ⁶⁄₈ time. To practice it, you need to accent the downstroke on the first eighth note, and the upstroke on the 4th eighth note. Try this pattern on any open string.

The disadvantage of this pattern is that you have to keep the ⁶⁄₈ accent pattern in your head as it shifts under your picking. However, this pattern has the advantage of being consistent with the way you already play. It also has no limitations of speed, while the first pattern may reach its maximum velocity fairly quickly since it requires two consecutive downstrokes.

WHICH PICKING SOLUTION DO I USE?

In order to stay consistent with most mandolin teaching and materials, the remaining examples will be written using Pattern No. 1 (down-up-down, down-up-down). You could easily adapt the examples to alternate picking until you decide which is right for you.

RHYTHM PLAYING FOR JIGS

The simplest rhythm pattern is similar to the "boom, chick" beat heard in bluegrass.

Jig Strum Pattern No. 1

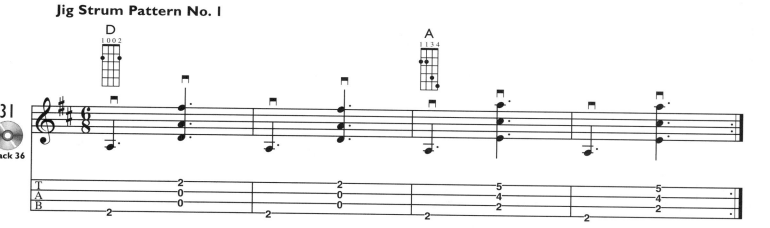

The next pattern uses constant eighth notes to create an insistent, galloping feel. Be sure to exaggerate the accents so that you can hear the compound meter clearly. Since all strings are strummed, no TAB is needed. Use the D and A chord fingerings shown in example 31.

Jig Strum Pattern No. 2

Here is a full-length jig to try in the key of D Major (page 104). As usual, you should work on this one bar, or even one beat at a time. This jig includes several arpeggios on D and A chords, which appear in many other tunes. It also ends each section on a G chord, which pulls you along to the next section, making you want to play it over again! Chords symbols are provided so that you can also practice your strumming. Use one of the strum patterns from page 135 (chord fingerings are shown on page 105).

MONEY IN BOTH POCKETS

Track 38

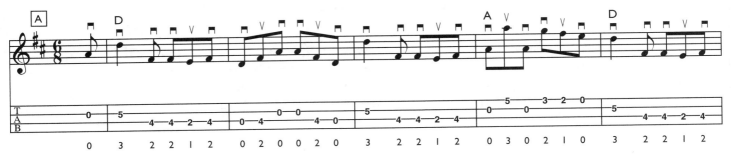

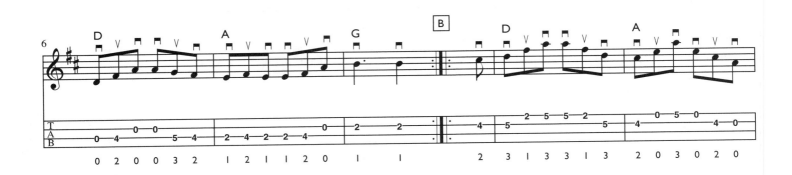

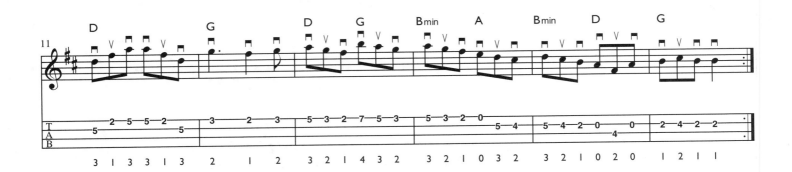

Here's another jig, this time in A Dorian (page 124). This jig has an addictive drive and a dark, bluesy sound. Musicians will often group tunes together into medleys. "D" tunes, for example, flow nicely into A Minor/modal tunes. "Scatter the Mud," for example, would make a good medley when preceded by "Money in Both Pockets." This version is inspired by the fiddling of Kevin Burke. Chords are indicated above the music and chord fingerings may be found on page 105.

SCATTER THE MUD

Track 39

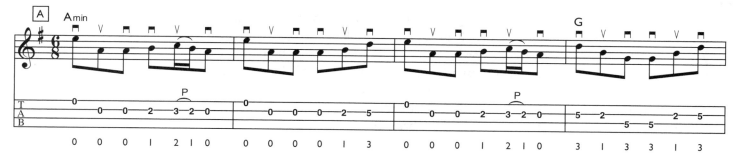

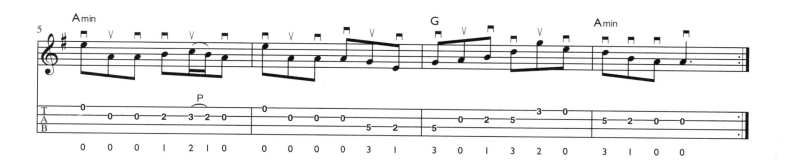

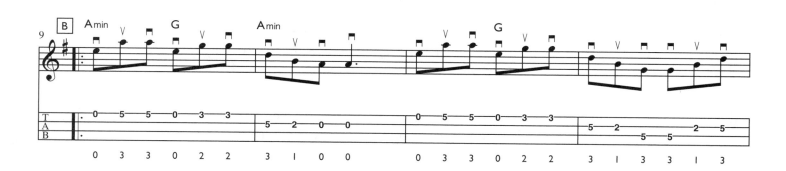

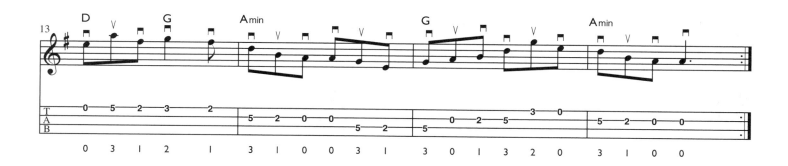

CHAPTER 5

Back to Bluegrass

LESSON 1: IMPROVING RHYTHM PLAYING

RETURN OF THE CHOP

On page 62, you learned some basic bluegrass strumming built around the chop. The chop is the rhythmic backbone of bluegrass mandolin. Using moveable chords (with no open strings), you strum a backbeat rhythm—chopping on beats 2 and 4. Your left-hand fingers control the percussive effect by relaxing pressure just after (or sometimes during) the downstroke of the pick. Keep your right-hand and wrist loose and drop the weight of your hand across the strings with a flick of the wrist. If your wrist is tight or you try to use a "cranking" motion, your chop will sound stiff and harsh. Here's a review of the basic chop strum.

BASIC CHOP STRUM

Sometimes, you will want to very simply chop on beats 2 and 4 as shown above. If there is a bass player playing on beats 1 and 3, you will be able to "lock together" into a great groove. In order to feel the bluegrass groove better, many mandolinists will add a quiet downstroke on the 4th string on beats 1 and 3. This creates the "boom-chick-boom-chick" rhythm familiar in this kind of music. Here's the trick: play the "boom" note softly on beat 1 or 3, and hold your hand on the chord until you've "chopped" it on beat 2 or 4.

You can also add upstrokes to your strum. Now that your hand is moving in a steady beat throughout the measure, you can throw in an upstroke every now and then to syncopate the rhythm, making it move more. Try the pattern in example 34. The fingerings shown are typical of Bill Monroe's rhythm playing.

ADVANCED CHOP STRUM

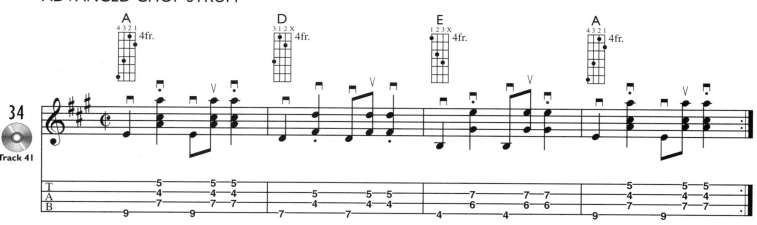

Here is a traditional song that will be used as the basis for this chapter. It was first recorded in 1927 by Dykes Magic City Trio, and has been a favorite ever since. The melody and structure are very close to many other bluegrass standards, especially "Rollin' In My Sweet Baby's Arms." "Free Little Bird" is originally in G Major, but has been set here in the key of A Major. Learn the melody and words, and for rhythm use the advanced chop strum with the chord fingerings from example 34 on page 138.

The performance on the recording for this book includes a vocal performance of the song with an accompaniment.

FREE LITTLE BIRD
Track 42

In bluegrass, there are three basic roles that an instrumentalist may play at any given point in the song.

- **Lead**: Playing a solo break or you are the featured melody instrument.
- **Backup, or Rhythm**: Playing chords as part of the rhythm section.
- **Lead Backup**: This is an in-between state, where you are playing a more active form of backup that may include chords, tremolo and melodic fills around the vocal part or another soloist.

FILLS

A *fill* is a short melodic idea or lick that occurs during a space in the vocal part or instrumental melody. Playing fills is not like playing a full solo break. You must listen carefully to what is happening, so that your fills add spice to the main melody, without playing all over it. Fills occur when a vocal note is held at the end of a phrase, or during empty spaces in the phrasing.

Fills are generally improvised using blues licks, ideas from fiddle tunes and anything else you can think of. The more melodies you learn, the more you have to draw from to create fills and solos. Rhythmically, a fill will very often lead to a strong *chord tone* (a root, 3rd or 5th of the chord being played) on the downbeat (beat 1) of the upcoming bar. Think of a drum fill in rock or jazz—the drummer improvises something exciting in the last bar of a phrase, and punctuates it with a cymbal crash on the first beat of the new phrase.

Here is a sample lead backup arrangement of "Free Little Bird." Above the mandolin music and TAB are the melody and lyrics from page 139. This will help you see how the lead backup part sits under, and then fills the spaces in the melody. On the CD that is available for this book, you will hear this lead backup along with a vocal performance and simple backup. The second time through is just the vocal and simple backup so that you can create and practice playing your own lead backup part.

FREE LITTLE BIRD—LEAD BACKUP

Track 43

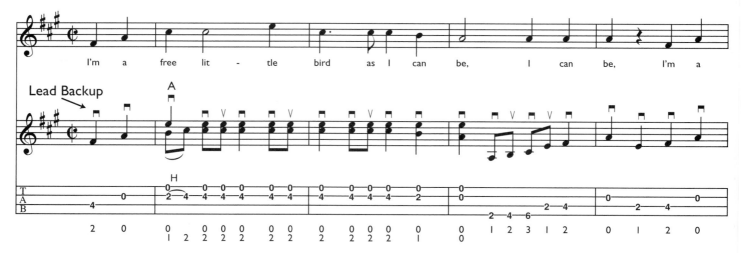

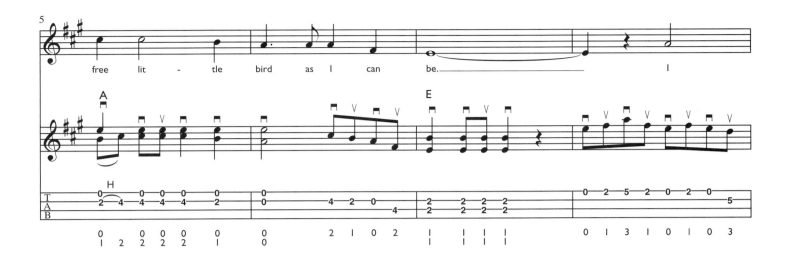

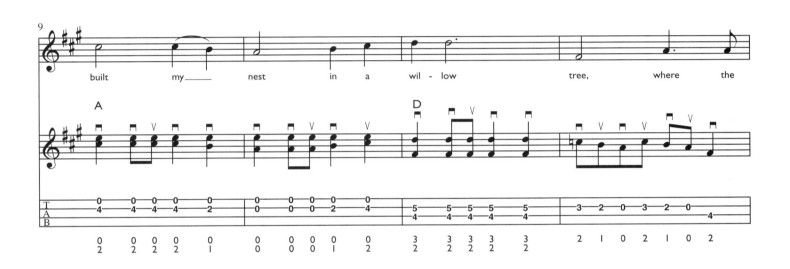

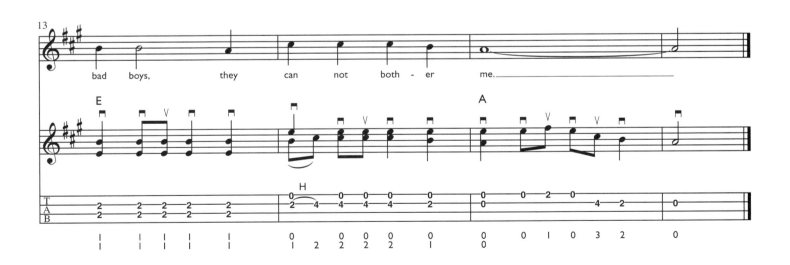

Bluegrass *breaks* (solos) are usually played over the verse and/or chorus of the tune itself. This allows you to take a couple of different approaches. On any given tune, you could play a *melodic break* or an *improvised break*.

> A **melodic break** is based on the melody of the song. This may be the vocal melody or, in the case of an instrumental, the main tune.

> An **improvised break** is based on the chord progression, but does not have to stick to the original melody. Lesson 4 (page 144) will cover improvised breaks.

TIPS FOR CONSTRUCTING MELODIC BREAKS

1. Learn a simple version of the melody of the song. This will give you a basic "skeleton" for your break. You can "flesh it out" with passing tones (page 39) between the main melody notes, and with harmony notes and fills.

2. Try imitating the voice with your mandolin. Sing the melody yourself, or work with a singer, and try to duplicate the rhythmic and melodic nuances you hear. This skill takes time to develop, so listen hard and be patient.

3. Though the melodic break is based on the melody, there are plenty of opportunities to improvise. You could syncopate rhythms, add blue notes (page 57) from the blues scale (♭3, ♭5 and ♭7, see fingering below), or improvise different passing tones.

4. Improvise or compose! Using the above tips, you can make up a new version of the melody on the spot. On the other hand, it is perfectly fine to work out specific breaks and practice them ahead of time so that you know what you're going to do when the man in the white hat turns around and says "Take it!"

Here is the A Blues scale. It incorporates the A Major scale (page 105) and the blue notes discussed above.

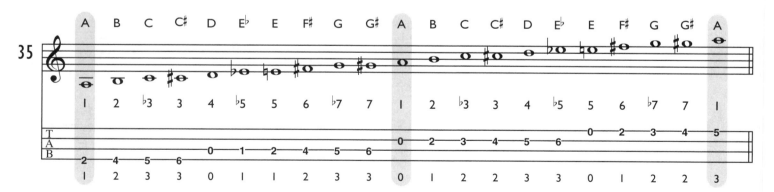

Here is a melodic break for "Free Little Bird." It incorporates hammer-ons, a unison slide (page 113), fiddle tune-style licks, tremolo (see page 110) and passing tones. There are also some blue notes. Remember the goal of a melodic break: even with all of the interesting things going on, you should still be able to hear the shape and structure of the main melody. It is as if the mandolin were "singing" the words of the song. On the recording for this book, you will hear the break with chords, then the chord progression will repeat so you can try your own break.

FREE LITTLE BIRD—MELODIC BREAK
Track 44

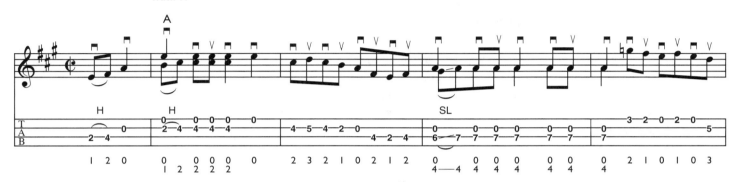

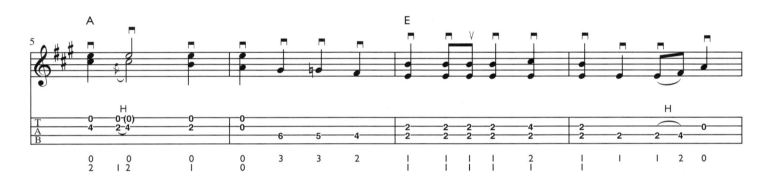

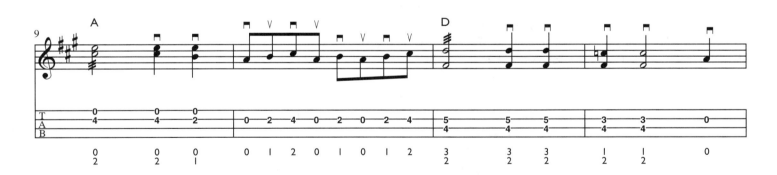

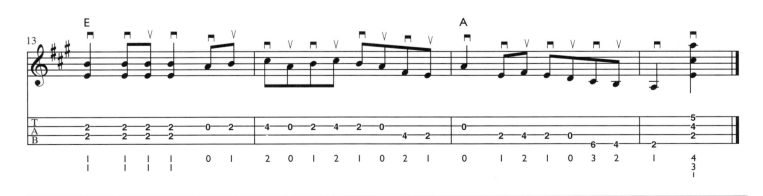

In an improvised break, you have total freedom to create new melodies and rhythmic ideas over the main chord progression. They can relate to the original melody, or go into whole new places. Insofar as improvised breaks are concerned, bluegrass is closely related to the blues and jazz traditions, where solos are an opportunity for the player to create something new on the spot that follows the chord progression the other musicians are playing.

TIPS FOR CREATING IMPROVISED BREAKS

- Use what you know. Every fiddle tune, folk song, bluegrass melody, or blues lick you have ever learned is available as inspiration for a break.

- Don't blow it all at once! Try using just a small number of ideas in your break. They can be repeated or altered through slight variations. This will help give your break a sense of tunefulness and structure, whereas just running unrelated scales and licks would likely not create a coherent solo. This will also help give each of your breaks for different songs their own identity and character.

- Experiment. Try new things all the time. If they don't work, find your way to something that will. This will lead you to sounds you never thought of that might be brilliant!

HOW TO MAKE THE MOST OUT OF A LITTLE

Here are some tips for "working" your ideas and licks to get the most out of them.

- **"Steal" the structure of the original melody.** One way to structure a break (or a phrase in a break) is to model it on the phrase lengths or rhythms of the original melody. In the following improvised break for "Free Little Bird" on page 145, the first two phrases (bars 1–8) mimic the original melody in that they start with the same basic notes, although they finish differently.

- **Reuse, recycle, renew!** While this is a sensible environmental policy, it's also a great musical policy. Try repeating a small two- or four-beat lick several times as the chords change in your break. You could repeat a lick two or three times and change how it ends the last time, or vary it as you go. Borrow licks from other tunes and sources. In the break on page 145, the third phrase (bars 9–12) borrows a melodic pattern you learned in the key of C Major for "Orville and Lloyd's Rag" (pages 132–133).

- **Patterns and sequences.** As mentioned above, the third phrase of the following example uses a rag-style lick on the A chord. It then repeats the lick one string lower on the D chord. The lick is used as a pattern that can be moved from chord to chord.

  Another way to use a pattern is as a sequence. In a sequence, a melodic idea is played, then its structure is duplicated starting on a different scale note (usually the adjacent note up or down). The sequencing can continue (up or down) for as long as you want. A great source for understanding sequences is the music of the Baroque master, Johann Sebastian Bach (1685–1750). An example of sequencing appears in bars 13–14 of the break on page 145.

Here is an improvised break for "Free Little Bird." On the recording for this book, you will hear this break first, then you will hear just the chords so that you can practice your own breaks.

FREE LITTLE BIRD—IMPROVISED BREAK

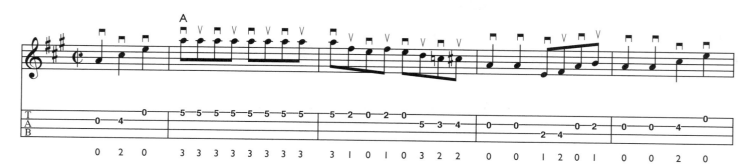

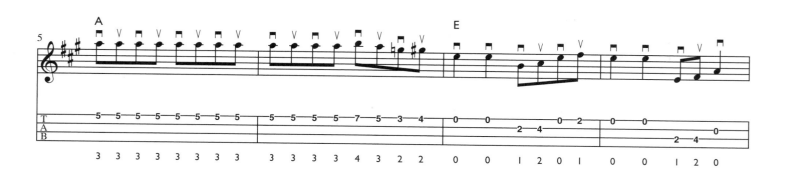

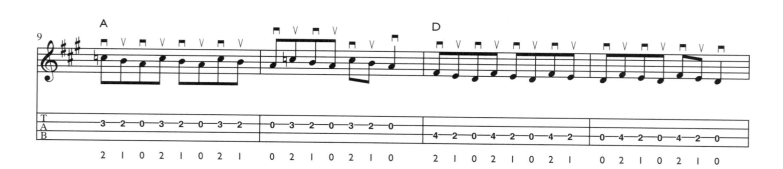

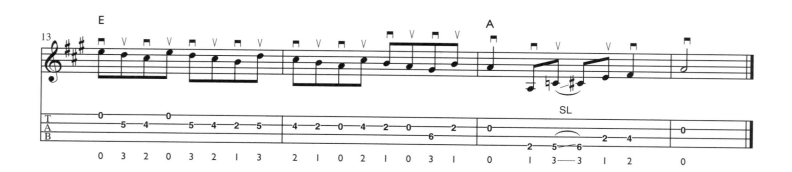

CHAPTER 6

Working Up the Neck

LESSON 1: MOVEABLE MAJOR SCALES

Whether you play bluegrass, jazz or rock, at some point you're going to want to play in something other than the easy open keys of G, D, A and C. The first step to playing in new keys is to learn how to play major scales that can be moved to any point on the neck (using no open strings).

As you learned on page 81, the major scale is the foundation of the language of music theory. It is the "default setting" or "home base" for the basic scale degrees of 1, 2, 3, 4, 5, 6 and 7. You will play many other scales and structures, but they will always be explained in terms that relate back to the original major scale structure of "whole step, whole step, half step, whole step, whole step, whole step, half step."

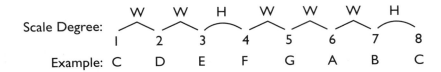

There are four basic fingerings for a one-octave major scale, one beginning on each of the left-hand fingers. This lesson will use the key of C Major to illustrate all four fingerings. While it is easy to play in C Major in an open position, this key is also useful for illustrating positions up the neck. The key of C Major has no sharps or flats, which makes it easy to keep track of the notes you are playing as you learn.

Moveable Major Scale, Start 1—Starting with the 1st Finger
Here is a C Major scale starting with the 1st finger at the 5th fret on the 4th string. This same pattern could also start an octave higher with the 1st finger at the 3rd fret of the 2nd string; the finger pattern would remain the same.

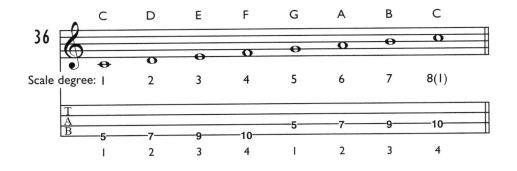

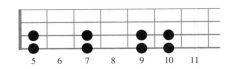

When you learn a new scale or fingering, it is important to spend time playing melodies and improvising within the fingering. This is how you will get to know it well. Here is an example to try using Start 1.

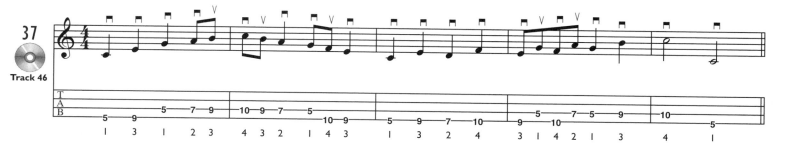

Moveable Major Scale, Start 2—Starting with the 2nd Finger

Here's the fingering for a C Major scale starting with the 2nd finger on the 5th fret of the 4th string. This pattern could also be played an octave higher starting with the 2nd finger on the 3rd fret of the 2nd string.

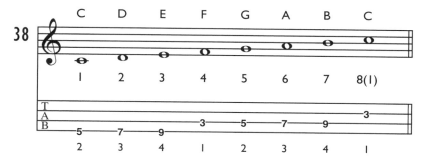

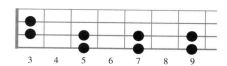

Here's an example to practice this fingering.

Here are the other two fingerings for a moveable major scale. Be sure to spend some time playing melodies and improvising licks in each fingering.

Moveable Major Scale, Start 3—Starting with the 3rd Finger

Here is the C Major scale starting with the 3rd finger on the 5th fret of the 4th string. This fingering could also start an octave higher with the 3rd finger on the 10th fret of the 3rd string.

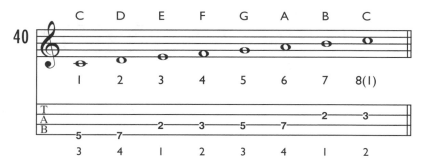
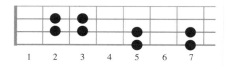

Moveable Major Scale, Start 4—Starting with the 4th Finger

Here is the C Major scale starting with the 4th finger on the 10th fret of the 3rd string.

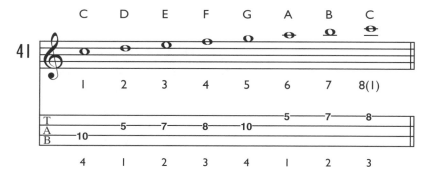
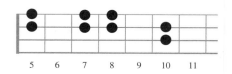

CONNECTING MAJOR SCALE FINGERINGS

Once you are familiar with the four one-octave fingerings, it is easy to string them together across the neck. There is even a formula you can use to remember the connections, just think "starting finger minus one." Here's how it works.

START 4 connects to START 3
START 3 connects to START 2
START 2 connects to START 1
START 1 connects to START 4

Start 4 Connecting to Start 3

Here is a C Major scale starting with the 4th finger on the 17th fret (way up there!) of the 4th string. The second octave begins with the 3rd finger on the 15th fret of the 2nd string. Do you recognize both patterns?

8va = Notes sound one octave higher than written

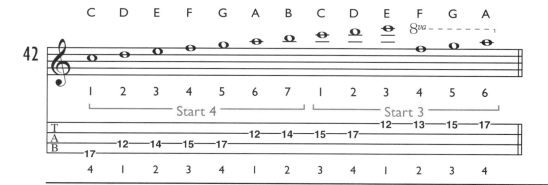
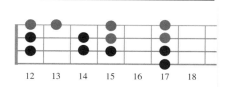

The finger-placement dots are shown in different colors to indicate where one fingering stops and another starts.

Start 3 Connecting to Start 2

This C Major scale starts with the 3rd finger on the 5th fret of the 4th string. The second octave begins with the 2nd finger on the 3rd fret of the 2nd string.

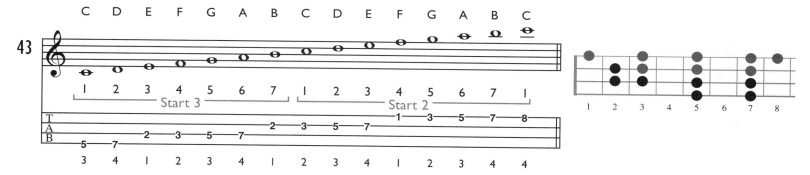

Start 2 Connecting to Start 1

Here is a C Major scale starting with the 2nd finger on the 5th fret of the 4th string. The second octave begins with the 1st finger on the 3rd fret of the 2nd string.

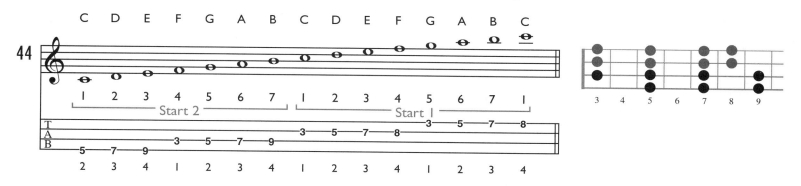

Start 1 Connecting to Start 4

This is a C Major scale starting with the 1st finger on the 5th fret of the 4th string. The second octave begins with the 4th finger on the 10th fret of the 3rd string.

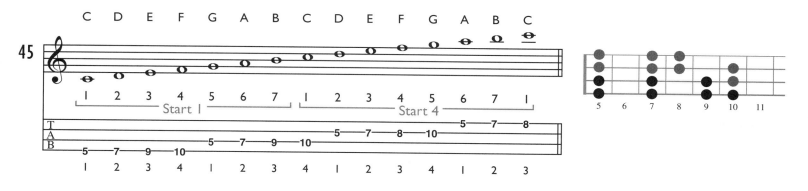

Another Approach: Start 1 Connecting to Start 3

Below is a fingering used very often in bluegrass and blues improvisation. When you reach the end of the first octave, slide your 3rd finger up from the 7th degree to the 1st degree of the next octave. This fingering connects two of the easiest, most agile one-octave fingerings.

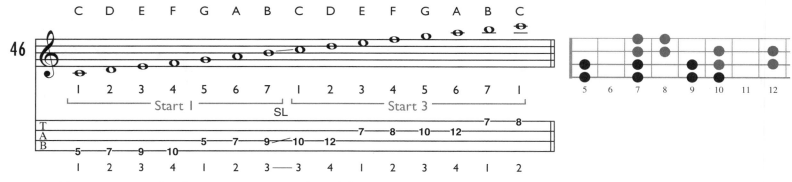

Here is an example of improvisation using Start 1 Connecting to Start 3. The chord progression is set to a bluegrass beat and is inspired by the bluegrass standard, "Nine-Pound Hammer." Chord fingerings may be found on page 105. On the recording that is included with this book, you will hear this example, then the chord progression is repeated so that you can practice improvising with this fingering and all of the other fingerings in this lesson. Watch the left-hand fingerings carefully!

THIS HAMMER'S STILL TOO HEAVY

Track 48

In order to prepare for the following lessons on double stops and arpeggios, it is important to review the chords that are produced using the notes of the major scale.

DIATONIC HARMONY IN MAJOR KEYS

On page 89, you learned about three kinds of triads and how they are used to harmonize the major scale. Triads are chords using three notes: a root, a 3rd (the third scale note above the root) and a 5th (the fifth scale note above the root). The three kinds of triads found in major keys are major, minor and diminished. Below is a C Major scale harmonized in triads. The triads that are formed using the notes of the scale create the *diatonic harmony* for the key. Diatonic means "of the key." Since it is difficult to play the triads as written, sample chord fingerings are shown above so that you can hear the basic sound of the chords.

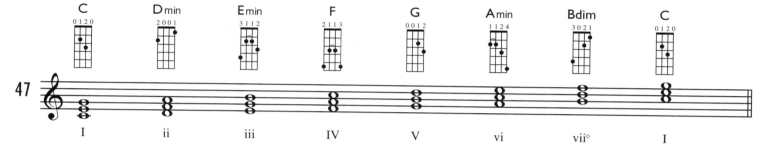

The triads are numbered with Roman numerals based on the scale degrees of the root notes. Upper-case Roman numerals designate major triads; lower-case numerals designate minor and diminished triads. Diminished triads are also marked with a small, open circle (○).

The major chords I, IV and V are considered the primary chords of the key. They impart the basic sound of the key, and are the most common chords in many blues, bluegrass and old-time tunes. You should memorize the primary chords of every key.

LEARNING THE CYCLE OF DIATONIC TRIADS IN ALL MAJOR KEYS

Let's call the diatonic triads for any major key played in numerical order *the cycle of diatonic triads*. The series can be memorized as: major–minor–minor–major–major–minor–diminished. Here are the diatonic triads in each major key.

Major Key	I	ii	iii	IV	V	vi	vii°
A	A	Bmin	C#min	D	E	F#min	G#dim
B♭	B♭	Cmin	Dmin	E♭	F	Gmin	A dim
B	B	C#min	D#min	E	F#	G#min	A#dim
C	C	Dmin	Emin	F	G	Amin	B dim
D♭	D♭	E♭min	Fmin	G♭	A♭	B♭min	C dim
D	D	Emin	F#min	G	A	Bmin	C#dim
E♭	E♭	Fmin	Gmin	A♭	B♭	Cmin	D dim
E	E	F#min	G#min	A	B	C#min	D#dim
F	F	Gmin	Amin	B♭	C	Dmin	E dim
G♭	G♭	A♭min	B♭min	C♭	D♭	E♭min	F dim
G	G	Amin	Bmin	C	D	Emin	F#dim
A♭	A♭	B♭min	Cmin	D♭	E♭	Fmin	G dim

LESSON 3: DOUBLE STOPS—3RDS

A double stop is two notes played simultaneously. The term comes from the violin family, where the maximum number of strings that can be played at once by the bow is two adjacent strings. The left hand fingers "stop" or finger the notes, hence the name "double stop."

Double stops are used on the mandolin to harmonize a melody. One way to harmonize a melody is in 3rds. To do this, you will need to be able to play major 3rds (M3) and minor 3rds (m3). For more on these and all of the other interval shapes, see pages 83–88. Here are the fingerings for major and minor 3rds on each adjacent pair of mandolin strings.

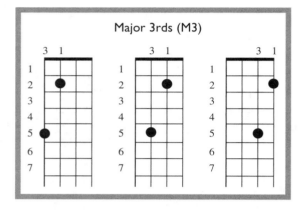

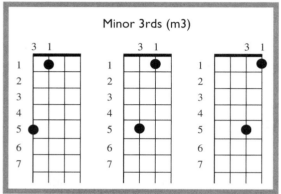

The most common way to harmonize a melody is to use the roots and 3rds of the cycle of diatonic triads. The melody note is the lower, or root note, and the harmony note is a 3rd above. You will know whether to use a major or minor 3rd by referring to the diatonic cycle: major–minor–minor–major–major–minor–diminished. The diminished chord uses a minor 3rd. Here is a D Major scale harmonized in 3rds on the first two strings.

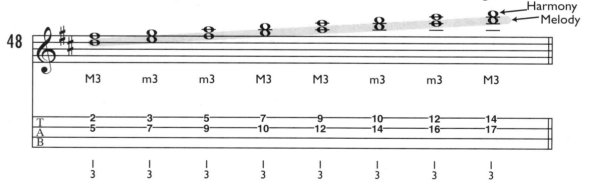

Try creating melodies that go up and down this cycle of 3rd intervals. Also try the same cycle of fingerings starting elsewhere on the neck (in other keys).

Here is a short exercise using double stops of major and minor 3rds. This should help you get used to the way the shapes cycle up and down the scale. This tune uses 3rds to evoke the music of Mexico and the American Southwest.

SAN ANTONIO SUNRISE

Track 49

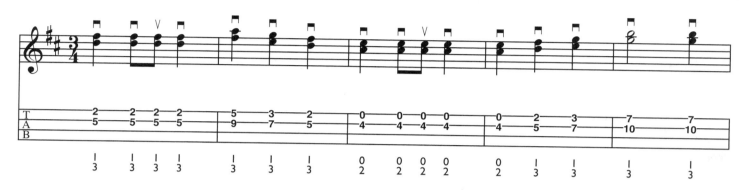

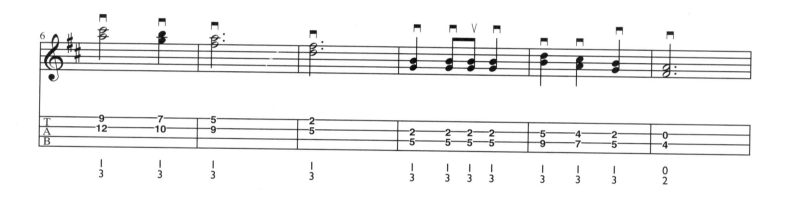

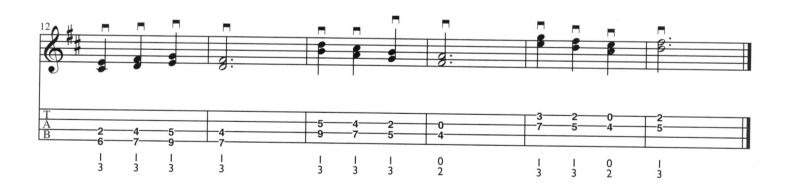

A WORLD TURNED UPSIDE-DOWN

A 6th is the inversion of a 3rd (for more on intervals and inversions, see pages 83–88). In other words, a 6th is a 3rd turned upside-down. For example, G to B is a major 3rd, while B to G is a minor 6th. When an interval is inverted, its quality (major or minor) is changed. So, keep in mind that *major* 3rds invert to *minor* 6ths, and *minor* 3rds invert to *major* 6ths. Here are fingerings for major 6ths (M6) and minor 6ths (m6).

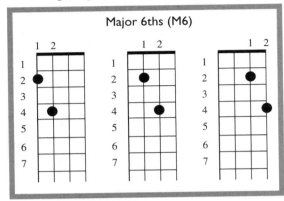

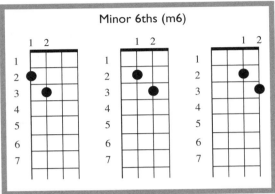

Below is a G Major scale harmonized in 6ths. The cycle still relates to the diatonic cycle. Now the roots are in the top voice, and the harmony is in the lower voice.

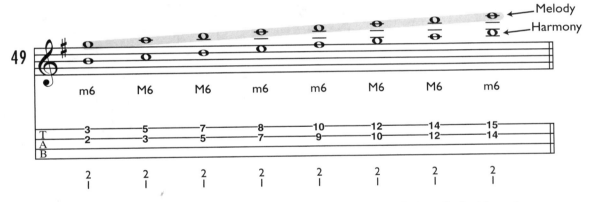

Harmonized 6ths have a more open, spread out sound than 3rds. Here is a move using 6ths that you can apply to any major chord. This is a very common sound on the mandolin. It is reminiscent of the guitar lick used in the intro to Van Morrison's "Brown Eyed Girl." Here it is shown for a G, C and D chord (I, IV and V in the key of G).

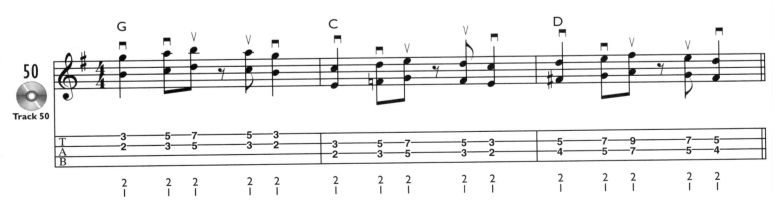

This tune uses 6ths played both simultaneously and broken up to evoke Hawaiian music and slide guitar. You will also slide 6ths from one position to another. This sound is also common in country, bluegrass and gospel. Notice the cool G6 chord at the end.

FINGERING ALERT: Sometimes you must adjust your fingerings to make the music flow better, or execute a move more comfortably. This exercise uses several ways of fingering the 6th shapes you have learned. Try them as written, or adapt your own fingerings to the TAB.

MANDOHULA SUNSET

Track 51

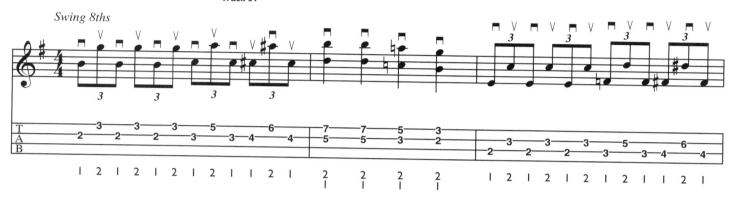

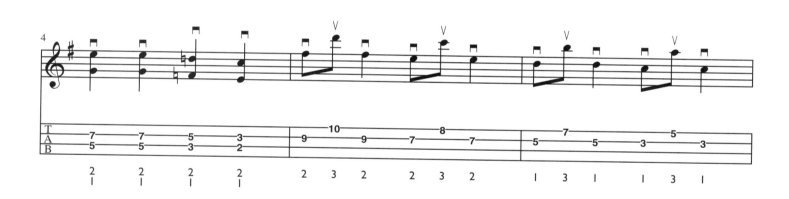

On page 77, you learned how to play open chords one string at a time to create arpeggio accompaniment patterns. In this lesson, you will learn how arpeggiated triads can spice up your improvisation and help you work up the neck.

The following arpeggio fingerings are shown for chords built on the root note C. This will help you see which notes are changing to form the different triads. Practice the fingerings going up and down, then try them on different root notes elsewhere on the neck. As you will see, these arpeggios are not the type played with each note on a different string.

MAJOR ARPEGGIO FINGERINGS

These fingerings for C Major arpeggios correspond directly to the scale fingerings you learned starting on page 146. The chord tones of root (R), 3rd (3) and 5th (5) are indicated.

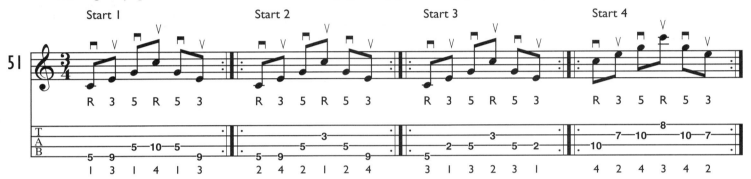

MINOR ARPEGGIO FINGERINGS

To make a C Minor triad arpeggio, simply lower the 3rds from the C Major arpeggios one half step to form minor 3rd chord tones (also called ♭3).

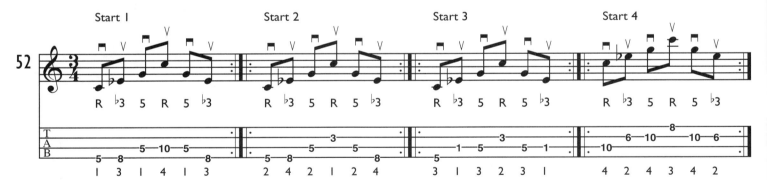

DIMINISHED ARPEGGIO FINGERINGS

Now try a C Diminished triad arpeggio. You must lower both the 3rd and 5th of a major triad to form the minor 3rd (♭3) and diminished 5th (♭5) chord tones.

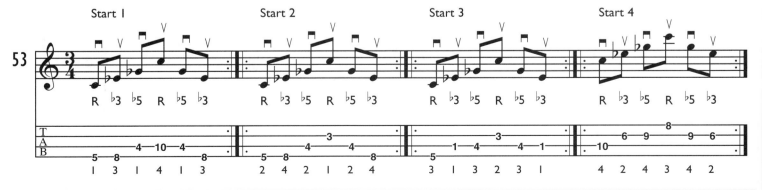

DIATONIC ARPEGGIOS IN C MAJOR

You can use the arpeggio fingerings you have learned to outline all of the triads in any major key. Here is one way to do the diatonic triads in the key of C. You will find many more possible fingerings if you try the chords on different strings starting with different fingers.

Arpeggios are used heavily in improvisation and within the melodies of tunes. Jazz and swing tunes often use arpeggios. Irish jigs are among the fiddle tunes that use arpeggios (see "Money in Both Pockets" and "Scatter the Mud" on pages 136 and 137). Even one of your first fiddle tunes, "Soldier's Joy" (page 38) is built on a D Major arpeggio. Here's a tune that will give you a chance to practice arpeggio fingerings.

SATURDAY NIGHT AT THE GULAG ARPEGGIO

Track 52

---

* The chord symbols are gray because while they are here to indicate which chord is being arpeggiated, they do not imply that an accompaniment is needed or present.

LESSON 6: ARPEGGIOS—AUGMENTED TRIADS AND SEVENTH CHORDS

There is one more triad type yet to learn: the *augmented* triad. Augmented triads do not occur in the diatonic cycle of a major key, but they are sometimes used to add a new flavor to a chord progression. An augmented triad is constructed with two major 3rds stacked on top of the root. In other words, an augmented triad is a major triad with a raised 5th (♯5). Here are the fingerings for augmented arpeggios built on C.

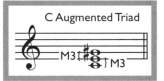

AUGMENTED ARPEGGIO FINGERINGS

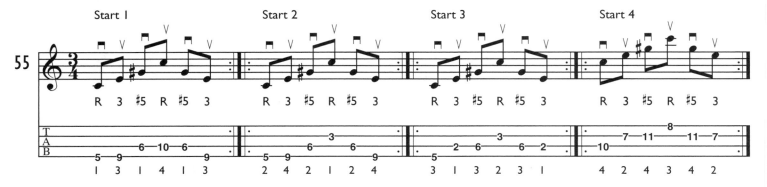

7TH CHORDS

When you add one more 3rd to your triad stack (root–3rd–5th), you get a seventh chord (root–3rd–5th–7th). There are five types of 7th chords. Here they are shown built on the root note C.

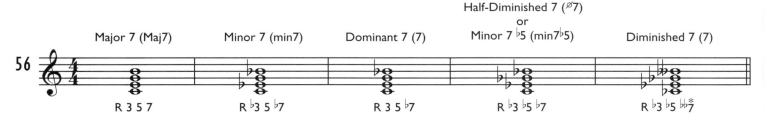

7th chord arpeggios are very important in blues, jazz and Brazilian mandolin music. This lesson will cover the three most common 7th chords: the major 7 (Maj7), minor 7 (min7) and dominant-7 (7) arpeggios. You can use your knowledge of the other chord structures shown above to adapt these fingerings for half-diminished and diminished 7 chords.

MAJOR 7 ARPEGGIO FINGERINGS

Major 7 chords use the root (R), 3rd (3), 5th (5) and 7th (7) from the major scale. Here are fingerings for a CMaj7 arpeggio. Major 7 chords occur on the I and IV chords of a major key.

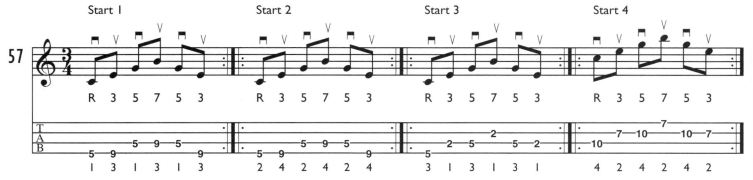

MINOR 7 ARPEGGIO FINGERINGS

Minor 7 chords (min7) are made with a minor triad plus a minor 7th interval. The structure is root (R), minor 3rd (♭3), 5th (5) and minor 7th (♭7). Minor 7 chords occur on the ii, iii and vi chords of a major key (for example, Dmin7, Emin7 and Amin7 in the key of C). Below are fingerings for a Cmin7 arpeggio. Learn and compare them with the major 7 and dominant-7 fingerings.

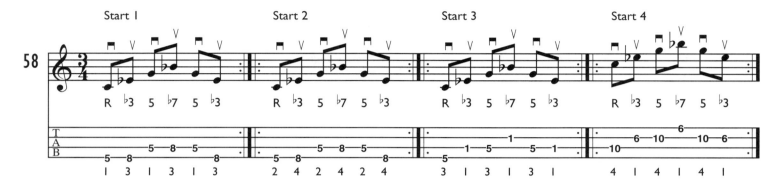

DOMINANT 7 ARPEGGIO FINGERINGS

The dominant 7 chord (indicated in music by the root and the 7, as in "C7") is a major triad plus a minor 7 interval. A dominant-7 chord is so named because it occurs on the V chord of a major key, which is also called the *dominant* chord. Here are the fingerings for C7 arpeggios. C7 is the V chord in the key of F, which has a key signature with one flat (B♭).

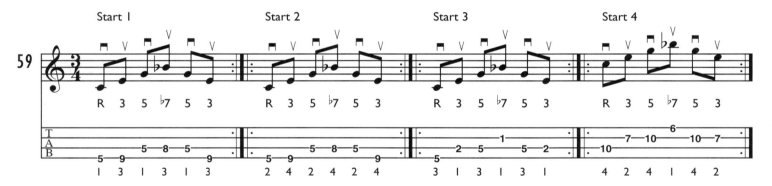

Here is a short chord progression using arpeggios for CMaj7, Amin7 and G7.

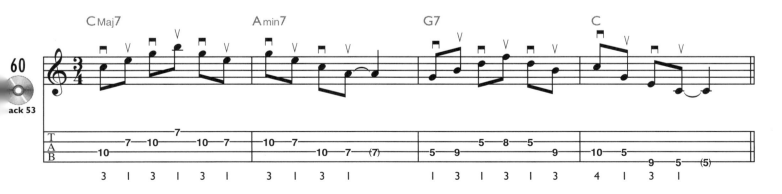

LESSON 7: THE NATURAL MINOR SCALE AND THE RELATIVE MINOR

On page 71, you learned that a natural minor scale is made by lowering the 3rd (♭3), 6th (♭6) and 7th (♭7) of a major scale. There are many other possible types of minor scales. The natural minor scale, one of the most common minor scales, has two other names: the *relative minor* scale and the *Aeolian mode*. All three of these names denote the same scale.

The natural minor scale can be formed by starting on the 6th scale degree of a major scale. For example, in a C Major scale, the 6 is A. By starting a new scale on A, using the same notes, you create an A Natural Minor scale.

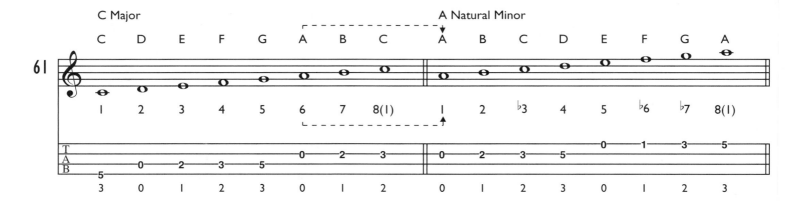

HANGING WITH THE RELATIVES AROUND THE BIG CIRCLE

Since the A Natural Minor scale and the C Major scale have the same notes, they are said to be *relative minor* and *relative major* to one another. All major keys have a relative minor starting on the 6th note of the scale. Likewise, all minor keys have a relative major starting on the 3rd note. Here is the circle of 5ths (see page 82) shown with major and relative minor keys and the key signatures they share.

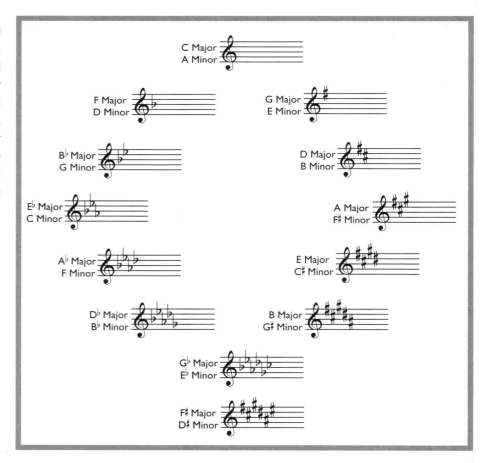

Now let's look again at the A Natural Minor scale. It helps to compare it to the A Major scale. We see that the A Major scale has a C#, an F# and a G#. The A Natural Minor scale, since it shares notes with C Major, has C♮ F♮ and G♮. In other words, the natural minor scale has a lowered 3rd (♭3), a lowered 6th (♭6) and a lowered 7th (♭7) when compared to a major scale built on the same note (called the *tonic*). Here is one octave for each scale for you to compare.

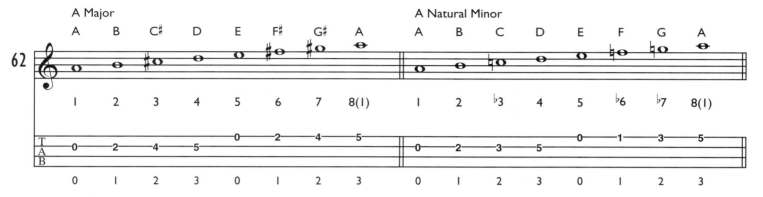

DIATONIC HARMONY OF THE NATURAL MINOR SCALE

Here is an A Natural Minor scale shown with triads built on each note. Sample mandolin fingerings are shown above the chords. The fingerings do not produce the chord tones exactly as written, but will help you hear the sound of the chord cycle. This cycle (minor–diminished–major–minor–minor–major–minor) is found in every natural minor key.

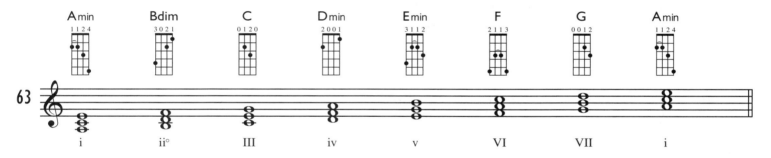

You can form moveable minor scales by lowering the 3rd, 6th and 7th of your major scale fingerings from page 146–150. Here is a short tune using the A Natural Minor scale in open position (shown in example 62, above). Chords are indicated, use a simple bluegrass strum for rhythm (page 138) with the fingerings shown in example 63, above.

TOULOUSE LAUTREC

Track 54

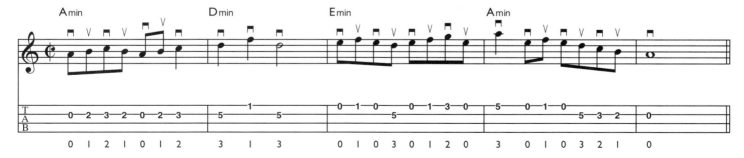

CHAPTER 7

Blues and Bluegrass Improv Up the Neck

This chapter will use the blues and bluegrass to help you work on your improvisation skills up the neck. You will learn how to use the minor pentatonic and major pentatonic scales in the key of B Major, with fingerings that can be moved to any other key on the neck. Work through this chapter even if you are interested in styles other than blues or bluegrass, as the scales, chords and skills involved are fundamental to all styles of music.

LESSON 1: MOVEABLE DOMINANT 7 CHORDS

On page 158–159, you learned arpeggio fingerings for dominant 7 chords. A dominant 7 chord includes a root (R), major 3rd (3), perfect 5th (5) and minor 7th (♭7). Below are some good moveable mandolin fingerings for dominant 7 chords. They can be moved all over the neck to form any dominant 7 chord. Simply move the fingering up or down to any root you desire. For example, a B7 chord could be moved up one half-step (one fret) to form a C7 chord or down one fret to form a B♭7.

The top row of fingerings are very common and easy to play. The fingerings in the bottom row are a bit more challenging, but can come in handy in some tight situations.

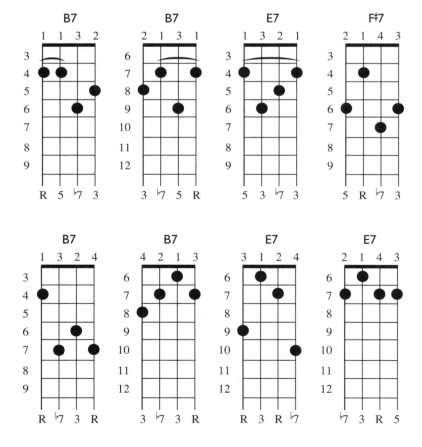

Below is a blues shuffle strum in swing 8ths. Try it with any of the fingerings shown on page 162.

Blues Shuffle Strum

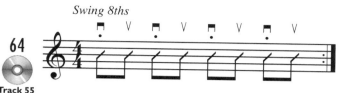

Now try this 12-bar blues (page 53) using dominant 7 chords in the key of B. On pages 158–159, you learned that the dominant 7 chord only occurs on the V chord of a major key. The blues, however, plays by different rules. Because of the addition of extra "blue" notes to the major scale, the dominant 7 chord can be used on the I, IV and V chord as you like.

Suggested chord voicings are shown. You can use the blues shuffle strum above, or try it with a bluegrass rhythm. The I, IV and V chords are marked below the staff to help you memorize the 12-bar blues form.

Track 56

BLUES IN MY BEE BONNET (OR, BEES IN MY BLUE BONNET)

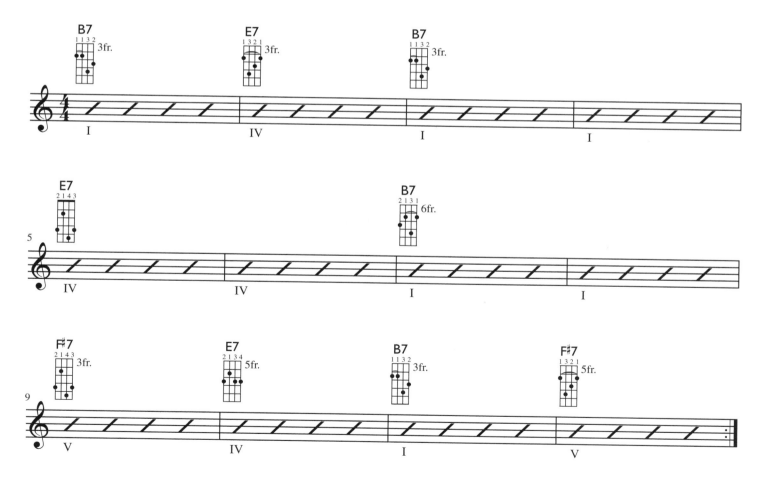

The minor pentatonic scale was introduced as a good scale for modal fiddle tunes (page 45) and for blues improvisation (page 57). Pentatonic means "five notes." The minor pentatonic scale has five scale degrees: 1, ♭3, 4, 5 and ♭7 (as always, the numbers correspond to notes in the major scale). This scale does not have scale degrees 2 or 6. Here is a comparison of the notes and intervals found in the B Major and B Minor Pentatonic scales.

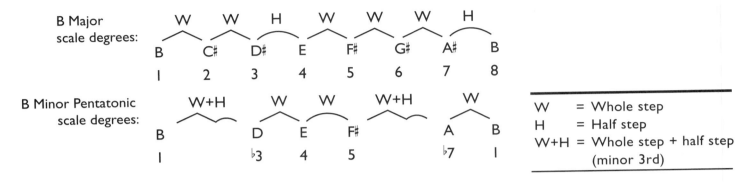

THE MINOR PENTATONIC INTERVAL SERIES

The minor pentatonic interval series is made up of whole steps and minor 3rds (whole step plus half step, W+H). The series found in the minor pentatonic scale (W+H–W–W–W+H–W) is very common in folk music from many cultures. Some of the earliest melodies known are in pentatonic scales.

USING PENTATONIC FINGERINGS AS "LANDMARKS"

By mastering the pentatonic fingerings shown in this lesson and the one on Major Pentatonic Scales (page 170), you can develop a "skeleton" or "outline" approach to learning the fretboard. The notes in the pentatonic scales become like landmarks, or basic tones common to many scales. This makes it easier to fill in the gaps with other scale tones you will learn about in the future.

WHEN TO USE THE MINOR PENTATONIC SCALE

Minor Keys: The minor pentatonic shares notes in common with many minor scales, particularly the natural minor (see page 160) and the Dorian mode (page 124). So the minor pentatonic will fit well in most minor keys (songs where the tonic chord (i) is minor).

Major Keys with Blue Notes: The ♭3 and ♭7 notes of the minor pentatonic could also be considered blue notes, or notes from a minor scale played against chords in a major key. This adds an emotional mood to the melody, which is part of the blues sound. This is also what puts the "blue" in "bluegrass." Whether or not this is the sound you want for a particular musical moment is a matter of taste and experimentation.

The fingerings in this lesson are shown starting on B, but can be moved to other keys by simply playing the pattern starting on other notes. Be sure to practice improvising and constructing melodies with each fingering. You could also use "Blues in my Bee Bonnet" (page 163) as a backup progression to practice improvising over.

Moveable Minor Pentatonic, Start 1—Starting with the 1st Finger

Below is a B Minor Pentatonic scale starting with the 1st finger on the 4th fret of the 4th string. The pattern can be used in higher octaves by starting with the 1st finger on the 9th fret of the 3rd string or with the 1st finger on the 2nd fret of the 2nd string.

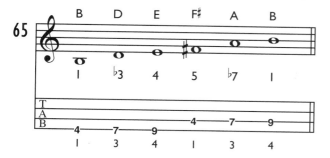

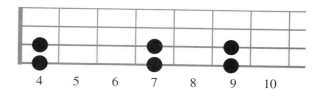

Improv Tip: Keep Track of the Tonic Note (Scale Degree 1)

A good way to start building licks in new scales is to construct licks that come to rest on the 1st scale degree. This helps you hear how the other notes in the scale are relating to the key. Using this concept, build small musical thoughts that end on 1 and then wait a bit before beginning the next thought. Here are a couple of examples.

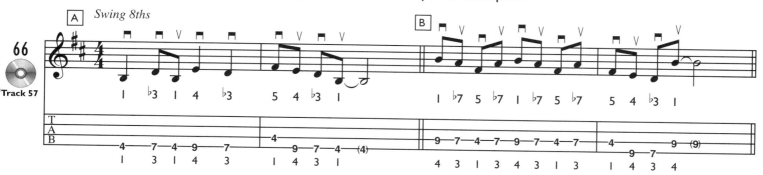

Moveable Minor Pentatonic, Start 2—Starting with the 2nd Finger

Below is a B Minor Pentatonic fingering starting with the 2nd finger on the 4th fret of the 4th string. The pattern can be used in higher octaves by starting with the 2nd finger on the 9th fret of the 3rd string or the 2nd finger on the 2nd fret of the 2nd string.

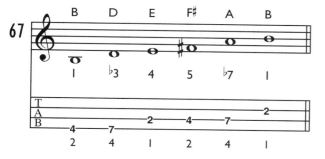

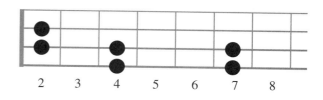

Here's a bluegrass style example. Chords are shown so that you can see how the licks fit over the chords. To play the chords, use the fingerings you learned on page 162.

Moveable Minor Pentatonic, Start 3/4—Starting with the 3rd or 4th Finger

Here is a B Minor Pentatonic fingering starting with the 3rd finger on the 9th fret of the 3rd string.

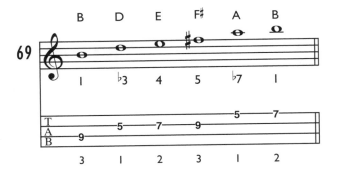
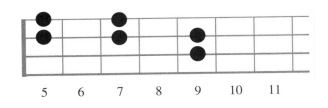

> **FINGERING ALERT: Two Fingerings for the Price of One!** The Start 3 fingering of the minor pentatonic scale can also be fingered starting with the 4th finger. Following is the B Minor Pentatonic Start 4 fingering.

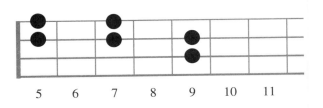

This example is set over chords in the key of B Minor (the relative minor of D Major, hence two sharps in the key signature). Chord fingerings are shown. Notice how the character of the scale changes depending on the quality (major or minor) of the backup chords. This example uses the Start 3 fingering, but you can also try it with Start 4.

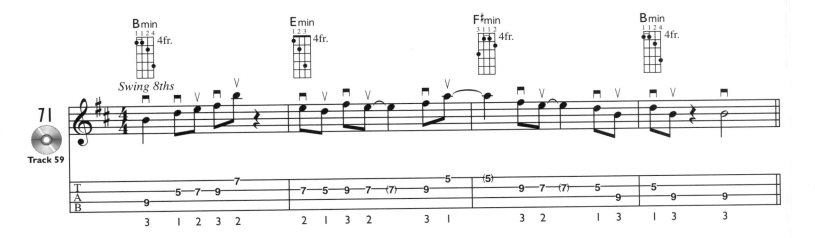

Track 59

To create two-octave scale fingerings that go across the strings, you can connect the one-octave fingerings you have learned.

START 1 CONNECTING TO START 3/4

The most common way to extend the Start 1 fingering is to use a position *shift* (change) with the 3rd finger. This is shown in the TAB as a slide, but does not have to be articulated that way (it doesn't have to *sound* like a slide). Another way to finger the scale is to start the second octave with the 4th finger. Both possibilities are shown below.

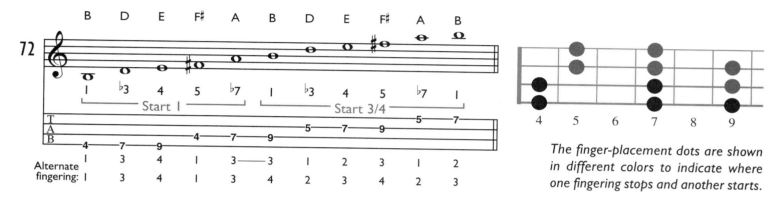

The finger-placement dots are shown in different colors to indicate where one fingering stops and another starts.

This example allows you to practice improvising over a simple bluegrass progression using the I, IV and V chords in B (B, E and F♯). On the recording for this book, you will hear the example as shown, then the chord progression will repeat so that you can practice your own improvisation.

START 2 CONNECTING TO START 1

Here, the B Minor Pentatonic starts with the 2nd finger on the 4th fret of the 4th string and connects with the fingering that starts with the 1st finger on the 2nd fret of the 2nd string.

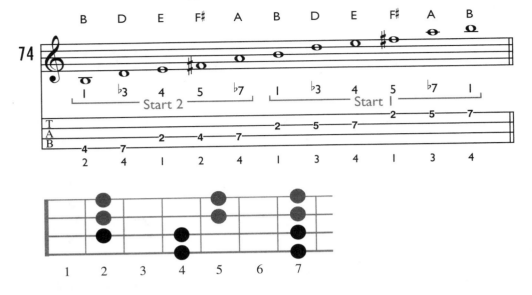

START 3 CONNECTING TO START 2

This fingering is not terribly convenient in the key of B, since it has to be placed so high on the neck. Once you learn the shapes of all these fingerings, try them in different keys. Some fingerings suit certain keys better than others. This one starts with the 3rd finger on the 16th fret of the 4th string and connects to the fingering that starts with the 2nd finger on the 14th fret of the 2nd string.

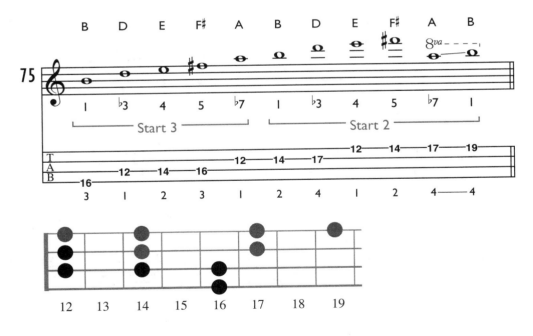

As stated earlier, you could use "Blues in My Bee Bonnet" (page 163) as a backup progression to practice your new scale fingerings. Here is a 12-bar blues in B Minor, using the minor i (Bmin), iv (Emin) and v (F#min) chords with a sample solo using some of the scale fingerings you have learned. On the recording for this book, this tune is set in a medium bluegrass tempo and the chord progression is repeated for you to practice improvising over. Also try it using other grooves and tempos you like.

YOU WON'T B-MINOR FOREVER

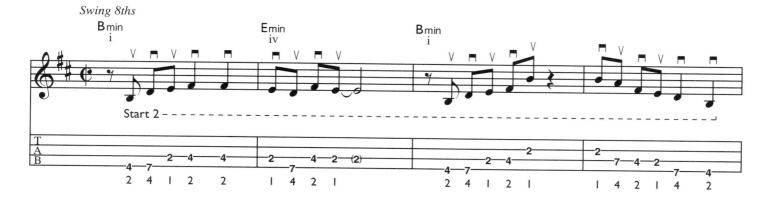

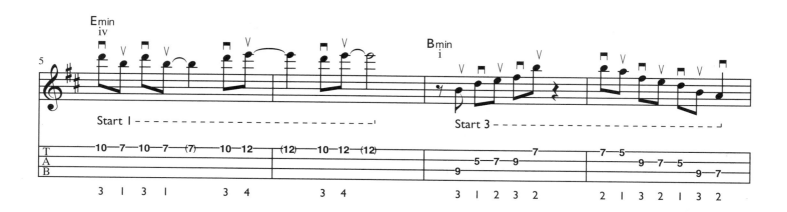

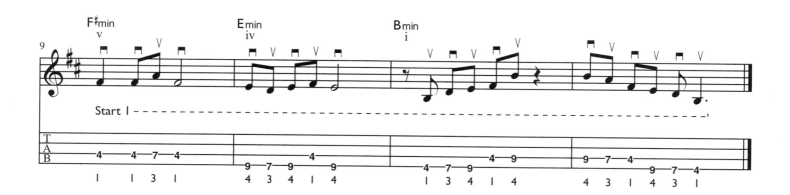

LESSON 4: THE MAJOR PENTATONIC SCALE

The *major pentatonic* scale is the friendlier, more optimistic sibling to the minor pentatonic scale. A huge number of vocal melodies used in folk songs and bluegrass songs are in the major pentatonic scale. The major pentatonic scale can be thought of as an "abbreviated" major scale. It contains scale degrees 1, 2, 3, 5 and 6, leaving out scale degrees 4 and 7. Here is a comparison of the interval structure and notes of the B Major scale and the B Major Pentatonic scale.

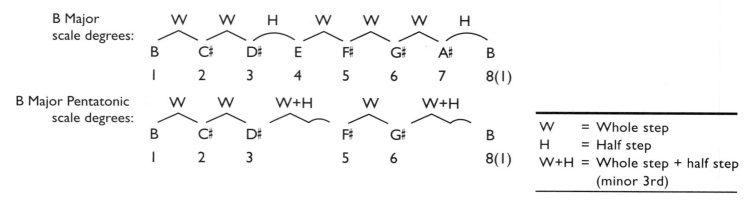

W	=	Whole step	
H	=	Half step	
W+H	=	Whole step + half step (minor 3rd)	

NOT JUST SIBLINGS, TWINS!

Look closely at the interval structure of the major pentatonic scale (W–W–W+H–W–W+H). If you rotate this series four places (in other words, start the series on the last W+H interval and repeat the series from there) you get the series that makes up the minor pentatonic (W+H–W–W–W+H–W). The major and minor pentatonic are just two expressions of the same basic pentatonic interval series. This will make the major pentatonic fingerings seem familiar, especially as you connect them together.

There's another way to look at this relationship. Below are the notes of the A Minor Pentatonic scale and the C Major Pentatonic scale. They have exactly the same notes! It's just like the relationship between the A Natural Minor scale and the C Major scale. The A Minor Pentatonic scale is the *relative minor pentatonic* scale to the C Major Pentatonic Scale.

A Minor Pentatonic	A	C	D	E	G	
C Major Pentatonic		C	D	E	G	A

WHEN TO USE THE MAJOR PENTATONIC SCALE

Major Keys: The major pentatonic scale suits songs where the tonic chord (I) is major. As you learn more scales, you will learn scales other than the major scale that also use a major I chord. The major pentatonic scale suits most of these scales as well. The major pentatonic scale has an open, tuneful sound heard in country and bluegrass licks. This grouping of notes makes a particularly good scale for improvisation because it avoids the 4th and 7th degrees, which occasionally clash with certain chords in the key.

Moveable Major Pentatonic, Start 1—Starting with the 1st Finger

You will recognize this fingering from its similarity to the Start 1 fingering of the major scale (page 146). Here it is in the key of B Major.

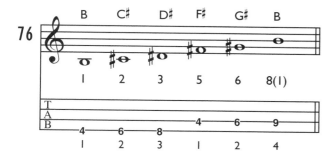

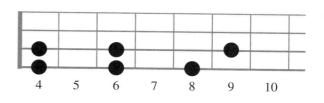

Here is a fiddle tune-style lick using the B Major Pentatonic Start 1 fingering.

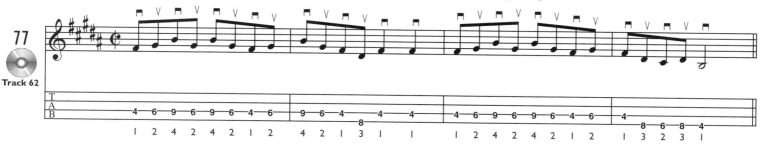

Moveable Major Pentatonic, Start 2—Starting with the 2nd Finger

Below is the B Major Pentatonic scale starting with the 2nd finger on the 4th fret of the 4th string. Note that this is just a slight variation of the Start 1 fingering, placing the final B-note (the start of the next octave) on the 2nd string instead of the 3rd string.

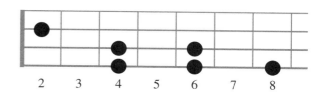

Try this example using Start 2.

Moveable Major Pentatonic Start 3—Starting with the 3rd Finger

This fingering is shown starting with the 3rd finger on the 9th fret of the 3rd string.

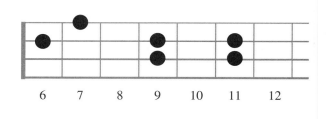

Notice how easily you can locate a major arpeggio (see page 156) within this fingering. Simply pick out the 1st, 3rd and 5th scale degrees. This example incorporates the B Major arpeggio using the B Major Pentatonic Start 3 fingering.

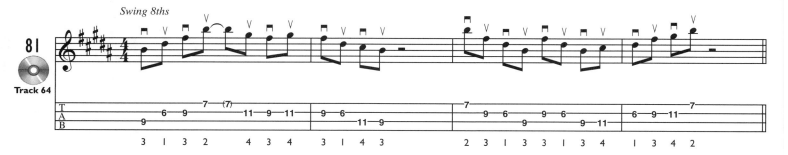

Moveable Major Pentatonic, Start 4—Starting with the 4th Finger

Here is a B Major Pentatonic scale starting with the 4th finger on the 9th fret of the 3rd string.

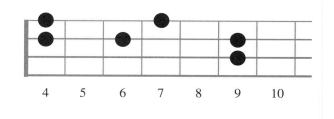

Try this example.

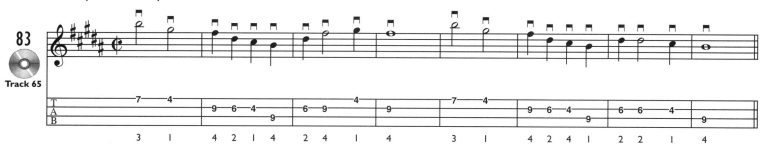

CONNECTING THE POSITIONS

The one-octave major pentatonic fingerings connect the same way the major scales did (page 148). Here are the two-octave moveable major pentatonic fingerings for the key of B Major. Practice them as scales going up and down, then use them to improvise and construct melodies.

Start 4 Connecting to Start 3

The finger-placement dots are shown in different colors to indicate where one fingering stops and another starts.

Start 3 Connecting to Start 2

Start 2 Connecting to Start 1

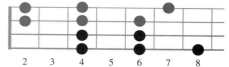

Start 1 Connecting to Start 4

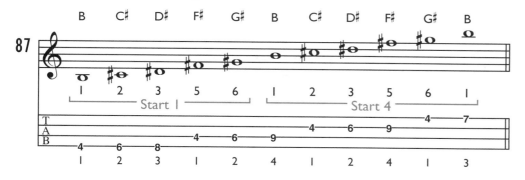

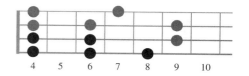

The sample solos in this lesson are based on an *8-bar blues* chord progression. There are several formulas used for the 8-bar blues. This particular progression can be heard in the blues standard "Key to the Highway" by Big Bill Broonzy. The chords are indicated and chord analysis shown so that you can play this progression in other keys. On the recording included with this book, each solo will be followed by a repeat of the chord progression so that you can practice your own soloing.

This solo uses the B Major Pentatonic in the "Start 1 Connecting to Start 4" fingering (page 173).

KEY TO THE HIGH SCHOOL—SOLO NO. 1 (MAJOR PENTATONIC)

Track 66

Try this solo over the same chord progression using the B Minor Pentatonic scale ("Start 1 Connecting to Start 3" fingering, page 167). Listen to how the blue notes in the scale change the emotional character of the solo.

KEY TO THE HIGH SCHOOL—SOLO NO. 2 (MINOR PENTATONIC)

Track 67

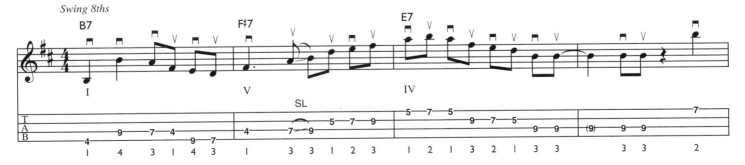

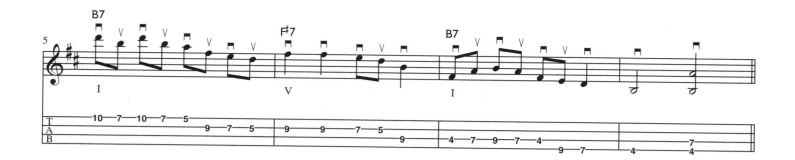

The next solo mixes the minor and major pentatonic scales in the same solo. Notice how the major pentatonic scale sounds great over the initial I and V chords, while the minor pentatonic helps lead the ear to the IV chord. This is because the ♭3 of the minor pentatonic scale (a D note in the key of B) is the same note as the ♭7 chord tone of the IV chord (a D note in the E7 chord). Also, the minor pentatonic scale includes the 4th scale degree, the root of the IV chord. While there is no rule that says the major pentatonic scale goes over the I and V, and the minor goes over the IV, it is interesting that the scales can suggest these changes because of the chord tones within the scale.

KEY TO THE HIGH SCHOOL—SOLO NO. 3 (MAJOR AND MINOR PENTATONIC)

Track 68

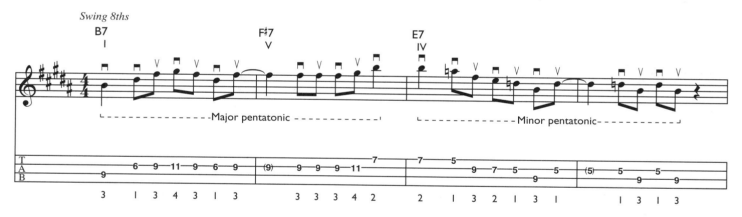

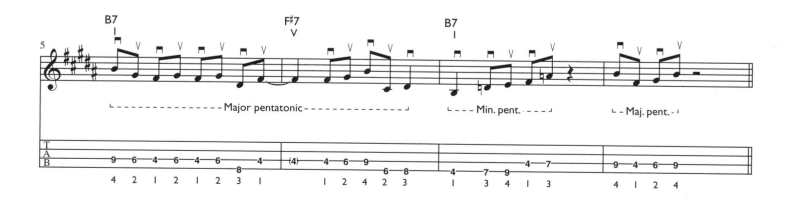

CHAPTER 8

A Taste of Swing and Jazz Mandolin

The mandolin has always had a foothold in the world of swing and jazz music. The black string bands of the early 20th century often had mandolinists playing their vast repertoires of dixieland, swing and other jazz and blues tunes. Later players such as Dave Apollon used the mandolin as a vehicle for virtuosic improvisation. No single player has done more to bring together swing and the mandolin than David "Dawg" Grisman. His patented "Dawg Music" sound incorporates influences from swing, bluegrass, Brazilian music and anything else to which Grisman takes a liking.

LESSON 1: SWING RHYTHM PLAYING

BASIC SWING STRUM

The most traditional swing rhythm pattern is to strum percussive, clipped (staccato) chords in a quarter-note rhythm. Guitarist Freddie Green was a master of this style. Try the following progression. The downstrokes are just like the bluegrass "chop" strum. Use your left hand to cut the chords short by slightly releasing the pressure on the strings. This strum also incorporates a soft upstroke at the end of the bar.

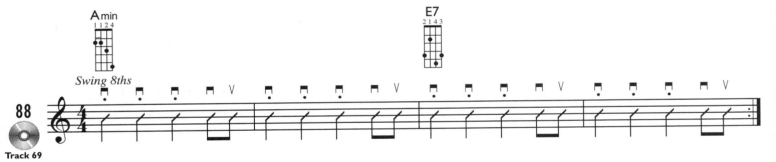

HOT GYPSY RHYTHM STRUM

This approach to swing rhythm draws inspiration from the "hot jazz" of gypsy guitarist Django Reinhardt.

THE 32-BAR SONG FORM

The *32-bar song form* is found in countless jazz tunes (known as *standards*). It is an old pop song form in which a melody lasting eight bars (the "A" section of the song) is played twice, then a contrasting "B" section of eight bars is played and finally followed by a repeat of the A section. This A–A–B–A form is repeated as many times as the musicians want, and is used for both the melody (called the *head*) and the improvised solos. In jazz lingo, each repetition is called a *chorus*.

Here is a chord progression using the strum patterns you have learned (watch out for a couple of variations!). It is a simple 32-bar song form. The return of the A section is indicated by *D.C. al Fine*, which means to repeat from the top until the finish (*Fine*).

SWING BY YOUR THUMBS (SIMPLE RHYTHM CHORDS)

Track 71

Now that you've got the basic sound of "Swing By Your Thumbs" in your ears, it's time to spice things up with some more colorful chords. Jazz players add 7ths, 6ths and even more extended chord tones to basic triads to make the harmony more rich and complex. Some of the great swing players change chord voicings on nearly every beat!

MAJOR 7 CHORDS

As you learned on page 158, a major 7 chord (Maj7) is constructed using the root (R), 3rd (3), 5th (5) and 7th (7) of a major scale. You can find voicings for major 7 chords on your mandolin by using your regular major triad fingerings. Find a root in the fingering, and lower it by one half step. This note is the major 7th chord tone. Here are some moveable fingerings with the chord tones shown under the diagrams. Some of these fingerings are very tricky. Learn the ones that work best for you.

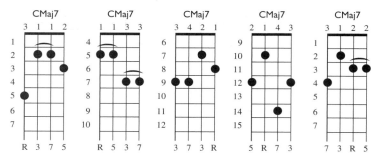

MINOR 7 CHORDS

The minor 7 chord (min7) construction is R–$\flat$3–5–$\flat$7. You can add a minor 7 to a triad by lowering a root one whole step, or raising a 5th by three half steps. Here are some moveable fingerings.

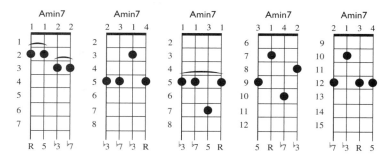

MAJOR 6 CHORDS

A major 6 chord (6) colors a major triad by adding the 6th to the R–3–5. To form a major 6, find a 5th in your chord voicing and raise it one whole step. Below are some moveable fingerings. You may recognize some of these from the minor 7 fingerings. This is because a minor 7 chord has the same notes as a major 6 chord built on a root a minor 3rd higher. For example, an Amin7 has the same notes (A–C–E–G) as a C6 (C–E–G–A).

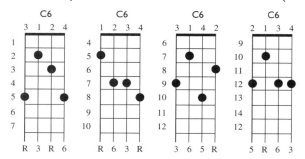

Now try a more colorful version of "Swing By Your Thumbs" using some of the chords you have just learned, plus some new variations. One new trick is the use of anticipation in the 7th measure. The C6 from measure 8 is anticipated, or played a half-beat early (on the "&" of beat 4, bar 7). You should also try finding different voicings for these chords using the fingerings on page 178. In this case, play the repeat and the D.C. al Fine!

SWING BY YOUR THUMBS (COOL SWING CHORDS)

Track 72

Mastering jazz improvisation can be a life's work, but having fun with it can start right away. As the melodies, rhythms and chords become more developed, the possibilities for what you can do with them widens. Each progression offers new implications for scales, while each melody can be harmonized many ways. Still, jazz improvisation has some of the same roots as blues and bluegrass. Solos can range from slight variations of the melody to advanced, extended explorations of uncharted territory. The chord progression of "Swing By Your Thumbs" offers several opportunities to try new scales and techniques.

"SWING BY YOUR THUMBS" A SECTION—CHANGING SCALES:

The first line of the A section of "Swing By Your Thumbs" is in the key of A Minor. The Amin7 chord fits the natural minor scale (page 160). However, the E7 chord conflicts with this scale. The A Natural Minor scale (shown below) has a G♮ in it. The E7 chord contains a G♯. In order to accommodate the E7 chord, you could use a new scale called the *harmonic minor*. The harmonic minor scale is based on the natural minor scale but raises the minor 7 (♭7, or G) back up to a major 7 (7, or G♯). Here are both scales for you to compare.

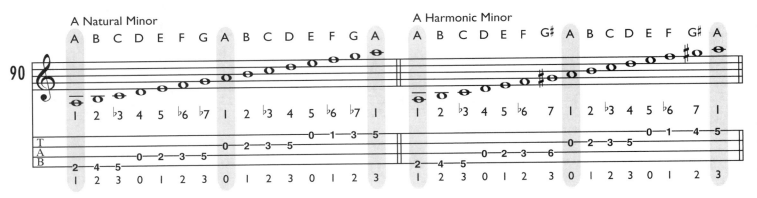

You could use the A Natural Minor scale on the Amin7 chord, then the A Harmonic Minor scale on the E7. The second line of the A section is in C Major (page 104), the relative major (page 160) of A Minor.

"SWING BY YOUR THUMBS" B SECTION: ARPEGGIOS

The B section of the tune changes chords quickly and moves through several possible keys. One easy way to deal with this improvisationally is to play arpeggios of the chords. You can use simple triad arpeggios (pages 156–157) or outline the 6th and 7th chords.

Here is a melody, or "head" for "Swing By Your Thumbs." In the A section, it uses the A Natural Minor scale, the A Harmonic Minor scale and the C Major scale. In the B section, it uses arpeggios of the many chords, with a short melodic run at the end. Don't forget to repeat the A section! On the recording included with this book, you will hear the melody, then a repeat of the chord progression for you to practice your own variations and solos.

SWING BY YOUR THUMBS (MELODY)

Track 73

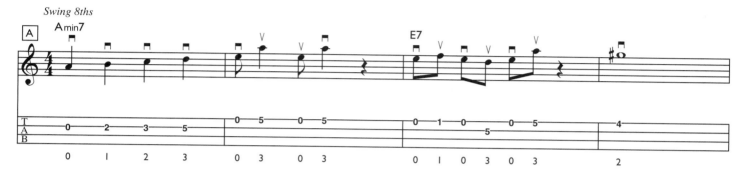

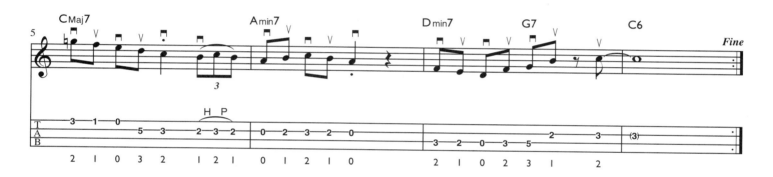

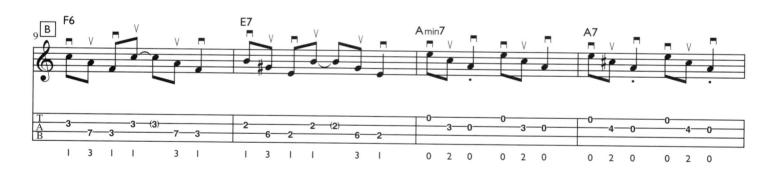

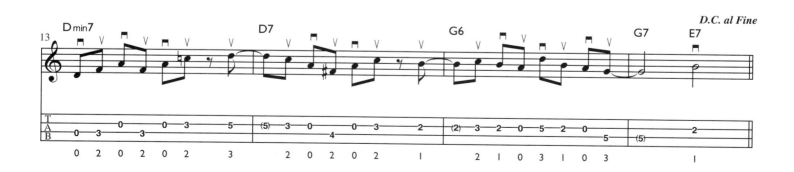

CHAPTER 9

New Rhythms and Sounds

LESSON 1: FUNK ON THE MANDOLIN

Funk music, pioneered by electric artists like Sly and the Family Stone, the Meters, James Brown and George Clinton, uses every instrument in the band like a drum. Layers of rhythm are built up from simple, repeated, interlocking patterns. The mandolin makes a great funk rhythm instrument. Its tight, percussive chop and high pitch makes it sit perfectly in a groove.

SIXTEENTH-NOTE STRUMMING

The foundation of funk strumming technique is sixteenth notes. As you know, there are four sixteenth notes in each beat, counted "1–e–&–ah, 2–e–&–ah" and so on. Try this counting, strumming and foot tapping exercise.

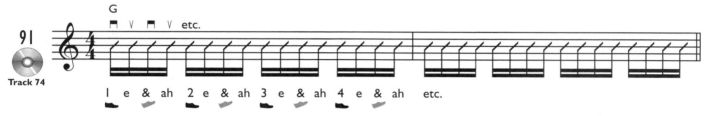

LEFT-HAND MUTING ("SQUEEZING AND SCRATCHING")

The secret of funk strumming is to keep the right hand moving in a steady, down-up sixteenth-note rhythm while the left hand controls the rhythmic accents of the chords. The left hand presses down to sound the chord ("squeeze") and releases the pressure just enough to create a muted, scratching sound. Make sure you don't lift your fingers all the way off the strings. This works best with moveable chord forms that use no open strings.

First, make the A7 chord shown. Then practice "scratching" (indicated by an ✕ instead of a notehead ● or a rhythm slash ╱). Try to set the pressure of your left hand so that no open strings or notes are sounding at all, just the scratch.

✕ = Mute or scratch

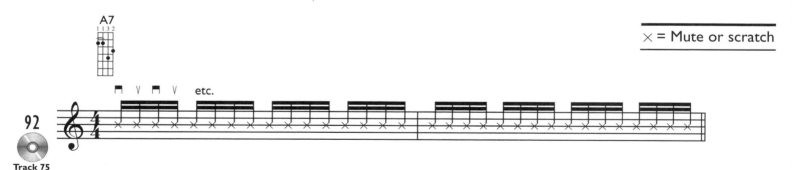

Now try "squeezing" the chord on the first sixteenth of each beat (shown with a slash ╱), relaxing for the other sixteenths. Use the same A7 fingering shown above.

In the following rhythm, squeeze the first two sixteenths and scratch the second two. In the second bar, reverse the pattern.

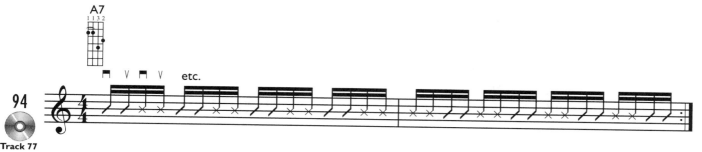

Try this funk-blues progression. You may want to practice it first with the simpler strums in examples 92–94, then try the funk groove shown. Keep your hand moving in a steady rhythm. Notice that in the first beat of every bar, you will strum a dotted eighth/sixteenth rhythm. Strum down on beat 1, hold the chord through "e-&" and strum up on "ah."

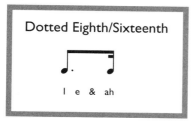

Remember, a dot increases a note's value by half. Since an eighth note is equal to two sixteenth notes, half of its value is one sixteenth note. Therefore, a dotted eighth note is equal to three sixteenth notes ("1–e–&").

OOH, THAT SOME FUNKY MANDO!

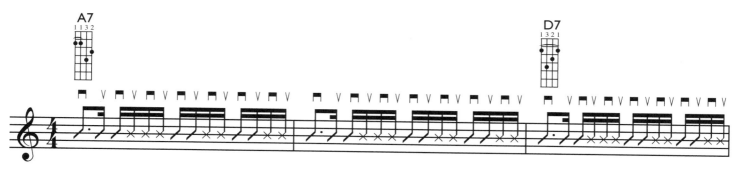

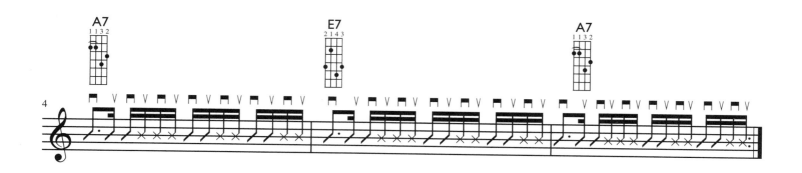

CROSS RHYTHMS AND THE NEW ORLEANS INFLUENCE

In an earlier lesson on ragtime playing (page 132), you learned how to accent eighth notes in groups of three within a simple meter. This sound, sometimes called a cross rhythm, is fundamental in rock, funk and blues music. The music of New Orleans, from the earliest "Dixieland" jazz through modern funk and Zydeco, rests on the foundation of simple meter (such as cut time C or) with eighth notes grouped in threes.

CLAP THE CLAVE

The *clave* (pronounced KLAH-vay) is an important percussion rhythm born out of the influence of African traditions in the Caribbean, Central and South America. The clave rhythm is traditionally played on wooden sticks called—believe it or not—claves. This rhythm and many variations of it are found in the rhythms of New Orleans jazz and funk. This example shows the clave as a two-bar rhythm in cut time. Remember that in cut time, your foot only taps on beats 1 and 3!

PLAY THE CLAVE

Try strumming the clave rhythm using the "squeezing and scratching" technique you learned on page 182.

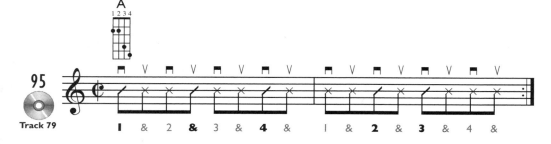

THE BO DIDDLEY BEAT

This is a variation of the clave rhythm made famous by guitarist Bo Diddley. It has been borrowed by Buddy Holly, the Rolling Stones, the Grateful Dead and countless others. David Grisman used it to occasionally break up the bluegrass backbeat of Old and In the Way's "Midnight Moonlight." It looks harder on paper than it is. If you're having trouble, break it down one or two beats at a time.

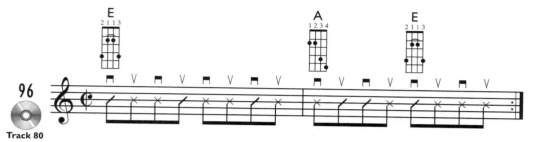

Here is a 12-bar blues in E built on the Bo Diddley beat. Watch out for the simpler bluegrass groove in the third line!

BO MAN DIDDLEY BLUES

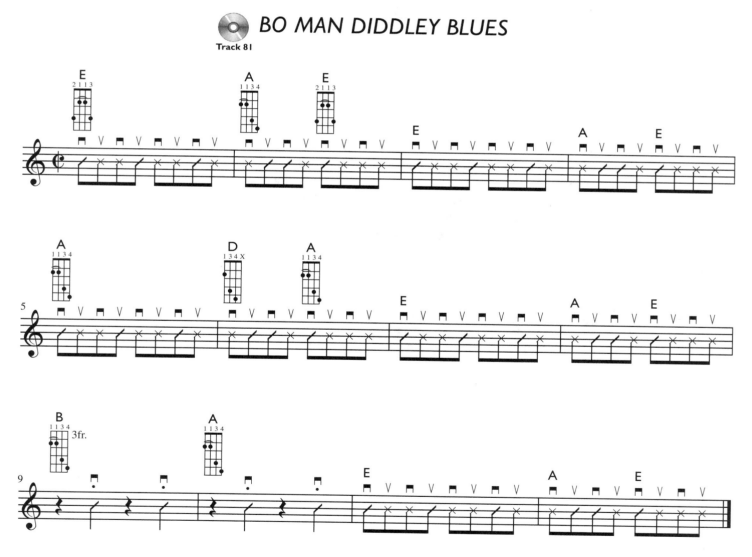

Reggae is the politically charged, infectiously danceable pop music of Jamaica. It combines Caribbean rhythms with the influence of classic American soul music. Modern mandolin pioneer Sam Bush brought the influence of reggae to the mandolin in his solo work and with his band, Newgrass Revival. Bush's rhythm playing was deeply influenced by the guitar techniques of reggae master Bob Marley.

REGGAE STRUMMING

The Reggae Backbeat

Like bluegrass, reggae's foundation is on the backbeat (beats 2 and 4 of a $\frac{4}{4}$ measure). The pace is generally more relaxed in reggae, and the strum often includes the upstroke on the "&" of the beat. Try this pattern using a swing eighth groove.

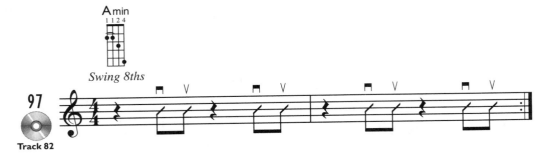

The Bob Marley Backbeat

Bob Marley's guitar technique was marked by clipped, percussive strums that sounded more like a percussion instrument than a chord instrument. He did it by using a variation of the funk squeezing and scratching technique you learned on page 182. Marley would often finger chords, but not quite squeeze them down all the way, just pulsing his fingers on the strings. These finger pulses are marked in this example using staccato eighth notes.

Adding Triplet Fills

When you have the basic groove going, you can vary the groove by adding "scratched" triplets during the rests in the bar. Example 99 adds a triplet on the first beat of bar 1 and the third beat of bar 2.

99
Track 84

Reggae Arpeggios

Here is a reggae-style tune using the rhythms you have learned. The second part of the tune uses reggae-style arpeggios. These often place a rest on the first beat, causing the arpeggio to sound more syncopated and spacious.

Track 85

HOW A'YOU GONNA PLAY DAT MANDO-LEEN?

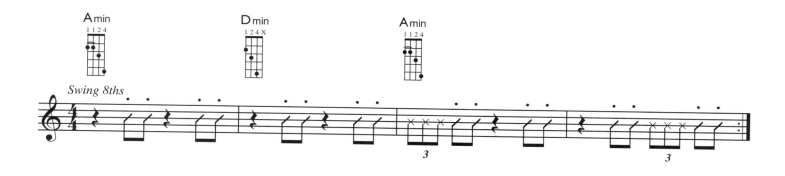

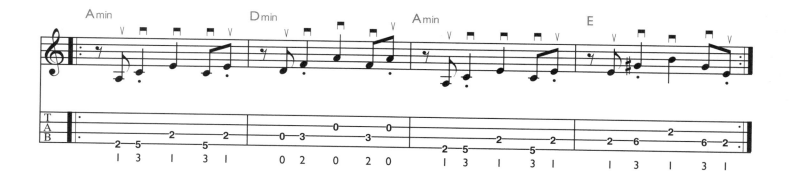

CHAPTER 10

A Taste of Brazil

The music of Brazil has had a huge influence on modern mandolin playing through players such as David Grisman and Mike Marshall. The chief influence comes from the Brazilian musical tradition called *choro*. Choro has its roots in the late 1800s, similar to American ragtime music and it has gone through many declines and revivals since then. It is played by small ensembles featuring string instruments, percussion and wind instruments and is known for unpredictable, leaping melodies, adventurous chord progressions and extremely virtuosic improvisation.

One of the great masters of choro was Jacob do Bandolim (the stage name of Jacob Pick Bittencourt). He was a terrific player of the Portuguese mandolin, called a *bandolim*. Jacob's recordings from the 1950s and '60s are still sought after as wonderful examples of the joy, passion and emotion of choro mandolin. The bandolim is usually teardrop shaped (like an A-style mandolin, but a bit bigger) with a flat or slightly arched top, a round soundhole and a deeper body than American mandolins.

LESSON 1: BRAZILIAN-STYLE RHYTHM PLAYING

In traditional choro music, the following rhythms are played by the *cavaquinho*, the Portuguese ancestor of the ukelele. The bandolim (mandolin) is considered a lead melody instrument. You can get some of the sound of the cavaquinho by learning the strum rhythms shown below. The rhythms in this lesson are drawn from rhythms heard in recordings by Jacob do Bandolim.

Brazilian rhythms are very highly syncopated, and carry the influence of the clave rhythm you learned on page 184. Here is a strum pattern in cut time based on a variation of the clave.

BRAZILIAN STRUM RHYTHM NO. 1—CLAVE VARIATION (SON CLAVE, 3–2)

Below is another common, yet extremely syncopated rhythm. Try tapping all four beats of each bar for a while before trying it in cut time. This one's a whole lot of fun, but you have to work to keep track of the beat!

BRAZILIAN STRUM RHYTHM NO. 2

Here is a chord progression for a tune written in the style of Jacob do Bandolim. It is set in a two-part form (like a fiddle tune) with repeated A and B parts, and includes a new strumming rhythm in the A part.

MANDOLIN JAKE (CHORDS AND RHYTHM)

Track 88

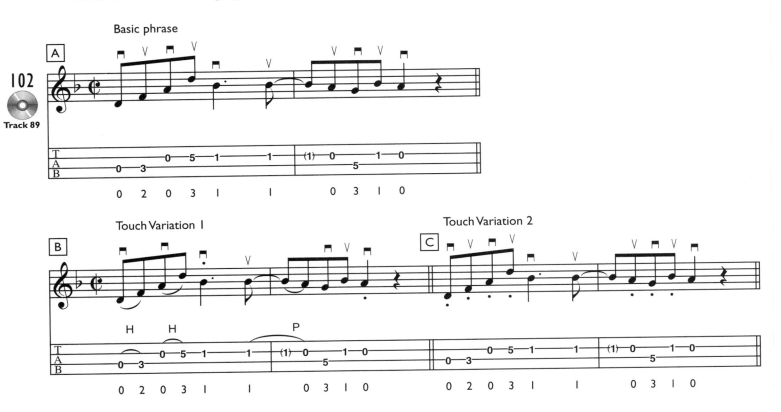

LESSON 2: BRAZILIAN-STYLE LEAD PLAYING

While choro music includes a great deal of improvisation and soloing, the main melodies are so sophisticated that they almost sound like improvised solos themselves. The tunes are full of 7th chord arpeggios, wide melodic leaps, sudden key and scale changes and syncopation.

THE IMPORTANCE OF "TOUCH"

One form of improvisation that is rarely discussed is the improvisational varying of touch. "Touch" refers to the way you articulate a note: You can use a downstroke, upstroke, accent it, play it legato (smooth and connected to other notes) or staccato (clipped and separated from other notes). Touch also includes slides, hammer-ons, pull-offs and any other form of articulation you can think of. Jacob do Bandolim was a master of the subtleties of touch. He would change the way he articulated a melody each time he played it.

Here is the first phrase of the melody of "Mandolin Jake" (page 191) shown with two additional variations based on changing the touch used.

On page 191 is the full melody of "Mandolin Jake." It is full of arpeggios, syncopation, and *chromatic passing tones* (notes outside of the scale that connect notes in the scale, generally in half steps). Specific touch markings have not been indicated; choose your own articulations as you master the tune.

MANDOLIN JAKE (MELODY)

Congratulations! You have completed the *Intermediate* section. Don't stop now—we'll see you in the *Mastering* section!

MASTERING MANDOLIN

WAYNE FUGATE

This book was acquired, edited, and produced
by Workshop Arts, Inc., the publishing arm of
the National Guitar Workshop.
Nathaniel Gunod, editor
Nathaniel Gunod, acquisitions, managing editor
Ante Gelo, music typesetter
Timothy Phelps, interior design
Audio tracks recorded at Grinning Deer Studios, Knoxville, TN

CONTENTS

PART THREE—RHYTHM

PART FOUR—PUTTING IT ALL TOGETHER

MP3 CD

00

Track 1

An MP3 CD is included with this book to make learning easier and more enjoyable. The symbol shown at bottom left appears next to every example in the book that features an MP3 track. Use the MP3s to ensure you're capturing the feel of the examples and interpreting the rhythms correctly. The track number below the symbol corresponds directly to the example you want to hear (example numbers are above the icon). All the track numbers are unique to each "book" within this volume, meaning every book has its own Track 1, Track 2, and so on. (For example, *Beginning Mandolin* starts with Track 1, as does *Intermediate Mandolin* and *Mastering Mandolin*.) Track 1 will help you tune to this CD.

The disc is playable on any CD player equipped to play MP3 CDs. To access the MP3s on your computer, place the CD in your CD-ROM drive. In Windows, double-click on My Computer, then right-click on the CD icon labeled "MP3 Files" and select Explore to view the files and copy them to your hard drive. For Mac, double-click on the CD icon on your desktop labeled "MP3 Files" to view the files and copy them to your hard drive.

ABOUT THE AUTHOR

PHOTO · DR. GEORGE PALMER

Mandolinist Wayne Fugate has developed a reputation for his versatility, having mastered musical styles as diverse as bluegrass, jazz and classical. Wayne studied extensively with mandolin virtuoso Barry Mitterhoff and credits him as being one of his primary musical influences. He further developed his technique under the tutelage of Mike Marshall.

He has performed with a host of bluegrass and acoustic music's finest artists including Tony Trischka, Hazel Dickens, Walt Michael & Co and Winfield guitar champion, Mark Cosgrove. Wayne has also been a member of The New York Mandolin Orchestra, an orchestra comprised solely of mandolin family instruments with an 80-year (plus) tradition of performing classical music.

Wayne's recording credits include contributions to Ben Freed's critically acclaimed CDs *Suite For Bluegrass Banjo*, *Speed Of Sound* and *Sugar Tree Stomp*, Lisa Gutkin's beautiful *Sidewalk Angel*, folksinger/songwriter Dean Friedman's *Songs for Grownups*, Bob Green's *Bluegrass & Other Traditional Music*, Tom Hanway's *Bucket of Bees*, Wretched Refuse String Band's self-titled CD and others. Wayne is also featured on mandolin, mandola, guitar, vocals and hammered dulcimer with his New York-based band, "Out To Lunch."

Wayne keeps a busy schedule by teaching mandolin and performing frequently with the incredibly talented Barebones & Wildflowers and Lisa's Pieces, a band that unites long-time friends Lisa Gutkin, Mark Murphy, Michael Sassano and Wayne.

Wayne Fugate has performed in a variety of venues ranging from coffee houses to festival stages. He performed as a co-soloist with Barry Mitterhoff at New York's Weill Recital Hall and at Carnegie Hall as a member of "The Clef Club" orchestra, under the direction of Maurice Peress. This concert enjoyed a sold out performance, a highly complimentary review in the New York Times and was later broadcast on National Public Radio with narration provided by Wynton Marsalis.

This book is dedicated with love and gratitude to Wayne's family,
"extended family" and band mates in "Out to Lunch"
and to his teachers, Barry Mitterhoff and Mike Marshall.

INTRODUCTION

Welcome to *Mastering Mandolin*, the final part of *The Complete Mandolin Method*. This section goes deeper into the concepts and techniques introduced in the *Beginning* and *Intermediate* sections.

WHO THIS SECTION IS INTENDED FOR

This section is designed for advanced students; to get the most out of it, you should be familiar with the construction of the major scale, triad structures, open chords, major and minor moveable chords, the circle of 5ths, key signatures, playing in a variety of time signatures including at least $\frac{4}{4}$, $\frac{3}{4}$, $\frac{2}{4}$ and double stops. These topics are covered in either the *Beginning* or *Intermediate* sections. You do not need to be able to read music to use this book as TAB (tablature) is provided. However, a basic knowledge of music reading is highly encouraged and will aid your ability to understand the scales, chords, rhythms and modal keys discussed. Being able to read music is the single biggest gift you can give yourself as a musician. The basics are covered in the *Beginning* and *Intermediate* sections, and there are many other books and study aids available should you want to increase your music reading proficiency.

HOW TO USE THIS SECTION

This section is organized into four main parts:

Harmony

This part covers new chords that extend beyond basic triads and 7th chords. You will also learn how to organize these new chords into popular chord progressions, create inversions of these chords, substitute chords appropriately, and finally, how to craft chords into a chord/melody solo.

Melody

This part covers the five basic scale types that every mandolin player should know, the modes of the major scale, pentatonic scales, the blues scale, whole tone scales and the chromatic scale.

Rhythm

This part reviews and introduces a variety of time signatures. You will learn how to vary tunes by changing the time signature and how to create a limitless number of variations on a melody through rhythmic variation.

Putting It All Together

This part brings together all of the concepts you've learned and presents a methodology for learning how to improvise. There is also a brief chapter about music from around the world.

Mastering Mandolin is designed so that you can study the harmony, melody and rhythm sections simultaneously or sequentially. The last chapter brings together many of the skills and concepts learned in previous parts and should be saved for last.

WHERE TO GO FROM HERE

This three-section method was designed to give you a foundation of technique and improvisational theory to help you play virtually all types of Western music with a special focus on bluegrass, Celtic and jazz. You can build your understanding by applying the lessons in this method to other keys and positions, trying your hand at creating your own compositions and by continuing your study using the many books, recordings, and videos that are available.

CHAPTER 1

Warm-Ups

This chapter includes some warm-up exercises from the ridiculously talented mandolin player, Mike Marshall. They focus on both the right and left hands and will help your flexibility, finger independence and right-hand coordination if practiced routinely.

No matter how advanced a player you are, it is always beneficial to spend a few minutes running through some warm-ups that include scales, arpeggios and a few exercises like those included in this chapter. Even the most basic exercises (such as the first few for the right hand on page 202) can pay big dividends since they help train both muscle and mind in good basic technique, which becomes all the more important as you start to take on more challenging material. Don't make the mistake of playing these exercises "flat," without feeling or musicality. Instead, do your best to put some feeling into each note you play.

FOCUS ON THE RIGHT HAND

Watch your pick direction and experiment with the tone. Picking closer to the bridge has one affect, picking farther away from the bridge has another. Be sure to keep your grip on the pick loose— just tight enough to be able to hold on to it. Gripping the pick like a vice would put all of the muscles you need to play quickly, fluidly and with good tone at a huge disadvantage. Imagine trying to run a marathon with all the muscles in your lower body clenched tight—you probably wouldn't make the first mile marker!

FOCUS ON THE LEFT HAND

Look for any wasted movement and practice good basic technique. Keep your fingers nicely curved and floating close to the frets. Economy of motion in your left hand becomes increasingly important as the material you challenge yourself with increases in difficulty and speed.

PHOTO COURTESY OF MIKE MARSHALL

Mike Marshall's touring and recording career began as a member of the original David Grisman Quintet in 1979. Since those days Mike has been at the center of the acoustic music scene and can be heard on hundreds of recordings of acoustic music. His mastery of mandolin, guitar and violin and his ability to swing gracefully between jazz, classical, bluegrass and Latin styles is rare in the world of American vernacular instrumentalists. He has performed and recorded with some of the top acoustic string instrumentalists in the world including Stephane Grappelli, Mark O'Connor, Bela Fleck, Edgar Meyer, Montreux and Joshua Bell.

In 1986 Mike founded a classical string quartet of mandolin family instruments (two mandolins, mandola and mandocello). This group, the Modern Mandolin Quartet, released four recordings for Windham Hill Records, which redefined the mandolin in a classical music setting. In 1995 the Quartet made its Carnegie Hall debut and in 1996 received a "Meet the Composer" grant from the Lila Wallace Foundation.

Example 1 is a great exercise for stretching your left hand. Bear in mind that a little goes a long way. Don't overdo it—especially if you start to feel any discomfort or pain! When you complete this exercise, it's a good idea to (literally) shake your left hand out and let it relax before continuing with your practice.

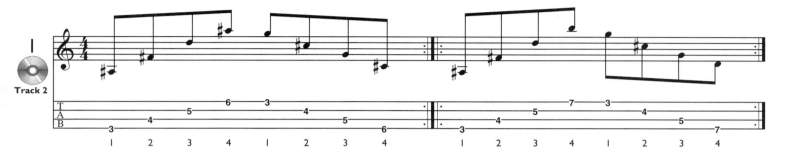

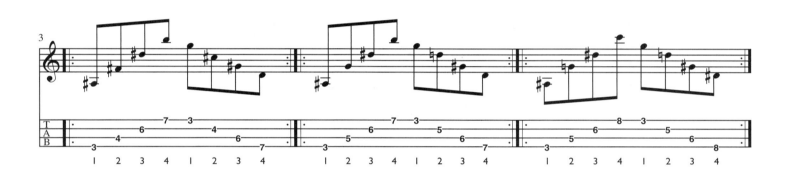

Example 2 is a great exercise for increasing independence between the fingers of your left hand. It starts out in a relatively simple fashion, using just your 1st and 2nd fingers. As you progress through the exercise, where you are working with just your 3rd and 4th fingers, you may find that it becomes more of a challenge.

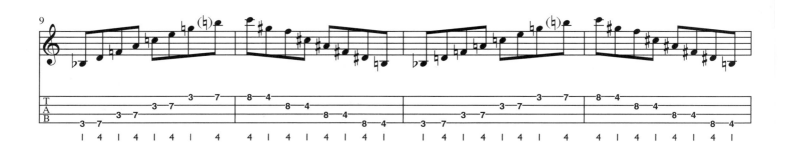

PART ONE—HARMONY

CHAPTER 2

Important Chords

In working through the first two books in this series, you learned how the basic chords are constructed. As an advanced mandolin player, you will take on more challenging material and so your understanding of chords (harmony), melodic devices (scales and modes) and rhythm will need to expand as well.

EXTENDED MAJOR CHORDS

Melody doesn't exist in a vacuum. It relates very closely to the underlying harmonic structure. A discussion of extended and altered chord forms is a logical place to begin our exploration of advanced mandolin playing.

Here is a C Major scale shown over two octaves. The numbers under each tone describe the position, or scale degree, of that note in the scale. Beginning at the second octave (8), the notes have the same letter names but the numbers increase to show their respective distances from the 1st degree or tonic of the scale (C).

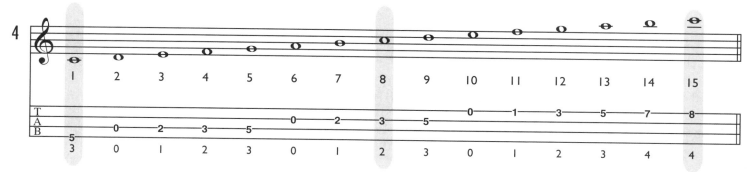

Extended chords can be built from this scale by applying a numerical formula to the C Major scale in much the same way that basic chords are constructed. For example, to construct a basic C Major triad we simply stack 3rds by using every third note in the C Major scale starting from tonic:

- Start with 1 (C)
- Skip 2 (D)
- Include 3 (E)
- Skip 4 (F)
- Include 5 (G)

We wind up with 1–3–5 of the scale, which are the root, 3rd and 5th of the chord, respectively. When played together, these tones create a basic C Major triad.

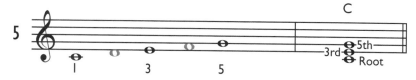

We can use this same simple concept approach to expand into the world of 7th chords, and by picking the appropriate scale tones, create a wealth of new chords. For example, to create a C Major 7 (CMaj7) we simply use 1–3–5–7 of the major scale.

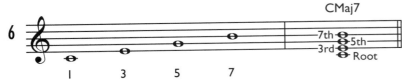

We can now continue into the realm of extended chords, which are chords that include tones beyond the 7th. To make a major 9th chord, such as C Major 9 (CMaj9), we use 1–3–5–7–9 of the C Major scale.

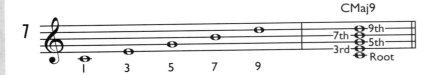

To make major 11th (Maj11) and 13th (Maj13) chords we use 1–3–5–7–9–11 and 1–3–5–7–9–11–13, respectively, like this:

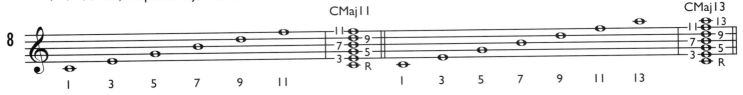

R = Root

The chart below organizes all the notes of all the major scales in the order required for the construction of major 7th chords and their extensions. At the top, across the first row, we see the root of each chord. Then, reading down the chart we can see the notes required to construct major 7th, major 9th, major 11th and major 13th chords. Notice that the keys of D♭ and G♭ can be enharmonically respelled to C# and F#, respectively.

MAJOR CHORD EXTENSION CHART

1st (root)	C	F	B♭	E♭	A♭	D♭/C#	G♭/F#	B/C♭	E	A	D	G
3rd	E	A	D	G	C	F	B♭	D#	G#	C#	F#	B
5th	G	C	F	B♭	E♭	A♭	D♭	F#	B	E	A	D
7th	B	E	A	D	G	C	F	A#	D#	G#	C#	F#
9th (Same as 2nd)	D	G	C	F	B♭	E♭	A♭	C#	F#	B	E	A
11th (Same as 4th)	F	B♭	E♭	A♭	D♭	G♭	C♭	E	A	D	G	C
13th (Same as 6th)	A	D	G	C	F	B♭	E♭	G#	C#	F#	B	E

SAMPLES
FMaj9 = F–A–C–E–G
AMaj11 = A–C#–E–G#–B–D

Let's use this chart to construct a CMaj13 chord. You can see that we would need the 1st, 3rd, 5th, 7th, 9th, 11th and 13th tones in the C Major scale—the notes C, E, G, B, D, F and A. To create an A9 chord, you can see that we would need the 1st, 3rd, 5th, 7th and 9th tones in the A Major scale—the notes A, C#, E, G# and B.

EXTENDED MINOR CHORDS

The 13th chord is the farthest possible extension of the basic major triad. After that, the scale tones starts to repeat themselves and no new chords result.

Even though we can't extend these chords any farther we can *alter* them. In fact, to create virtually every other type of chord available in Western music (minor, dominant, half-diminished, diminished) we must alter the major scale.

MINOR CHORDS

To build a basic minor triad, all we need do is alter our major scale by lowering the 3rd degree of the scale one half step (♭3).

Altering the Major Scale to Create a Minor Triad

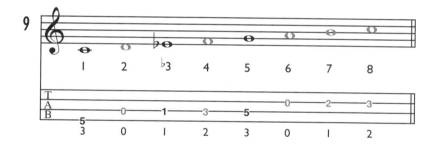

Using our system of stacking 3rds to build a triad, we would choose the 1–♭3–5 (C, E♭, G) to build a basic C Minor (Cmin) triad. However, to build minor chords beyond this basic triad, we'll employ a slightly more altered scale that lowers the 7th tone (♭7) in the scale by one half step.

Altering the Major Scale to Create Extended Minor Chords

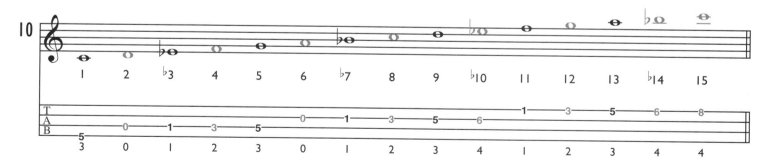

Using this scale with our system of stacking 3rds, we can extend the basic minor triad and build new chords just as we did with the major triad. Our chart for minor chords takes the ♭3 and ♭7 into consideration.

MINOR CHORD EXTENSION CHART

1st (root)	C	F	B♭	E♭	A♭	D♭/C#	G♭/F#	B/C♭	E	A	D	G
♭3rd	E♭	A♭	D♭	G♭	C♭*/B	F♭*/E	A	D	G	C	F	B♭
5th	G	C	F	B♭	E♭	A♭	D♭	F#	B	E	A	D
♭7th	B♭	E♭	A♭	D♭	G♭/F#	C♭/B	E	A	D	G	C	F
9th (Same as 2nd)	D	G	C	F	B♭	E♭	A♭	C#	F#	B	E	A
11th (Same as 4th)	F	B♭	E♭	A♭	D♭	G♭	C♭	E	A	D	G	C
13th (Same as 6th)	A	D	G	C	F	B♭	E♭	G#	C#	F#	B	E

SAMPLES
Fmin9 = F–A♭–C–E♭–G
Amin11 = A–C–E–G–B–D

* These tones are often enharmonically respelled.

EXTENDED DOMINANT CHORDS

To build a basic dominant 7th chord, all we need do is alter our major scale by lowering the 7th degree of the scale one half step.

Altering the Major Scale to Create Extended Dominant Chords

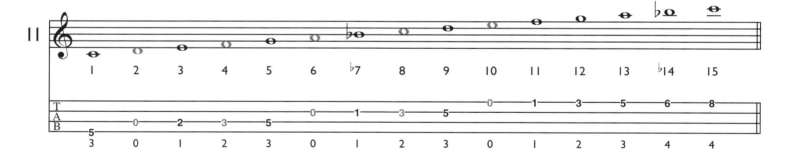

Using our system of stacking 3rds to build a basic dominant 7th chord, we choose the 1–3–5–♭7 of the scale (C, E, G, B♭) to build a C Dominant 7 (C7) chord. We can extend this basic dominant 7th chord and build new chords using the method we've employed for the major and minor chords. The chart for dominant chords (top of page 207) takes the ♭7 into consideration.

DOMINANT CHORD EXTENSION CHART

1st (root)	C	F	B♭	E♭	A♭	D♭/C#	G♭/F#	B/C♭	E	A	D	G
3rd	E	A	D	G	C	F	B♭	D#	G#	C#	F#	B
5th	G	C	F	B♭	E♭	A♭	D♭	F#	B	E	A	D
♭7th	B♭	E♭	A♭	D♭	G♭/F#	B	E	A	D	G	C	F
9th (Same as 2nd)	D	G	C	F	B♭	E♭	A♭	C#	F#	B	E	A
11th (Same as 4th)	F	B♭	E♭	A♭	D♭	G♭	C♭	E	A	D	G	C
13th (Same as 6th)	A	D	G	C	F	B♭	E♭	G#	C#	F#	B	E

SAMPLES
F9 = F–A–C–E♭–G
A11 = A–C#–E–G–B–D

DIMINISHED 7TH CHORDS

MINOR 7♭5 CHORDS

There are two types of 7th chord based on a diminished triad. One of these types of chords is the *minor 7♭5*. This type of chord is also referred to as a *half-diminished* chord.

Minor7♭5 chords are built by lowering the 3rd and 7th tones of the scale by one half step (just like the minor 7th scale). In addition, the 5th of the scale is also lowered by one half step to create a ♭5.

Altering the Major Scale to Create Minor 7th ♭5 Chords

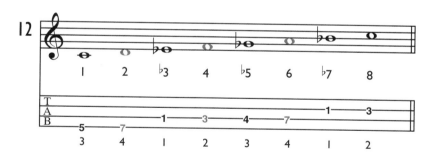

This type of chord is rarely extended beyond the 7th.

In summary, to construct a minor 7th ♭5 chord, we use 1–♭3–♭5–♭7.

MINOR 7♭5 CHORD CHART

1st (root)	C	F	B♭	E♭	A♭	D♭/C#	G♭/F#	B	E	A	D	G
♭3rd	E♭	A♭	D♭	G♭	C♭/B	F♭/E	A	D	G	C	F	B♭
♭5th	G♭	C♭/B	F♭/E	A	D	G	C	F	B♭	E♭	A♭	D♭
♭7th	B♭	E♭	A♭	D♭	G♭/F#	B	E	A	D	G	C	F

SAMPLES
Fmin7♭5 = F–A♭–B*–E♭
Amin7♭5 = A–C–E♭–G

DIMINISHED 7TH CHORDS

Another chord that is built on the diminished triad is the *diminished 7th* (dim7) chord. Diminished 7th chords are built with these tones: 1–♭3–♭5–♭♭7. That's right, the 7th tone of the scale is *double flatted* (or lowered one whole step).

Altering the Major Scale to Create Diminished 7th Chords

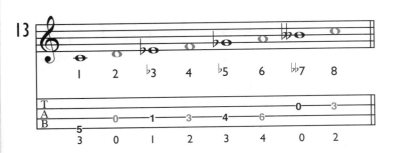

This type of chord can't be extended beyond the 7th because it repeats itself.

One unique thing about the diminished 7th chord is that all of the stacked 3rds are a minor 3rd (a whole step plus a half step) apart.

DIMINISHED 7TH CHORD CHART

1st (root)	C	F	B♭	E♭	A♭	D♭/C#	G♭/F#	B	E	A	D	G
♭3rd	E♭	A♭	D♭	G♭	B	E		A	D	G	C	F	B♭
♭5th	G♭	B	E	A	D	G		C	F	B♭	E♭	A♭	D♭
♭♭7th	A	D	G	C	F	B♭		E♭	A♭	D♭	G♭	B	E

SAMPLES

Fdim7 = F–A♭–B–D
Adim7 = A–C–E♭–G♭

OTHER IMPORTANT CHORDS

6TH CHORDS

6th chords are built by simply adding the sixth tone of the major scale to a major or minor triad. With few exceptions, such as the 6/9 chord, 6th chords do not involve extensions into the next octave. To build a major 6th chord (6), we use 1–3–5–6 (C, E, G, A). To build a minor 6th chord (min6), we use 1–♭3–5–6 (C, E♭, G, A).

Major 6th Chord Chart

1st (root)	C	F	B♭	E♭	A♭	D♭/C#	G♭/F#	B/C♭	E	A	D	G
3rd	E	A	D	G	C	F	B♭	D#	G#	C#	F#	B
5th	G	C	F	B♭	E♭	A♭	D♭	F#	B	E	A	D
6th	A	D	G	C	F	B♭	E♭	G#	C#	F#	B	E

SAMPLES
F6 = F–A–C–D
A6 = A–C#–E–F#

Minor 6th Chord Chart

1st (root)	C	F	B♭	E♭	A♭	D♭/C#	G♭/F#	B/C♭	E	A	D	G
♭3rd	E♭	A♭	D♭	G♭	C♭/B	F♭/E	A	D	G	C	F	B♭
5th	G	C	F	B♭	E♭	A♭	D♭	F#	B	E	A	D
6th	A	D	G	C	F	B♭	E♭	G#	C#	F#	B	E

SAMPLES
Fmin6 = F–A♭–C–D
Amin6 = A–C–E–F#

SUSPENDED 4TH CHORDS

Suspended 4 chords (sus4) are made up of the 1st, 4th and 5th tones in a scale. Notice that suspended chords are chords that have the fourth scale degree instead of the third. The chord is neither major nor minor.

Suspended 4 chords are most typically used to make a smooth transition from a major scale to a minor scale. All in all, it's an extremely versatile and nice sounding chord.

Suspended 4 Chord Chart

1st (root)	C	F	B♭	E♭	A♭	D♭/C#	G♭/F#	B/C♭	E	A	D	G
4th	F	B♭	E♭	A♭	D♭	G♭	B	E	A	D	G	C
5th	G	C	F	B♭	E♭	A♭	D♭	F#	B	E	A	D

SAMPLES
Fsus4 = F–B♭–C
Asus4 = A–D–E

SUSPENDED 2ND CHORDS

The suspended 2nd chord (sus2) consists of 1–2–5. In the same way that the 4th replaces the 3rd in a sus4 chord, the 2nd replaces the 3rd in a sus2 chord. Therefore, just like a suspended 4 chord, it is neither major nor minor.

Suspended 2 Chord Chart

1st (root)	C	F	B♭	E♭	A♭	D♭/C♯	G♭/F♯	B/C♭	E	A	D	G
2nd	D	G	C	F	B♭	E♭	A♭	C♯	F♯	B	E	A
5th	G	C	F	B♭	E♭	A♭	D♭	F♯	B	E	A	D

SAMPLES

Fsus2 = F–G–C

Asus2 = A–B–E

ALTERED CHORDS

So far in this chapter, we've covered all the basic chord types and their extensions. Familiarity with these types of chords will cover you in most playing situations. Be aware, however, that beyond what we've covered here there are an almost infinite number of additional alterations that can be applied to these chords.

Additional chord alterations usually center on either lowering or raising the 5th, 9th, 11th and 13th. These chords might have names such as Maj7♯5 (or ♭5), Maj7♯9 (or ♭9), Maj9♯11(or ♭11), Maj11♯13(or ♭13). The same alterations could apply to minor or dominant chords as well resulting in names like min7♭9 or 11♯9, to name just two. One of the most common altered chords is a simple *augmented triad*: 1–3–♯5.

Even beyond these alterations, multiple alterations can be applied to create very complex chords such as 7♯9♭13 or 7♭5♭9♭13, again, to name just two. Many fine books cover the almost infinite possibilities of chord construction, such as *Theory for the Contemporary Guitarist*, or *Jazz Keyboard Harmony* (both published by Alfred and the National Guitar/ Keyboard Workshop), and, although not written specifically for mandolinists, you can learn much from them.

CHORD REFERENCE CHARTS

The chord charts on the following pages are provided to familiarize you with one way of fingering some common chords in each of the 12 keys. As you play through each of these forms, try to be conscious of where each scale tone in the chord is and how raising or lowering the 5th, 9th, 11th or 13th by a fret changes the name and sound of the chord.

C CHORD FAMILY

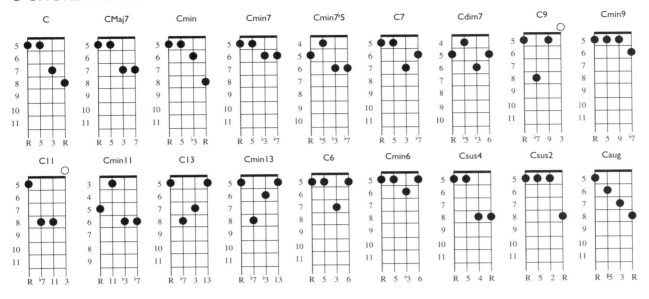

D CHORD FAMILY

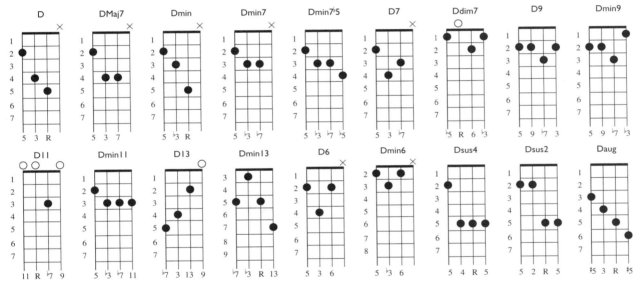

G CHORD FAMILY

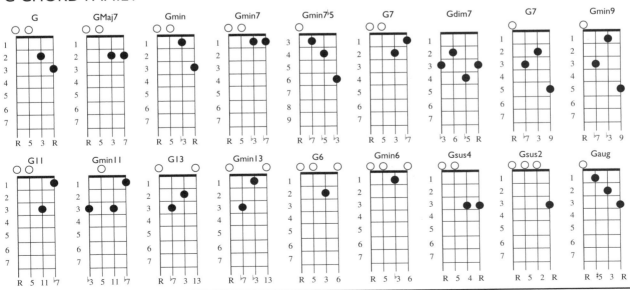

A CHORD FAMILY

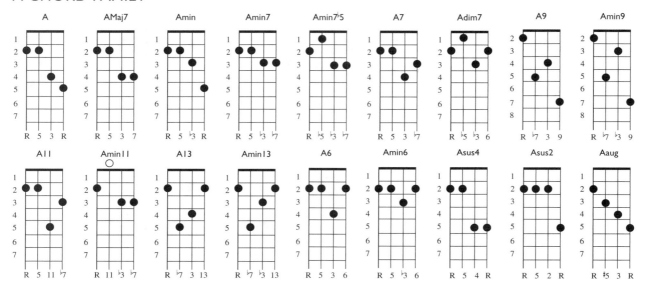

E CHORD FAMILY

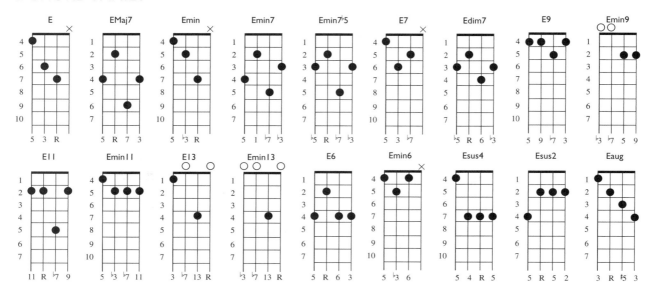

B CHORD FAMILY

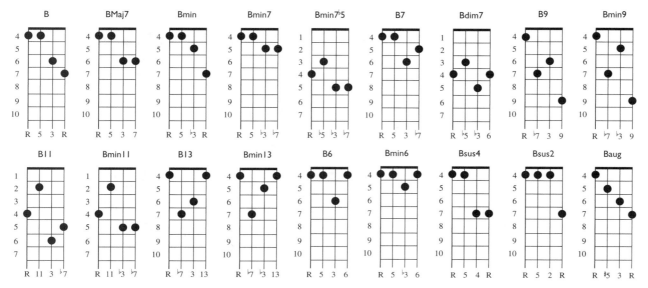

F♯ CHORD FAMILY (ALSO G♭ CHORD FAMILY)

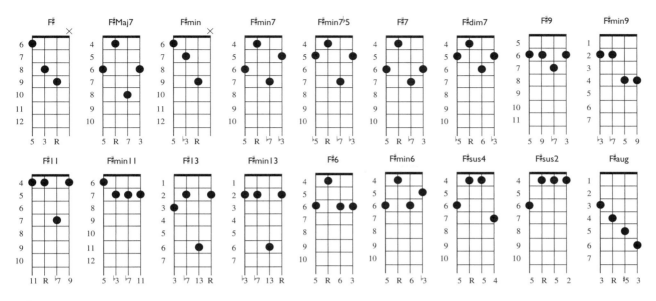

D♭ CHORD FAMILY (ALSO C♯ CHORD FAMILY)

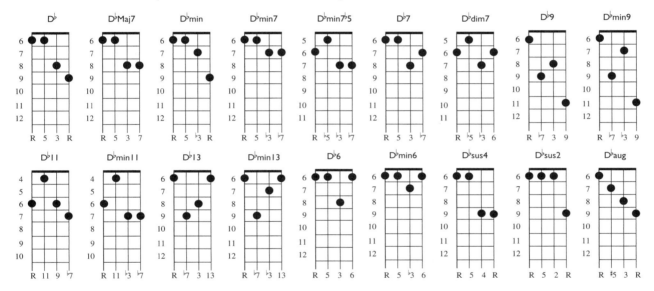

A♭ CHORD FAMILY (ALSO G♯ CHORD FAMILY)

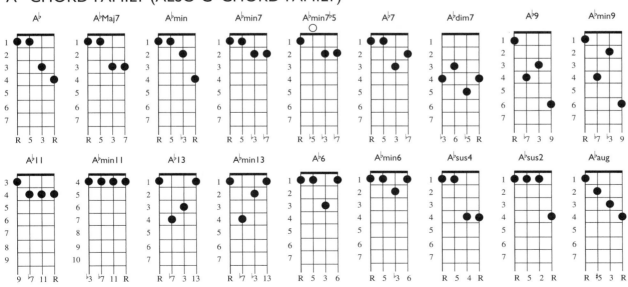

E♭ CHORD FAMILY

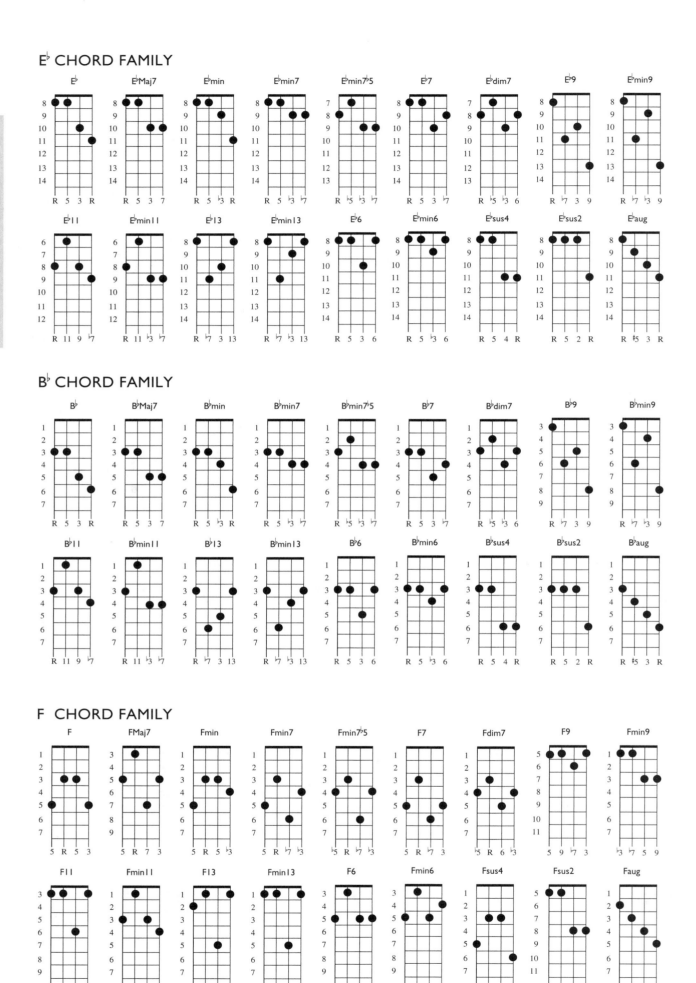

B♭ CHORD FAMILY

F CHORD FAMILY

FINDING OTHER VOICINGS

In the preceding charts, only one way of playing each chord was shown. Now that you know how chords are constructed, you are also no doubt aware that there are many different ways to play them on the fretboard. Try to create your own alternate *voicings* (arrangements of chord tones) for these chords. To do this, you need to know which tones are most important to each chord and which are disposable. After all, you've only got four strings and theoretically, any extended chord has more than four notes. You can usually toss the root and the 5th, unless the 5th has been altered in some way. You will usually want to keep the 3rd, the 7th and any notes beyond the 7th that convey the "color" of the chord.

Finally, here is a neat trick from the amazing mandolin player, Barry Mitterhoff, for learning new voicings up and down the fretboard. Let's start with this simple open C Major chord voicing.

The trick is to find the next higher note in the chord on each string. For example, looking at this chord from 4th to the 1st string, the lowest note in this voicing is an open G-note (the 5th of the chord). Looking farther up the fretboard we find that the next note that occurs in a C Major chord on the 4th string is a C (the root). Continue this process for each string as shown in the chart at the right.

Strings	1	2	3	4
Original voicing	G	E	C	G
	↓	↓	↓	↓
Next voicing	C	G	E	C

This creates a new position of the C Major chord. Finding a comfortable way to play these chord tones further up the neck gives you the "new" C Major chord beginning on the 5th fret. The original voicing had the 5th on the lowest string (*2nd inversion*). The new one has the root on the lowest string (*root position*).

If we follow this process again, beginning from the C-note on the 4th string, we wind up with yet another C Major chord beginning on the 9th fret. This one has the 3rd on the lowest string (*1st inversion*).

You can apply this process to virtually any chord and dramatically expand both your vocabulary of chords and your knowledge of the fretboard.

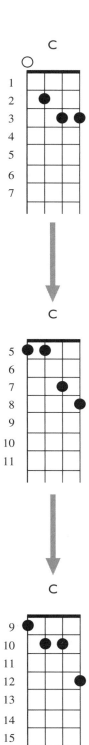

CHAPTER 3

Chord Progressions

Many tunes in all styles of music make use of the extended and altered chords covered in the last chapter. Now that you have a vocabulary of these chords, the next task is to put them into *chord progressions* (series of chords that comprise a piece of music). Certain chord progressions are used by most musicians in many styles of music. Chief among these are the blues progressions.

BLUES FORMS

Blues progressions are widely used as the basis for blues, bluegrass, rock and jazz tunes. There are 8-, 12-, 14-, 16- and 24-bar blues progressions, all based on combining the I, IV and V chords (see pages 89–90 for a full explanation of diatonic harmony) in a prescribed form. Here is the simplest blues progression—*the 8-bar blues*.

8-BAR BLUES
Track 5

The most common blues form is the *12-bar blues*. There are many examples of this type of progression in all styles of music. The alternate IV chord in bar 2 is a common variation called a *quick 4*. It is found both ways.

12-BAR BLUES
Track 6

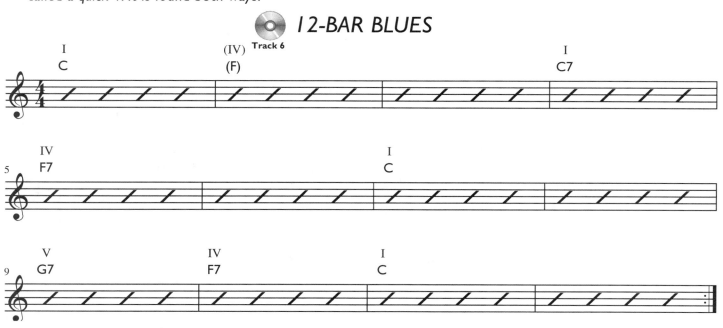

There are at least two variations of the *16-bar blues*. This one is created by repeating bars 5–8 of a 12-bar blues.

16-BAR BLUES (1ST VARIATION)
Track 7

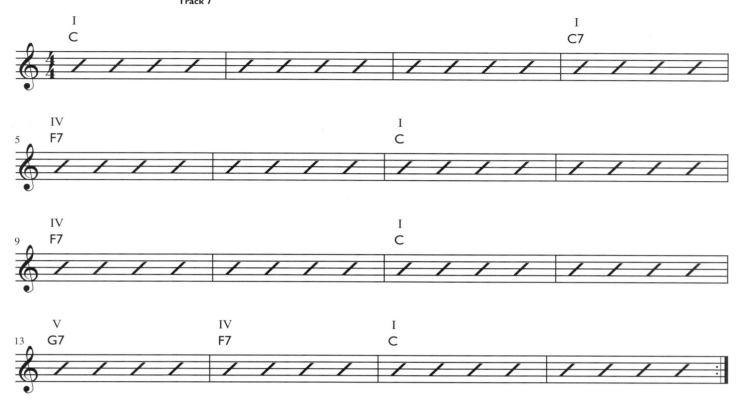

Another variation of the 16-bar blues is simply the 8-bar structure with all chords doubled over twice the number of bars.

16-BAR BLUES (2ND VARIATION)
Track 8

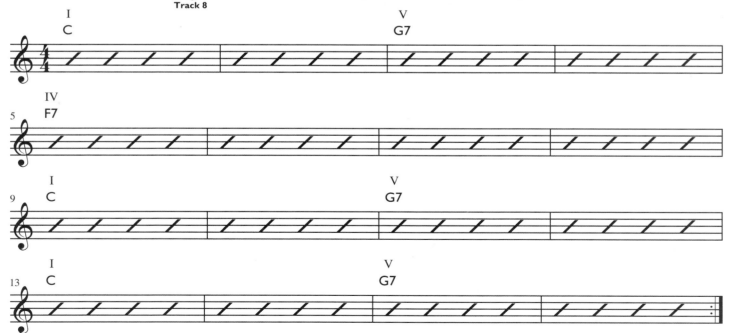

If you double the bars of a 12-bar blues, just as we did in creating the 16-bar blues (2nd Variation) from an 8-bar blues, the result is a 24-bar form. Notice the alternate chord (IV) in bars 3 and 4. You will hear this IV chord substituted for the I chord frequently in this particular form. This is just a larger version of the quick 4 discussed on page 216.

24-BAR BLUES

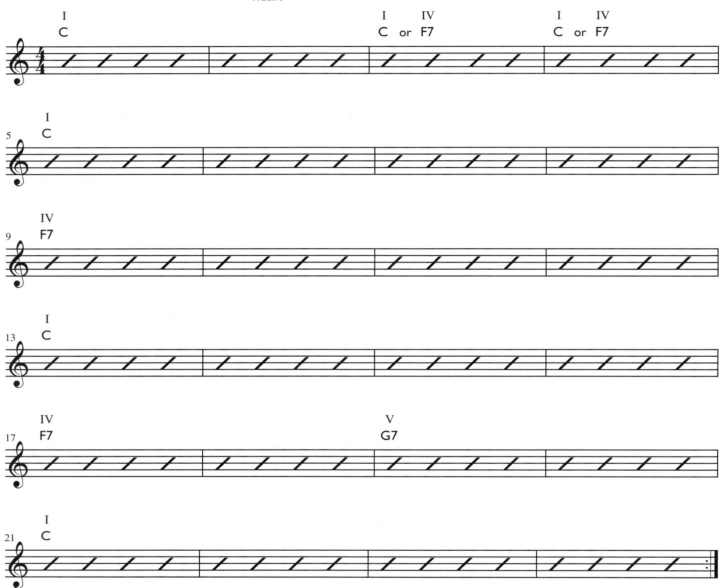

Blues chord progressions can be played in any key, so there is an incentive for learning all the chords (and scale material from Part Two—Melody) in all twelve keys.

Following are a few tunes that make use of blues progressions. First, here's a pretty straight forward 12-bar blues in the key of G Major.

12-BAR BLUES IN G

Track 10

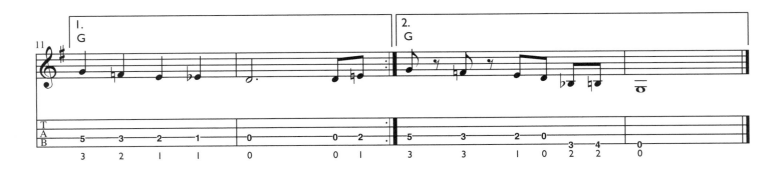

Here is a 12-bar blues again, this time in the key of F Major, using chords that might be used by a jazz player such as Charlie Parker. Notice the *sixteenth-note triplet* in bar 9. This is three sixteenth notes played in the time of two (half a beat). In this case, the first triplet sixteenth note is tied to the eighth note from the previous bar and thus not struck.

ALMOST TIME

Track 11

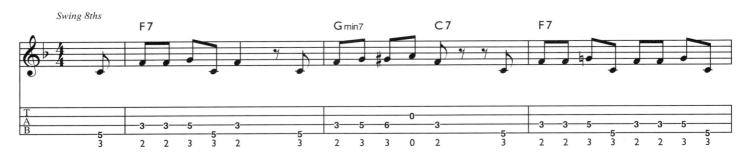

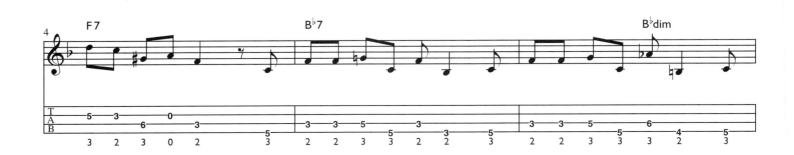

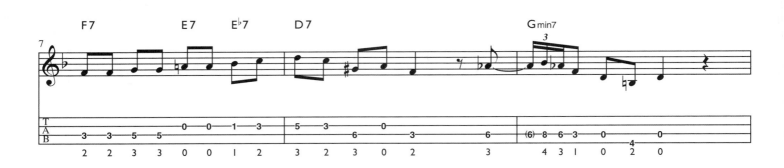

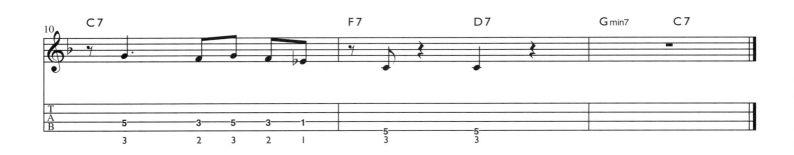

And finally, here is an example of how Bill Monroe, the bluegrass master, might approach a
12-bar blues in the key of D Major.

BLUES GRASS RAMBLE

Track 12

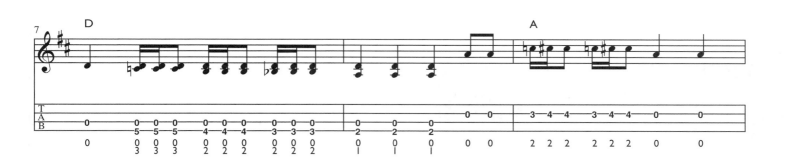

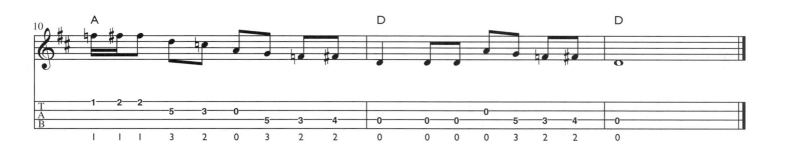

JAZZ—RHYTHM CHANGES

Another very common type of chord progression frequently used in jazz but also used in other styles is referred to as *Rhythm Changes*. The term Rhythm was coined in the late 1940s by bebop musicians referring to the chord progression, or *changes*, used in the 1930 George Gershwin tune, "I Got Rhythm."

After the blues, this structure, more than any other single chord progression, serves as the basis for more bebop and post-bebop tunes than any other. Countless jazz tunes have been written over this chord progression, including such classics as:

Song	Composer
"Anthropology "	Charlie Parker
"Celebrity"	Charlie Parker
"Dexterity"	Charlie Parker
"Good Queen Bess"	Duke Ellington
"Lester Leaps In"	Lester Young
"Oleo"	Sonny Rollins
"Red Top"	Lionel Hampton
"Rhythm-a-ning"	Thelonius Monk
"Straighten Up and Fly Right"	Nat Cole

...and a list of others that almost seems to be without end.

Rhythm Changes has a 32-bar harmonic structure following the A–A–B–A song form using the diatonic progression I-vi-ii-V7 in the A section. The remainder of the A section progression (the only part that is not I-vi-ii-V7, beginning at bar 5) is I–I7–IV–$^{\sharp}$iv°7. The $^{\sharp}$iv is a chord built on a root one half step higher than IV, and in this case is a diminished 7 chord.

Rhythm Changes are typically played in the key of B♭ but they are also played in various other keys, commonly F, E♭ and A♭. Once you have mastered these keys, move this progression through all of the other keys.

Keep in mind that this first example is the most basic version of Rhythm Changes. Many interesting variations exist, some of which we will investigate on the following pages.

George Gershwin (1898–1937) wrote hundreds of songs, several hit musicals and the opera Porgy and Bess (1935).

RHYTHM CHANGES (BASIC)

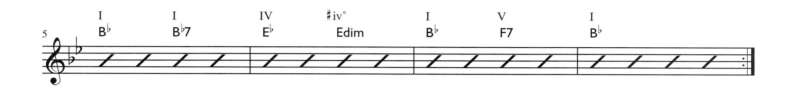

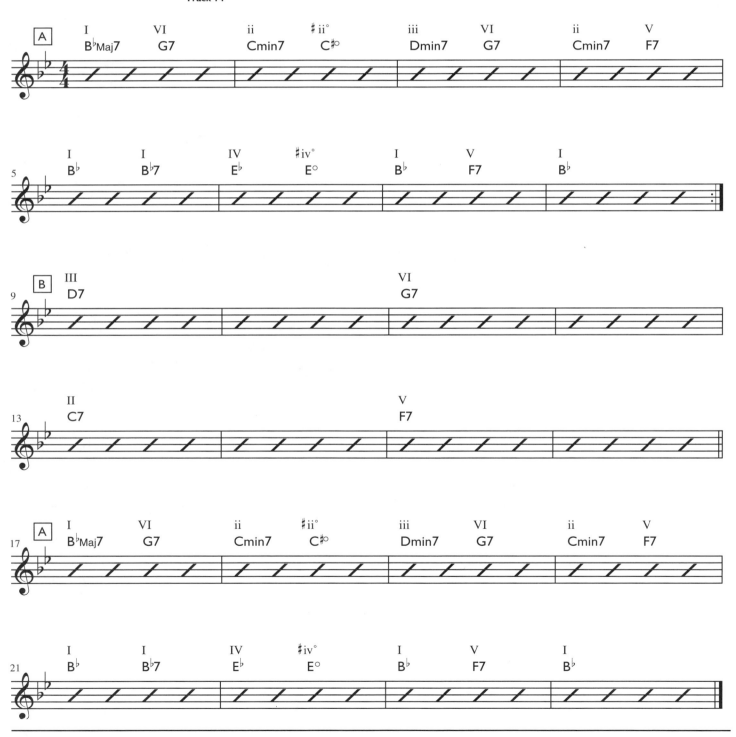

A few variations on Rhythm Changes follow. Over the years, jazz musicians used *chord substitutions* to create almost countless variations of Rhythm Changes in support of the many different melodies that have been played over the progression. In a chord substitution, a different but related chord is used instead of the original, basic chord to give a different effect. You should try analyzing each of these variations and do your best to try this material in all 12 keys. If you are interested in playing lots of jazz, you will need to study every jazz harmony book you can get your hands on and master the practice of chord substitution.

This first variation is typical of the way Rhythm Changes was played during the swing era (the 1930s).

RHYTHM CHANGES—SWING

Track 14

As swing gave way to the bebop era in jazz (the 1940s), Rhythm Changes might have been played as shown below. Note that bebop players liked to play 7th and 9th chords. They also liked to alter some of the extensions in dominant chords (note the use of #11s and ♭9s). Also notice that they created a little more motion in the tune by using the Fmin7 leading to the B♭7 in bar 5.

In the B section, notice that each dominant 7th chord changes to a min7 chord leading to the next dominant 7th chord. The movement of the min7 to the 7th chords can be analyzed as ii–V7. This pattern, in which each V chord becomes the ii of the next V chord, is often referred to as a *backcycle*.

RHYTHM CHANGES–BEBOP

Track 15

Still another more modern variation on Rhythm Changes often makes use of a type of substitution called *tritone substitution*. We'll be discussing this in more depth shortly, but for now try to listen for the *chromatic* (half step) movement that this type of substitution can produce. This is evident in bars 11–12 and 15–16.

RHYTHM CHANGES (TRITONE SUBSTITUTION)

Track 16

As you can see, there are many ways to reharmonize Rhythm Changes and we've just scratched the surface! This is one of the reasons that this progression has endured and proven so popular— it provides lots of options for an improviser.

Charlie Parker's (1920–1955) style relied on brilliant technique, surprising rhythms and sophisticated note choices, all of which contributed to a sound that was exciting but harder to dance to than the music of the swing era.

Let's apply a melody over a set of Rhythm Changes so you can get a better idea of how the chords function in supporting the melody. Here is a bebop tune composed in the style of Charlie Parker.

ANTHROMORPHOLOGY

Track 17

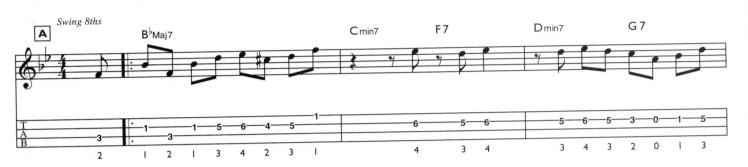

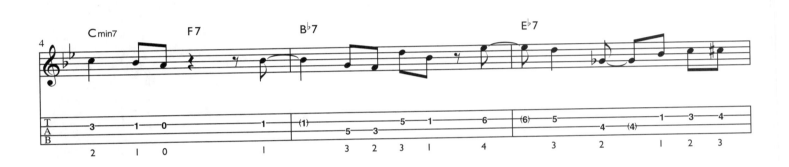

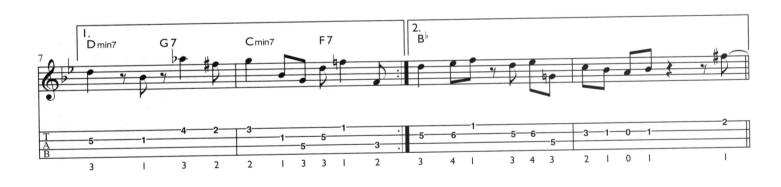

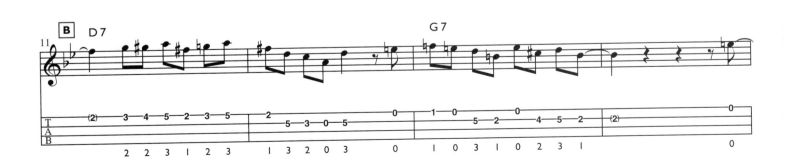

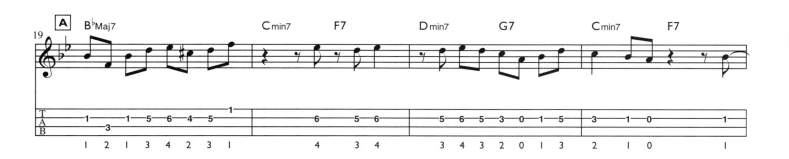

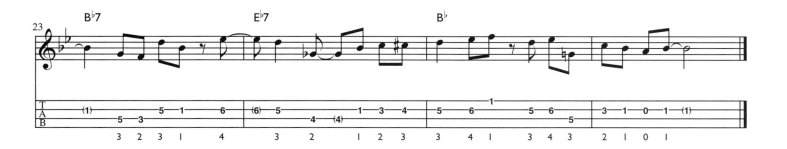

Here is another tune that makes use of some of the extended and altered chords that you've learned. Play along with the recording that is included with this book, with a friend or record the melody and play the chords along with yourself trying to focus on how the chords function to support the melody. Note the quintuplet in bar 13. This is five sixteenth notes in the time of four (one beat).

CRIMINAL SATISFACTION

Track 18

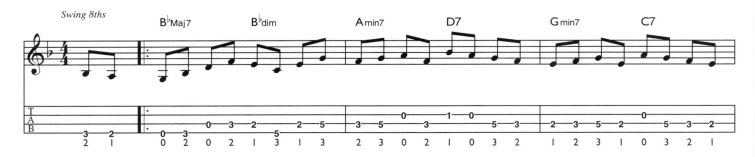

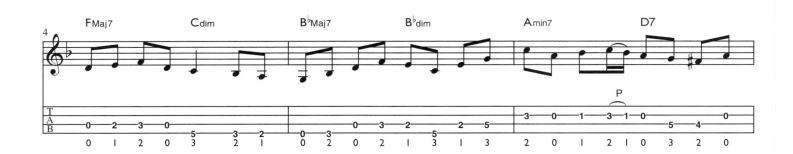

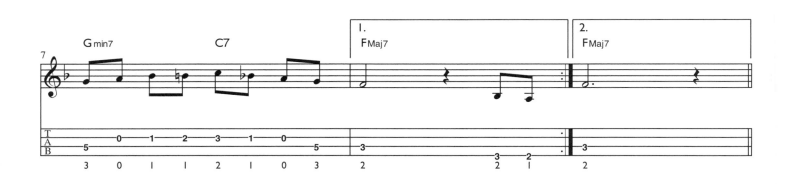

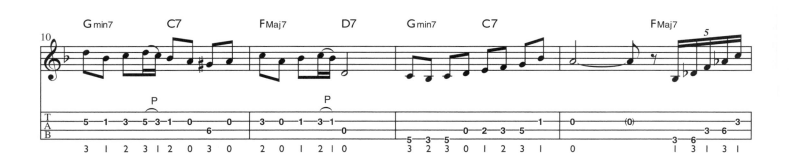

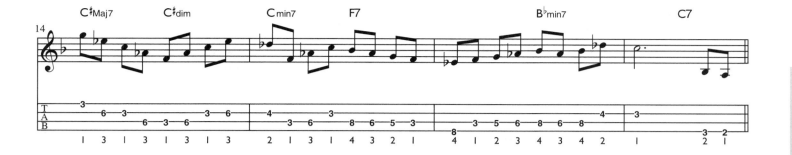

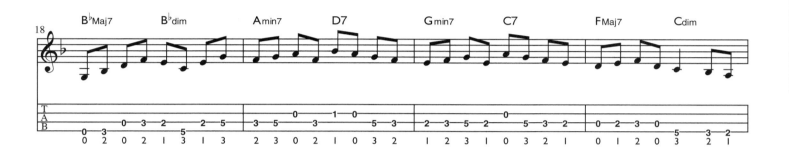

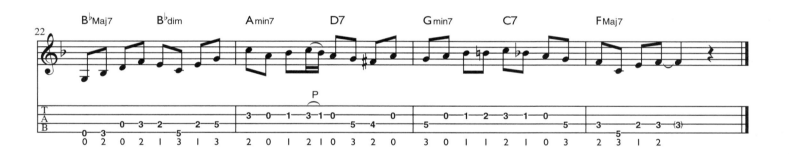

CHORD SUBSTITUTION

Chord substitution involves using a different, but musically valid, chord in place of the original chord. Chord substitution can involve something very simple, such as replacing a single chord with a different one, or it can be a vastly more complex process that involves reharmonizing an entire tune.

The art of chord substitution is based in part on knowledge and in part on taste. To truly present all the possible means and justifications for why one chord can function in place of another is a huge topic worthy of its own book. There are, however, a few guiding principles you can use to serve as a basis for further exploration.

Substitution Principle No. 1—Let Your Ear Be Your Guide
This one may be obvious but bears repeating. Let your ear and your taste guide you. Not all chord substitutions will sound good to you. It always depends on the context and the effect you're going for.

Substitution Principle No. 2—Use Chords With at Least Two Tones in Common
Chords that share several tones in common are likely to be good substitutes for one another. A good example is as follows: You can substitute the vi7 or the iii7 for the I chord of the same key. This is because those three chords share three common tones. For example, in the key of C, the I chord (CMaj7—C,E,G,B) shares the tones E, G and B with the iii7 chord (Emin7—E,G,B,D), and the tones C, E and G with the vi7 chord (Amin7—A,C,E,G).

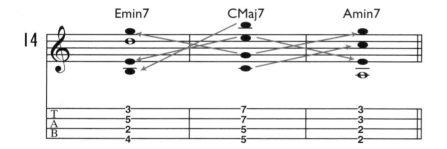

In practice, this chord progression ...

...can become this...

...or this.

Substitution Principle No. 3—Insert ii before V

In accordance with Substitution Principle No. 2, the ii7 chord may be substituted for the V7 chord. In C, ii7 is Dmin7 (D,F,A,C) and V is G7 (G,B,D,F); they have D and F in common. The point of this principle is that the ii7 can be inserted before its V7 chord, creating a ii–V chord progression. The ii–V progression is extremely common in jazz and lots of newgrass tunes as well. We saw it used in a backcycle in "Rhythm Changes—Bebop" on page 225.

This progression...

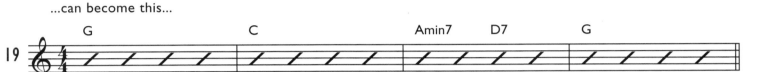

...can become this...

...or this.

Substitution Principle No. 4—Tritone Substitution

This rule states that you can replace a dominant 7th chord with another dominant 7th chord a *tritone* (an interval of three whole steps, or a ♭5) away.

The interval of a tritone, which gives the chord its characteristic sound, is found within every dominant 7th chord: the distance from the 3rd to the ♭7th. *Every tritone defines, and is shared by, two dominant 7th chords a tritone apart.*

Let's use a G7 chord as an example. Its tritone includes the notes B (3rd) and F (♭7th). A D♭7 chord, the dominant 7 chord that lies a tritone away from G7, also has a tritone that includes the notes B (♭7th, enharmonically respelled as C♭) and F (3rd).

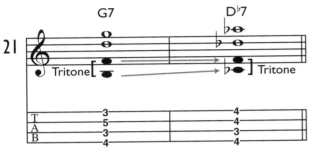

The important thing here is that the tritone B–F is present in both chords and, since these two notes give each chord its characteristic dominant 7th chord sound, they can be used interchangeably.

Here is an example of tritone substitution at work in a tune with chord changes for "Rollin' In My Sweet Baby's Arms." Here are the chords played "straight," without a tritone substitution.

ROLLIN' IN MY SWEET BABY'S ARMS (STRAIGHT)

Track 19

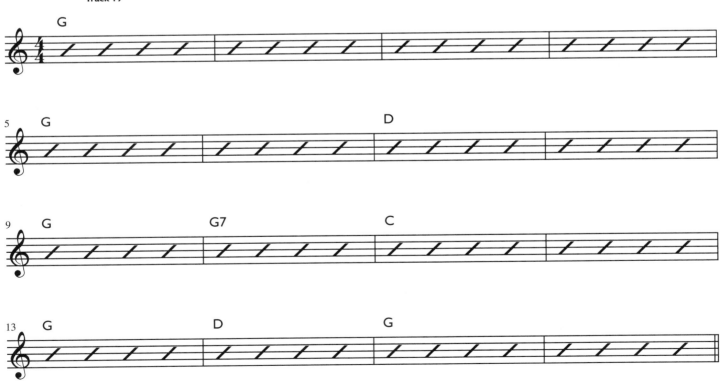

Here it is with a tritone substitution in bar 10.

 ROLLIN' IN MY SWEET BABY'S ARMS (TRITONE SUBSTITUTION)

Track 20

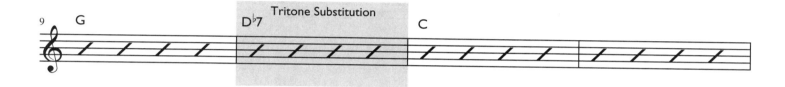

Substitution Principle No. 5—The Minor 3rd Substitution

Dominant 7th chords a minor 3rd apart can substitute for one another. Let's take another look at the chords to "Rollin In My Sweet Baby's Arms." In the 10th bar of this tune, we normally play a G7. We could use an E♭7 chord, which is a minor 3rd away, in place of the G7 for a different effect.

ROLLIN' IN MY SWEET BABY'S ARMS (MINOR 3RD SUBSTITUTION)

Track 21

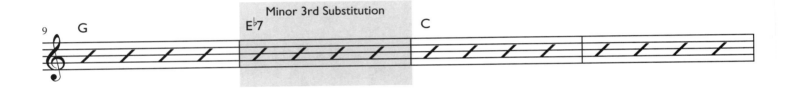

This same principle is true for min7 chords as well. Let's look at a basic ii-V-I progression where ii is Gmin7, V is C7 and I is FMaj7.

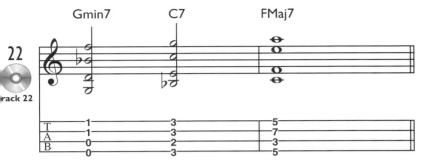

B♭min7 can substitute nicely for the Gmin7, since these chords have two tones in common, B♭ and F.

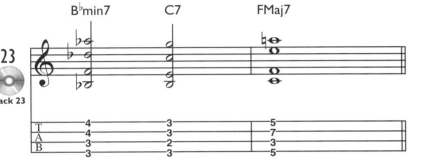

D♭min7 can substitute for the B♭min7, since these chords have two tones in common, D♭ and A♭.

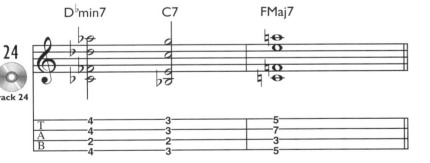

Emin7 can substitute for the D♭min7, since these chords have two tones in common, F♭ is respelled as E, and C♭ is respelled as B.

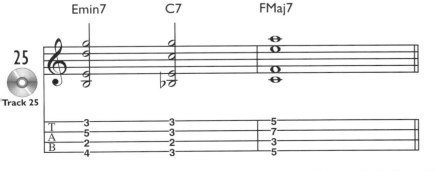

Substitution Principle No. 6—The Diminished Chord Substitution

A diminished 7th chord can substitute for any of four dominant 7th chords.

If you lower any note in a diminished 7th chord one half step you end up with a dominant 7th chord. For example, a Cdim7 uses the notes C–E♭–G♭–B♭♭. If we were to lower the C by one half step to B, the resulting chord would be a B7 chord (enharmonically respelled as B–D♯–F♯–A). The following chart shows how this works with each tone in the chord. The tone that has been lowered to create a dominant 7th chord is highlighted and enharmonic respellings are gray.

Original Diminished 7th chord	Cdim7	C	E♭	G♭	B♭♭
Dominant 7th Chords	B7	B	D♯	F♯	A
	F7	C	E♭	F	A
	D7	C	D	F♯	A
	A♭7	C	E♭	G♭	A♭

A Cdim7 chord can therefore act as a substitute for a B7, F7, D7 or A♭7 chord because three of its four notes will be in common with three of the notes in the dominant 7th chord it would be replacing. The "extra" note contained in the diminished chord used this way would be considered the ♭9 of the dominant chord. For example, if Cdim7 is used to substitute for B7, the C-note acts as the ♭9 of the B7. Many jazz musicians would think of the dim7 chord used this way as a *rootless* 7♭9 chord (Cdim7 is a rootless B7♭9).

Let's look at how this would work, again using the chord changes for "Rollin' In My Sweet Baby's Arms." The substitution in this example will again take place in bar 10.

 # ROLLIN' IN MY SWEET BABY'S ARMS (DIM7 SUBSTITUTION)

Track 26

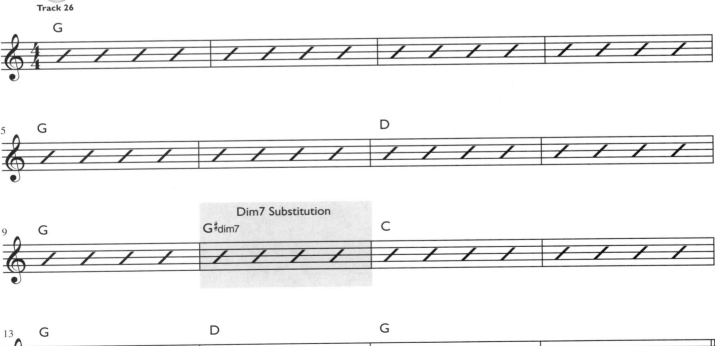

Substitution Principle No. 7—Minor ii Chord / IV Chord

The minor ii chord can act as a replacement for the IV chord. This is really an application of substitution Principle No. 2 and this works because ii and IV share tones in common. For example, in the key of G Major, ii is Amin (A, C, E) and IV is C (C, E, G); they have the notes C and E in common.

This progression...

...can become this.

Substitution Principle No. 8—V Chord / vii° Chord

The V7 chord (dominant 7) can act as a substitute for a vii° (min7♭5). Again, this relates back to Substitution Principle No. 2, as V7 and vii° share several tones in common. For example, in C, V7 (G7—G, B, D, F) and vii° (Bmin7♭5—B, D, F, A) have B, D and F in common.

This progression ...

...can become this.

CHAPTER 4

Chord/Melody

A technique popularized by jazz greats like guitarist Wes Montgomery was to actually fold a melody into a series of chords creating a chord/melody arrangement.

With your expanded knowledge of chords, you can employ this technique to great effect. This technique will put a wrap on our discussion of chords and provide a nice segue into our next main area of focus—melody.

Now that we've built a vocabulary of chords, let's see how they can be used to support a melody by constructing a chord/melody solo. The basic principle of chord/melody soloing on fretted instruments is to play the melody of a tune while simultaneously playing chords underneath it. All of the melody notes, or at least the majority of them, are chord tones. The all-time master of this style is mandolin legend Jethro Burns.

To do this we'll create a chord solo based on the melody of "Mississippi Sawyer," a popular fiddle tune.

First, let's establish a few rules that will guide our playing in this tune. These can be applied to any mandolin chord/melody solo.

- The melody note should always be the top note of your chord. This will help it stand out against the background of the chord tones.

- The top note does not always have to be on the 1st string. It can just as easily be played on the 2nd string or 3rd string.

- Always attempt to accent the melody notes in your picking. This may be something that you would tend to do naturally, but consciously focusing on it helps.

- Sometimes the melody note is a part of the basic chord (the root, 3rd or 5th of a major triad) and sometimes it is not. In jazz harmony, it may also be any one of the extended or altered tones (4th, 6th, 7th, 9th, 11th, 13th, ♭5th, ♯5th, ♭9th, ♯9th).

  Remember, since the mandolin has only four strings, it is important to know which notes can be dropped from a chord voicing in the event you're playing a chord with more than four notes. As a very general rule of thumb, the "keepers" are the 3rd and 7th of each chord along with the alteration(s).

- It is not necessary for every melody note to have an accompanying chord. This is determined both by what is physically possible for your fingers to do in time with the music, and by your personal taste.

- In the event of a long pause on one note, you may improvise your own melodic figure or chord sequence to fill in the musical space. Of course you can choose not to fill the space, too—sometimes it's nice to take a musical breath. Let taste be your guide.

Sometimes you will discover that it is necessary to go to great lengths to get the notes we want on top of our chord voicings. Perhaps you would have chosen slightly different voicings in some of these instances in the example that follows—that's fine. The trick is to find voicings that fit well with one another so that you can move from one chord to another in an efficient way while still getting the melody across.

With those rules in mind, let's look at the basic melody of the tune.

MISSISSIPPI SAWYER (MELODY)
Track 27

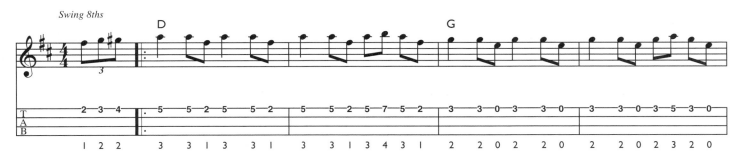

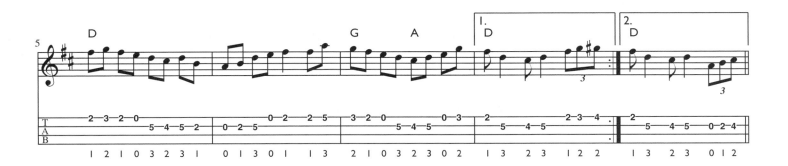

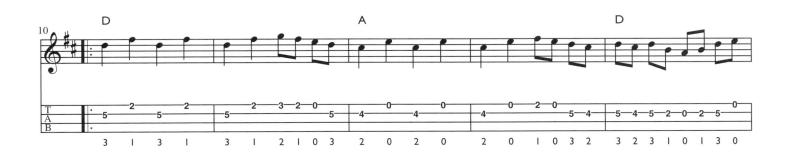

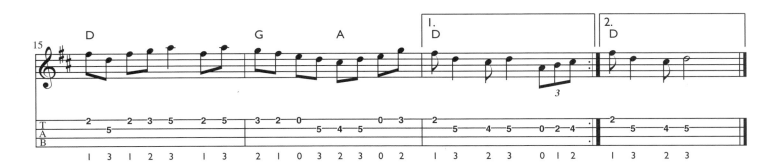

To create a chord melody from this tune, we first decide which are the most important notes in the melody and find interesting harmonies to put underneath.

- In the first two measures, the primary note used to convey the melody is the A. In measures three and four, the key melody note is the G, so we'll want to build our solo by using chords that keep those notes on top.

  We can keep the A-note on top in the first two bars and create a nice descending harmony underneath. The G-note stays on top with the same kind of descending harmony through bars 4 and 5.

- To keep the descending harmony going in bars 5 and 6 while keeping the F#, the melody note for the D chord, we use D, F#min, D7 and Bmin. Remember that the melody does not always have to have a chord supporting it.

- In the straight version, there was a G chord at the beginning of the end tag for the section in bar 7. By using the relative minor (Emin), we create a new harmonization that works for the same melody.

- In the beginning of the "B" section, bar 10, we outline the main melody notes, D and F#.

- The B♭dim chord allows us to nail the C- and E-notes in the melody in bars 12 and 13.

- In the remaining bars we tie it all up by going back to the key melody notes and the descending chord pattern that we used at the top of the tune.

MISSISSIPPI SAWYER (JETHRO STYLE)

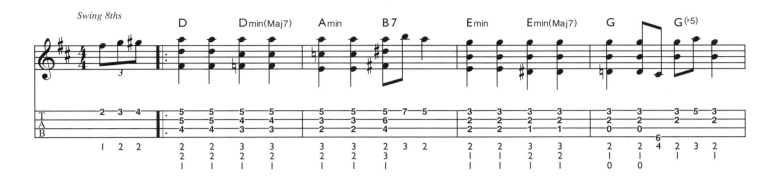

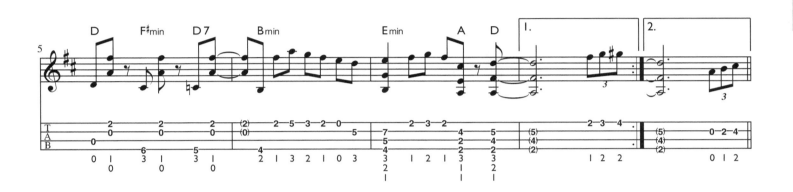

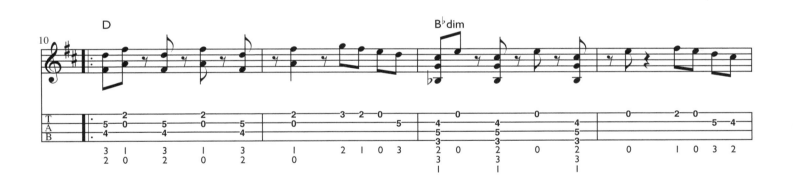

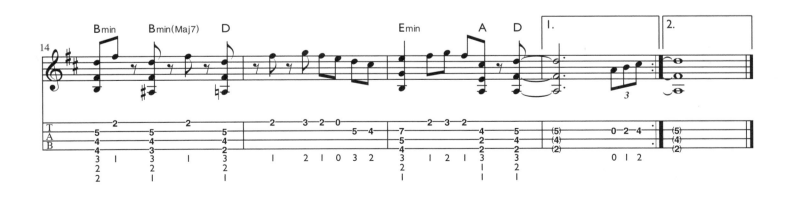

PART TWO—MELODY

CHAPTER 5

Scales and Modes

By performing a simple mathematical trick with the major scale, you can generate six more scales known as the *modes* of the major scale. Each of these scales has its own emotional quality, its own diatonic harmony and its own melodic sound.

The modes have Greek names that harken back to ancient music. They are heard in all styles of music, from folk and blues to jazz and rock.

Following is a brief, whirlwind introduction to the modes.

GENERATING THE MODES FROM A PARENT SCALE— THE RELATIVE VIEW

To generate the modes, follow these steps:
1. Write out the interval structure of a major scale using whole steps (W) and half steps (H). The major scale itself is also known as the first mode, *Ionian*. For now, let's work in C. We will generate other modes from this *parent scale*.

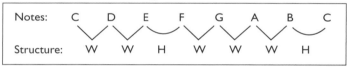

2. Think of the whole steps and half steps as a series. Rotate the first interval to the end of the series (move the first whole step to the end). This generates the second mode, *Dorian*.

3. Another rotation produces the third mode, *Phrygian*.

Notes:	E	F	G	A	B	C	D	E
Structure:		H	W	W	W	H	W	W

Below are the seven modes, shown with their interval structures and example scales using C as the parent scale. Try to memorize the names of the modes in order. You do not necessarily have to memorize the interval structures.

Mode #	Name	Structure	Example
1	Ionian	W W H W W W H	C D E F G A B C
2	Dorian	W H W W W H W	D E F G A B C D
3	Phrygian	H W W W H W W	E F G A B C D E
4	Lydian	W W W H W W H	F G A B C D E F
5	Mixolydian	W W H W W H W	G A B C D E F G
6	Aeolian	W H W W H W W	A B C D E F G A
7	Locrian	H W W H W W W	B C D E F G A B

244   Mastering Mandolin

THE PARALLEL VIEW

Another way to look at each mode is to compare it to the major scale in the same key as the mode. In other words, you would compare the mode to its *parallel major scale* and see which scale degrees stay the same and which change. For example, compare D Dorian and D Major.

D Major (D Ionian)

Notes:	D	E	F♯	G	A	B	C♯	D
Scale degrees:	1	2	3	4	5	6	7	8

D Dorian

Notes:	D	E	F♮	G	A	B	C♮	D
Scale degrees:	1	2	♭3	4	5	6	♭7	8

Notice that in D Dorian the 3rd and 7th degrees are one half step lower than they were in D Major. They are referred to as ♭3 and ♭7 (flat three and flat seven). This is a useful way to look at the modes, because it helps you quickly identify what is different about the sound of the scale.

Here is a list of the modes with their scale degrees and example notes using C as note number 1. The list starts with Ionian and then shows the modes *in order of closest similarity.*

MODE	SCALE DEGREES							IN C						
Ionian	1	2	3	4	5	6	7	C	D	E	F	G	A	B
Mixolydian	1	2	3	4	5	6	♭7	C	D	E	F	G	A	B♭
Dorian	1	2	♭3	4	5	6	♭7	C	D	E♭	F	G	A	B♭
Aeolian	1	2	♭3	4	5	♭6	♭7	C	D	E♭	F	G	A♭	B♭
Phrygian	1	♭2	♭3	4	5	♭6	♭7	C	D♭	E♭	F	G	A♭	B♭
Locrian	1	♭2	♭3	4	♭5	♭6	♭7	C	D♭	E♭	F	G♭	A♭	B♭
Lydian	1	2	3	♯4	5	6	7	C	D	E	F♯	G	A	B

Notice that each scale differs from the previous one by only one note. Lydian is placed at the end because it is actually like Locrian with a ♭1 (flat one). Since it would be illogical and confusing to lower your tonal center by one half step, the flats in Lydian are all cancelled out, leaving you with a ♯4 (sharp four).

DO NOT PANIC!

If you find all of this a bit mind-blowing, don't worry. Just use this introduction as a reference while you work on the upcoming material.

To learn more about all of the modes, check out *The Guitar Mode Encyclopedia* by Jody Fisher (#14445), also published by The National Guitar Workshop and Alfred, and *The Ultimate Guitar Scale Bible* by Mark Dziuba (#07-1009), published by The National Guitar Workshop.

The following material will help you play the modes on the mandolin. All of the scale construction, chord references and fingerings are in C, but are *fully transposable to any key.* Just move the root of the fingerings to the desired note and off you go.

IONIAN—Starts on the 1st degree of a major scale.
Sounds good when played over a I chord (CMaj7).

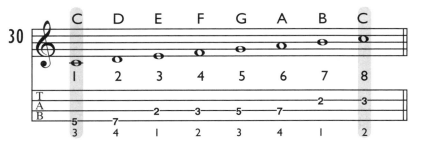
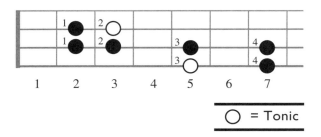

○ = Tonic

DORIAN—Starts on the 2nd degree of a major scale.
Sounds good when played over a ii chord (Dmin7). Has a gospel / bluesy feeling.

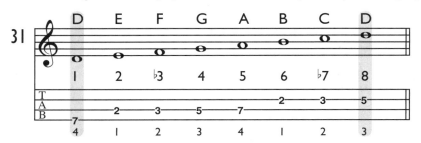
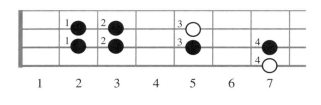

PHRYGIAN—Starts on the 3rd degree of a major scale.
Sounds good when played over a iii chord (Emin7). Has a Spanish or Middle Eastern flavor.

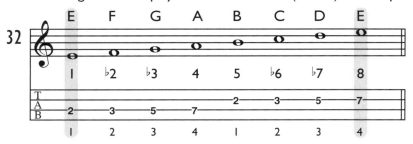
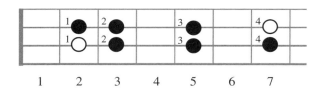

LYDIAN—Starts on the 4th degree of a major scale.
Sounds good when played over a IV chord (FMaj7). Very bright sound.

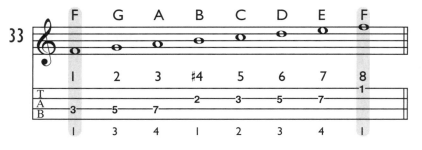
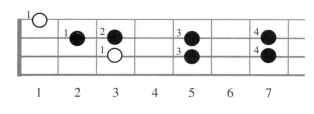

PART TWO—MELODY

MIXOLYDIAN—Starts on the 5th degree of a major scale.
Sounds good when played over a V7 chord (G7). Frequently used in fiddle tunes.

34

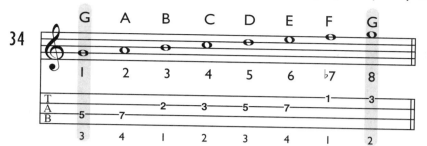
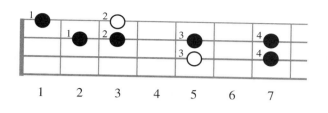

AEOLIAN—Starts on the 6th degree of a major scale.
Sounds good when played over a vi chord (Amin7). The same as the natural minor scale.

35

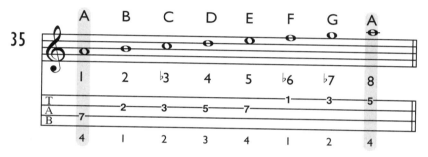
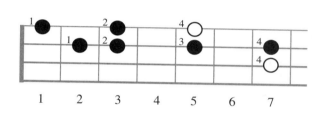

LOCRIAN—Starts on the 7th degree of a major scale.
Sounds good when played over a vii° chord (Bmin7♭5). Has an unresolved sound.

36

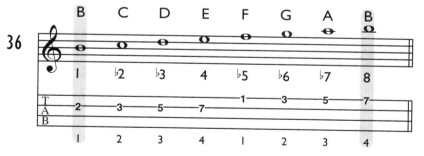
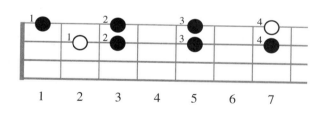

"Okay," you say, "I think I get it, but still, why use modes?"

A mastery of modes greatly increases the improvisational palette you have to work with (7 modes x 12 keys = 84 modes!). Each mode has a distinct quality, color and feel that can add lots of interest to your solos. Of course rote memorization of modes (or any other melodic device) is no replacement for creativity, but all great soloists have thoroughly learned these principles. Musicians who don't understand the scales, their modes and how they relate to the chord progressions usually wander around a lot in their solos, occasionally getting lucky in their note choices.

Knowing which chord types can be constructed from each mode will help you to apply the modes in an actual playing situation. The following chart will help you sort this out. Let's say, for example, that you encounter a Bmin7 chord. According to the chart, three different modes can be associated with a min7 chord: Dorian, Phrygian and Aeolian. This means that for Bmin7, you could play the B Dorian mode, the B Phrygian mode, the B Aeolian mode, or any combination of the three possibilities.

MODE	TRIAD	7	9	11	13
Ionian	Maj	Maj7	Maj9	Maj11	Maj13
Dorian	min	min7	min9	min11	min13
Phyrigian	min	min7	min7♭9	min11♭9	min11♭9♭13
Lydian	Maj	Maj7	Maj9	Maj7#11	Maj13#11
Mixolydian	Maj	7	9	11	13
Aeolian	min	min7	min9	min11	min11♭13
Locrian	dim	min7♭5	min7♭5♭9	min11♭5♭9	min11♭5♭9♭13

TIP FOR HEARING THE UNIQUE FLAVOR OF EACH MODE

Concentrate on the unique flavor of the mode when played against a drone. Either record yourself or have a partner play a "drone" consisting of the first note in the mode or even better, the appropriate chord. Play the mode against that drone. Create little melodic patterns from the notes in the mode and play them against the drone.

TIPS FOR INCORPORATING MODES INTO YOUR SOLOS

Accent or hold the tonic (first note) of the mode a bit longer where possible to emphasize the tonality.

Avoid using the Lydian mode and accenting the 4th degree while playing over I chords, unless you want a bit of dissonance (clashing sound).

There is an entire universe of harmonic and melodic possibilities waiting to be discovered within the modes of the major scale. Try working the modes through all 12 keys. The fingerboard diagrams of the scale fingerings (pages 246–247) will help. They represent one way of playing each mode in a closed position that can be moved throughout the fretboard to facilitate playing the modes in different keys.

To wrap up our discussion of modes, here are a few "modal" tunes for you to try. These tunes are representative examples of tunes that employ the most commonly used modes used in most types of folk music: Ionian, Dorian, Mixolydian and Aeolian.

We'll start with a great Irish tune in E Aeolian called "The Rights of Man." Note that although the tune's tonal center is in "E," it uses a C♮ instead of a C♯ as its sixth scale tone and has a single sharp as its key signature. This is the key signature for G Major, the parent scale of E Aeolian.

THE RIGHTS OF MAN
Track 29

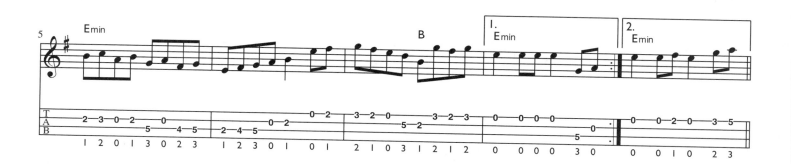

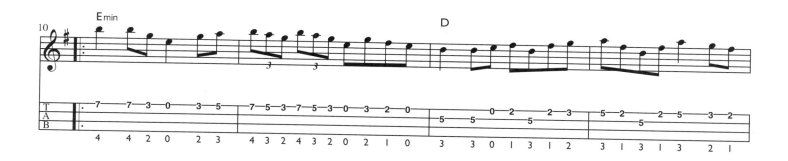

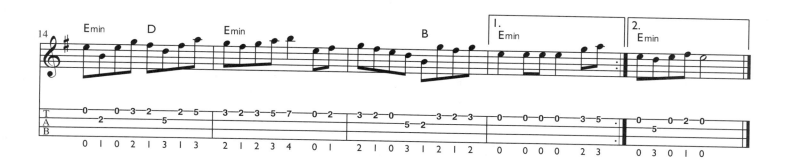

Here is another great tune from Ireland in several parts called "The Drunken Sailor." It is written in A Dorian. Note that this tune also has only a single sharp in its key signature, the key signature for G Major. Because the melody centers around A, the sound is Dorian and the harmonies shift from a focus on the G chord to a focus on Amin.

DRUNKEN SAILOR

Track 30

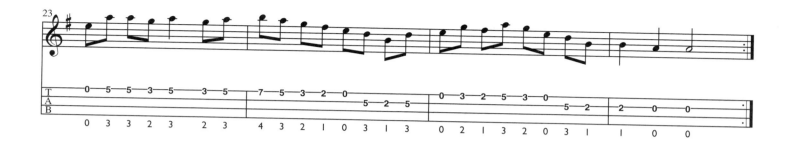

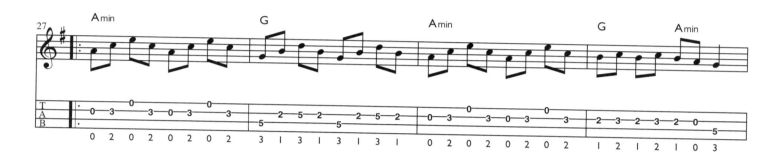

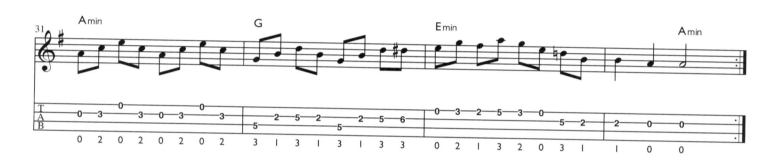

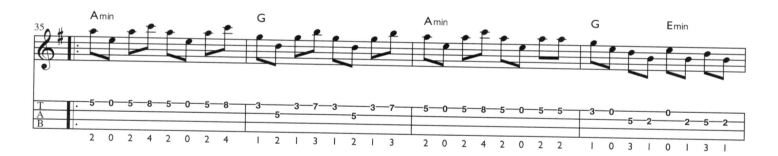

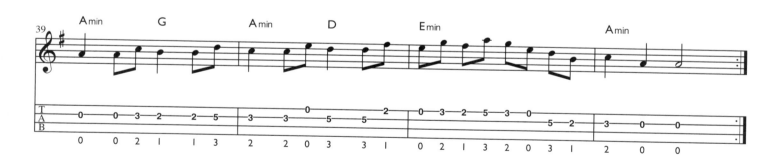

There are many, many examples of tunes written in the Mixolydian mode, the fiddle tune "June Apple" being just one of them. Following is a straightforward version of "June Apple." Listen to this tune and focus on the difference that the $^b7$ (G♮) makes in the melody. Also notice the key signature of two sharps (key signature for D Major). This would lead you to believe that the harmonization underlying the melody would also be based in a D tonality. Instead, the harmonization is based in an A tonality to support the A Mixolydian melody.

JUNE APPLE

Track 31

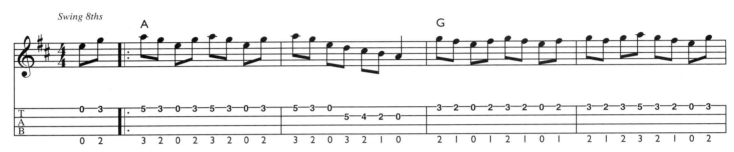

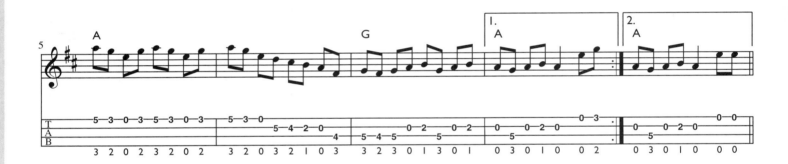

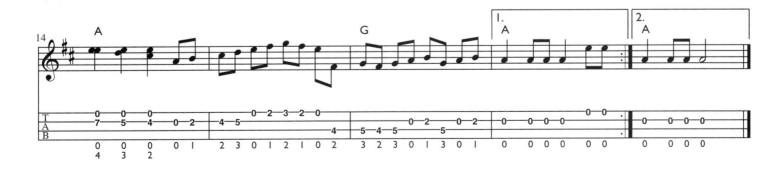

Sometimes you will come across a tune that makes use of mixed modes, with one mode used in one section and another mode used in another distinct section. The fiddle tune "Over the Waterfall" is a perfect example. The first part of this tune is written in D Mixolydian using a ♭7 (C♮) in the melody while the second part is written in D Ionian (D Major) using the ♮7 (C♯).

 ## OVER THE WATERFALL

Track 32

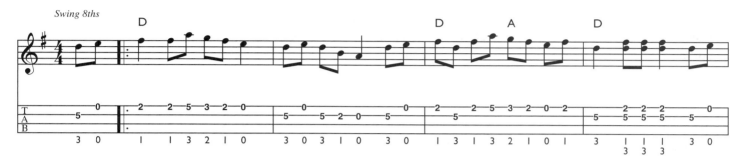

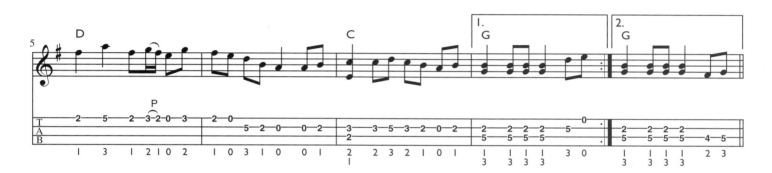

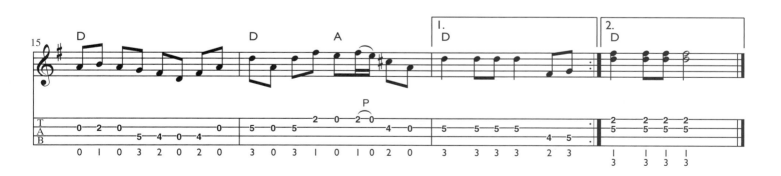

PENTATONIC SCALES

Dawg music is a style of music that blends bluegrass, jazz and other influences into a truly unique sound. Dawg music was popularized (some would argue created by) David Grisman whose nickname also happens to be "Dawg."

Since Grisman makes ample use of the pentatonic scale (first introduced on page 45) in his compositions and soloing, it is absolutely something you'll want to get under your fingers in order to play in this style. In fact, like so many of the other scales and modes we've learned, pentatonic scales are found in all kinds of tunes and improvisations, not only in Western music, but in music from all over the globe.

Pentatonic scales are five-note scales that come in three types: major, minor and dominant. The thing that makes these scales so cool is their incredible versatility. Look at the major pentatonic scale shown below. This scale is in the key of C. Now, either record yourself or see if you can enlist the aid of a musician friend and have them play a C Major chord while you play this scale. It will sound good. Next, try playing this scale over a Dmin chord. It will still sound nice. Next try playing it over an Emin chord. It still sounds good. Now try this scale over the F, G, Amin and Bmin7♭5 chords. Notes and patterns derived from this one five-note scale can be played (and sound good) over any chord that occurs naturally in the key of C Major.

What this means to an improviser is that they can play one scale over all the chord changes in a tune (providing of course that the tune doesn't modulate to another key) and not have to stress themselves out about the chord changes.

This process will work in any key.

Here is the C Major Pentatonic scale. As with the mode fingerings, the fingering pattern shown in the diagram can be moved to any desired note to use the scale in a different key.

C Major Pentatonic

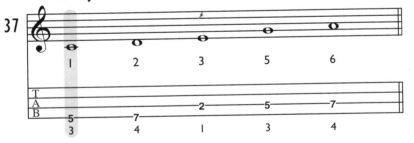

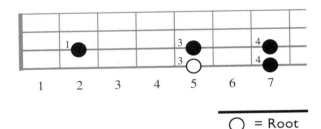

◯ = Root

Of course for variety, you can use the pentatonic scales that correspond to each chord in a given progression (for example, C Major Pentatonic over a C Major chord, F Major Pentatonic over an F Major chord and G Major Pentatonic over a G Major chord).

The minor and dominant variations on the pentatonic scale can be used over the appropriate corresponding minor or dominant chords.

C Minor Pentatonic

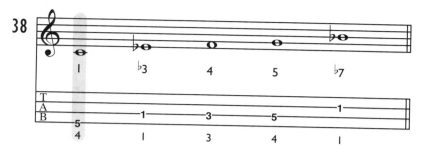
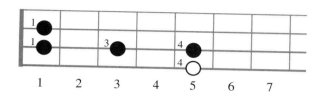

One important thing to note is the relationship between the major and minor pentatonic scales. As discussed on page 170, the two scales are relative. Using the key of C as an example, a C Major Pentatonic scale is C–D–E–G–A. The relative minor key of C Major is A Minor and the notes of an A Minor Pentatonic scale are A–C–D–E–G, exactly the same notes as C Major Pentatonic. So, not only can a pentatonic major scale sound correct when played over any naturally occurring chord in its key, but it can also sound correct when played over a progression in the relative minor key.

C Dominant Pentatonic

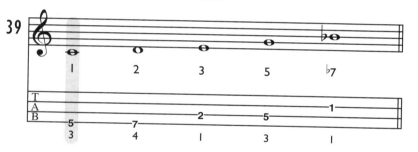
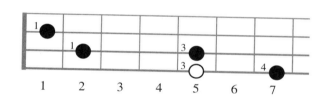

One cautionary note regarding pentatonic scales: There is a danger, especially with beginning improvisers, in developing a dependency on these scales because of their simplicity and versatility. An over-reliance on this type of scale, or any other melodic or harmonic device for that matter, would make your playing sound canned and boring quickly! Do use these scales, but as always, let your ear be your guide.

Use the fretboard diagrams to play these pentatonic scale types in all 12 keys.

Now that you have some familiarity with pentatonic scales and understand how they can be used, here is a great tune for you to try. This tune is composed solely from the notes contained in the G Major Pentatonic scale and provides a perfect example of how the scale can not only sound pleasing over different chords in a key but can be crafted into a very nice sounding tune too.

SPOOTISKERRY REEL

Track 33

THE BLUES SCALE

One of the most infallible ways for a beginning improviser to create pleasing solos is to use the *blues scale*. That's because all of the notes in the scale will sound good with almost any basic blues tune, in a major or minor key. The important thing is to use the scale with the same root name as the key you're playing in. Like the pentatonic scales we just discussed, the blues scale let's you play one scale over the entire chord progression with virtually no chance of playing a "wrong note."

You will notice right away that a blues scale bears an amazing similarity to the minor pentatonic scale. In fact, for all practical purposes, it is a minor pentatonic scale with an added a ♭5, making it a six-note scale.

Here is a C Blues scale. Use the movable fingering shown in the diagram to play the scale in any key.

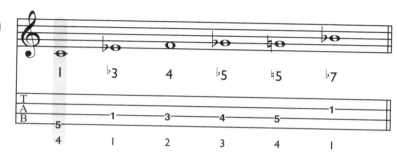

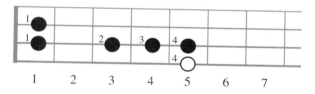

Yank Rachell (1910–1997) was one of the most prolific and influential blues mandolinists playing both electric and acoustic mandolins. His performing and recording career spanned seven decades and included work as a soloist with artists such as Sonny Boy Williamson and Sleepy John Estes.

PHOTO • MAUREEN DELGROSSO

THE WHOLE-TONE SCALE

Mandolin great Andy Statman is a great proponent of using *whole-tone scales* for improvisation. Because the whole-tone scale is rootless in nature, having no half steps between any of the notes, the material from these scales gives an improvised solo an "outside" edge with an "out-there-in-space" sound that is unanchored in any specific key or tonality.

There are only two whole-tone scales, neither of which have any tones in common with the other.

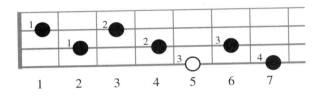

The whole-tone scale is best used for improvising over a 7#5#11 chord or any dominant 7th chord whose root is one of the tones in the scale. With that in mind, you could use the scale in the example above over these dominant chords (with or without extensions, altered or unaltered): C7, D7, E7, F#7, G#7 or Bb7.

Now let's look at the other whole-tone scale.

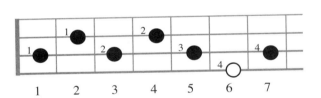

As you can see, this form of the scale shares no tones in common with the first. As was the case with the first version of the scale, this version is also best used when improvising over dominant chords whose root is one of the tones in the scale. So this version of the scale would best be used when improvising over Db7, Eb7, F7, G7, A7 or B7.

PART TWO—MELODY

THE CHROMATIC SCALE

The *chromatic scale* is simply a scale that includes all the adjacent half steps between two notes an octave apart. Since it uses all of the notes, there is really only one chromatic scale. Here it is.

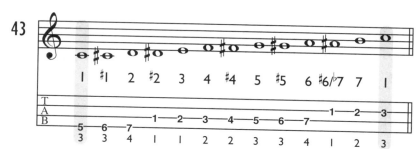

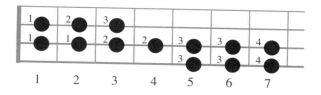

Chromatic scale material can be very useful in improvisation as a means of connecting two phrases or providing additional interest to a line. Be careful not to overuse chromatic material—your musical thought can get lost very easily in a sea of half steps if you aren't careful. Let your ear be your guide!

THE FIVE BASIC SCALE TYPES EVERY MANDOLIN PLAYER SHOULD KNOW

Thus far in this method you have learned how to create five basic types of 7th chords—Maj7, min7, (dominant) 7, min7♭5 and dim7—and that there are almost limitless ways to alter and extend those chords. A solid understanding of the five basic scales that correspond to and are supported by these chords is requisite knowledge for any advanced mandolin player. Getting these scales under your fingers will allow you to make better note choices as you improvise over chord changes in virtually any musical style.

For the sake of convenience, all five of these scales will be shown on these two pages. One of these scales is new, but you know most of them. The idea here is to emphasize the relationships of these important scales to the basic types of chords. In the examples below, chord tones are black, non-chord tones are gray.

Chord—Maj7; Scale—Major

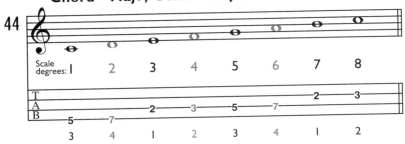

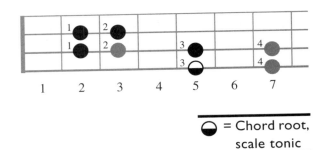

Remember, the scale fingerings are moveable. Simply move the pattern to the desired root and you can play them in any key.

Chord—min7; Scale—Dorian Mode

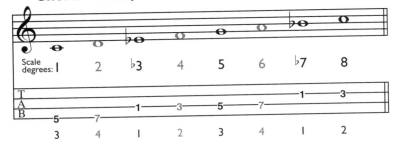

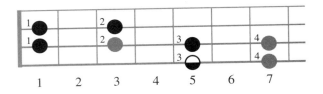

PART TWO—MELODY

Chord—7 (dominant); Scale—Mixolydian Mode

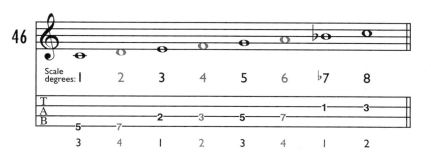

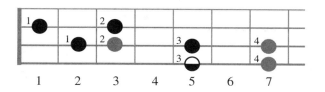

Chord—min7♭5; Scale—Locrian Mode

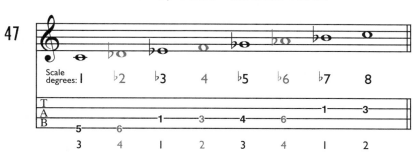

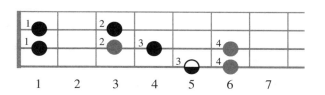

Here's the new scale.

Chord—dim; Scale—Whole/Half Diminished (Auxiliary Diminished)

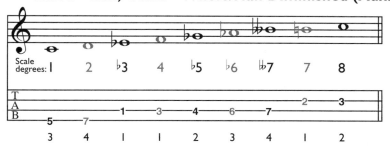

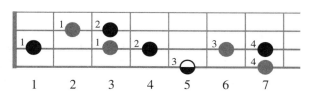

To fully master these scales, you should memorize the moveable fingerings and try each type of scale in all 12 keys.

CHAPTER 6

Exploring Time Signatures

In addition to the harmonic and melodic material we've discussed, you will need to develop another facet of your playing in order to truly "master" the mandolin. Rhythm, the organization of music in time, is the third major component of making music. Let's start by revisiting the organization of musical time into measures.

REVIEW OF COMPOUND METER

As you learned in Chapter 4 of the *Intermediate* section, ⁶⁄₈ time is most frequently associated with Celtic music—Irish "jigs" in particular. It is also used frequently in classical music and music from other parts of the globe as well. In ⁶⁄₈, there are six beats in each bar of music and an eighth note will get one beat. Tunes played in ⁶⁄₈ are rarely felt as six beats unless they are played very slowly. They are most often felt (and counted) as though each measure has two beats with three equal parts in each. This is referred to as a *compound meter*. Meter is the pattern of beats within a time signature.

You can see this in the example below. The eighth notes in each measure are beamed in two groups of three notes each. Each group of three eighth notes is equal to a dotted quarter note. Since many tunes in this meter move quickly, the natural tendency is to feel the tune in "2" rather than "6" and to think of the dotted quarter note as receiving one beat. A few things generally describe compound time:

1) The dotted quarter note receives one beat.

2) Each beat is subdivided into three equal parts.

3) The top number in the time signature is evenly divisible by three.

There is some debate among mandolin players as to how to "pick" with your right hand in ⁶⁄₈. This was covered on pages 134 and 135. To review, one school of thought says that you should continue to use the down–up–down–up pattern that you would normally use to pick a group of eighth notes. The other school of thought and the one recommended by mandolin players like Mike Marshall and Chris Thile is a pattern of down–up–down, down–up–down. This pattern works well because a downstroke falls on the first and fourth eighth notes (the onbeats) of the measure, giving them added emphasis.

Here's how this pattern would be applied to a group of eighth notes in ⁶⁄₈.

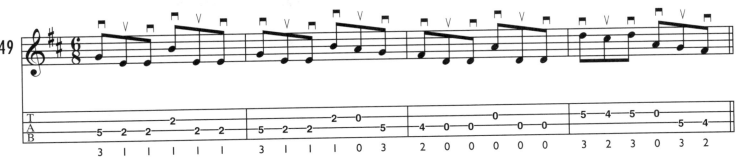

Try playing through a few jigs to make sure you are comfortable with this picking pattern.

A TRIP TO THE COTTAGE

Track 34

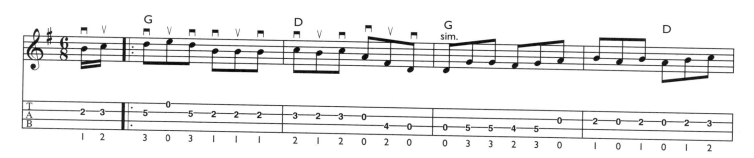

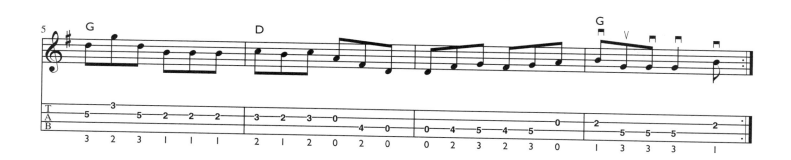

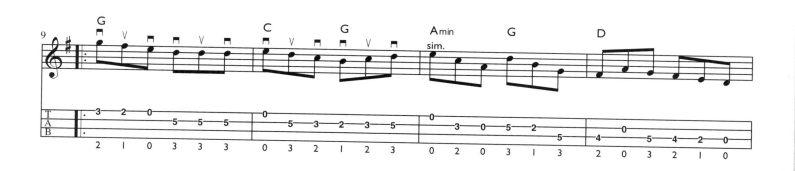

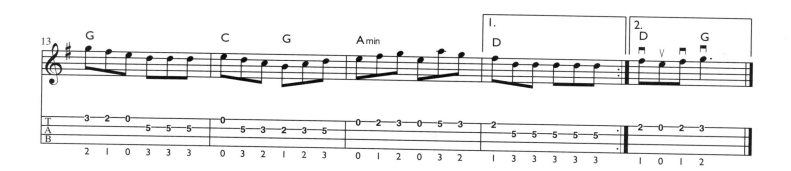

Here's another popular Irish jig. This tune is in three parts and will require you to pay close attention to your right hand, as the syncopations demand some adjustments to the ⊓–∨–⊓, ⊓–∨–⊓ pattern. Once you have this one comfortably under your fingers, grab hold of a friend and try playing it as a round (like "Row, Row, Row Your Boat")—it works really well!

BANISH MISFORTUNE

Track 35

264 Mastering Mandolin

Other compound meters you will encounter are $\frac{9}{8}$ (feels like three beats per measure) and $\frac{12}{8}$ (feels like four beats per measure). The following pieces will give you some practice reading in these time signatures.

This is a great Irish tune in $\frac{9}{8}$ that has been recorded by quite a few bands. One version that particularly stands out is the one recorded by The Bothy Band on their *After Hours* album.

THE BUTTERFLY

Track 36

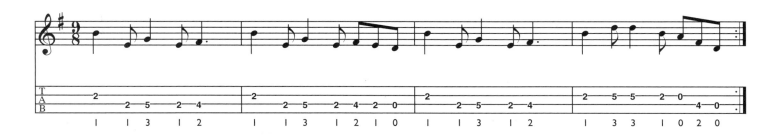

Here's another Irish tune, this time in $\frac{12}{8}$. As you play through this one and become comfortable with the counting, you'll notice that it has a jig-like quality even though it isn't in the usual jig meter of $\frac{6}{8}$.

DAN O'KEEFE'S SLIDE

Track 37

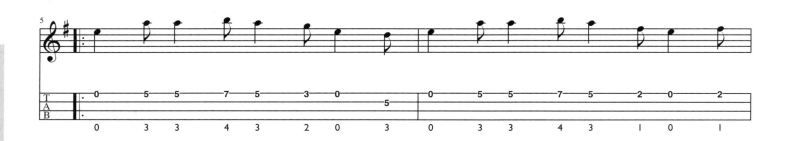

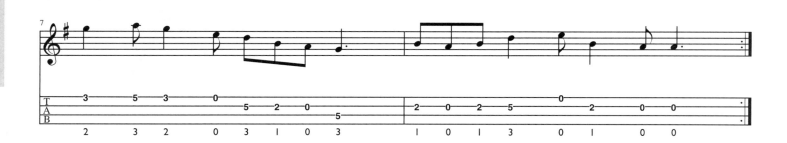

ODD METERS

In addition to compound meters, you may encounter some *odd time signatures*. An odd time is one where the number of beats per measure is not divisible by two or three. The most commonly used odd times are five and seven: $\frac{5}{8}$, $\frac{5}{4}$, $\frac{7}{8}$ and $\frac{7}{4}$.

Quite often an odd meter is actually felt as a combination of more basic units of time. For example, $\frac{5}{8}$ is most often either 2+3 or 3+2.

Here are some suggestions for counting odd meters.

COUNTING FIVE

Whether $\frac{5}{8}$ or $\frac{5}{4}$, five will most likely be felt one of two ways:

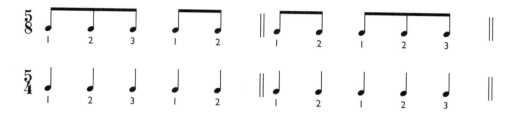

COUNTING SEVEN

$\frac{7}{8}$ or $\frac{7}{4}$ is counted either as 2+2+3 beats or 3+2+2:

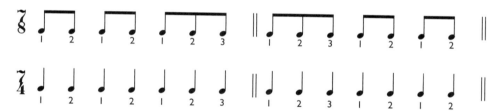

As you can imagine, other groupings are possible, but these are the most common.

When you encounter an odd time, immediately attempt to assess how the beats are grouped and practice counting it that way. This is the best way to understand and play in odd time.

On the following pages are pieces in odd time for you to play. Enjoy!

This first tune is in $\frac{5}{4}$ time. Once you've played through this and become comfortable with the odd meter, you should feel a bizarre almost waltz-like quality.

5-TIME WALTZ

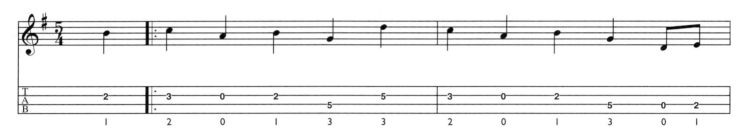

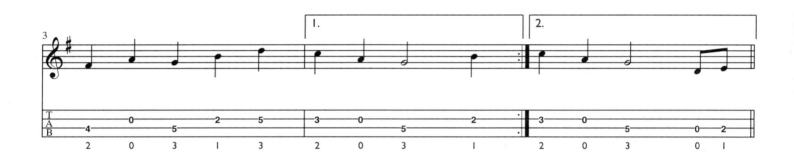

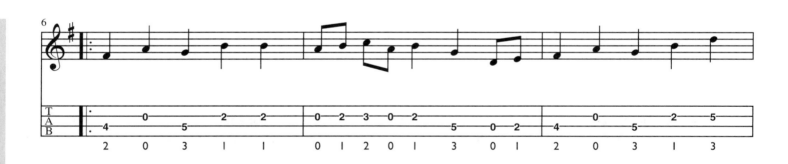

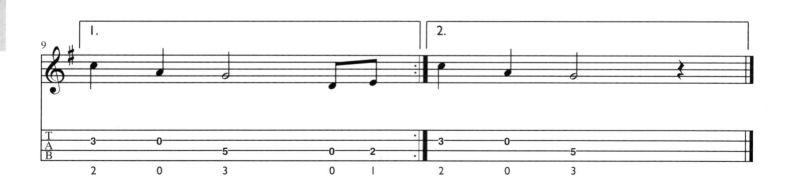

Here is a British tune in $\frac{7}{8}$. Accenting the first beat of each bar as you play this might help you become accustomed to the odd meter. Also, try counting 1–2–3, 1–2, 1–2 in most measures. Notice that the first and second endings, plus the final measure are 1–2, 1–2, 1–2–3.

SILLYFJORD
Track 39

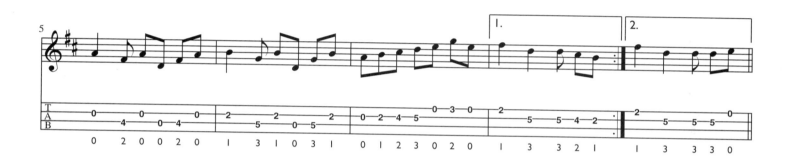

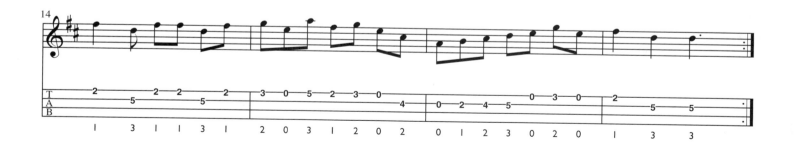

CHAPTER 7

Melodic Rhythm

As mandolin players we've all developed our rhythmic sense in playing chordal accompaniments. Bluegrass mandolin players have evolved their ability to play chord chops on the offbeats to provide a drum-like rhythmic accent (page 62). So certainly, from an accompaniment perspective, rhythm is very important. It would be a great idea for you to listen to some of the top mandolin players, such as David Grisman, Mike Marshall, Barry Mitterhoff, Chris Thile, Ronnie McCoury, Don Rigsby, Adam Steffey, Sam Bush, Tim O'Brien, Ricky Skaggs and the "man" himself, Bill Monroe (to name just a very few), paying particular attention to how they use the mandolin as a rhythm instrument when accompanying melodies.

Beyond rhythmic accompaniment, though, you will need to develop your sense of *how rhythm affects melody*. Understanding this concept will help you to move your improvisations away from a never-ending, steady stream of eighth notes and allow you to come up with all kinds of fresh, new approaches.

Two exercises you can use to begin to develop your sense of melodic rhythm follow. The first of these exercises involves taking a simple melody and changing the rhythm of the pitches in as many ways as you can dream up.

Let's use the first few bars of the popular fiddle tune, "Blackberry Blossom" as an example. Here is a straightforward version of the A section.

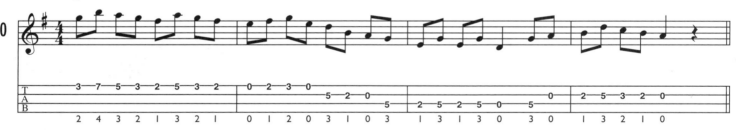

Now let's throw a few quarter notes into the mix and see what happens.

Same tune—different feel. In the second version there is a little more space between the notes and this provides a nice change.

Now let's vary the phrase by starting with some triplets. This variation is a little busier. You can still recognize the melody but it has a different feel.

Now let's vary the rhythm again using eighth notes and quarter notes. This one has more space in it yet still sounds different from the first variation we tried.

Here is yet another variation that uses quarter notes and triplets to create a nice effect. Just for the fun of it, let's throw some sixteenth notes in there, too.

Finally, let's syncopate the rhythm a little bit by throwing a few rests into the mix.

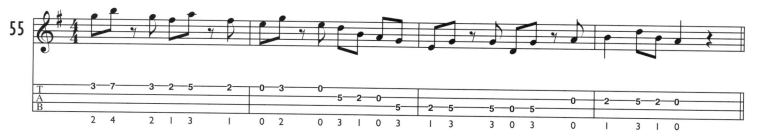

You can see by this exercise that, without trying very hard, we were able to come up with several interesting variations on the basic "Blackberry Blossom" phrase by simply altering the rhythm of the pitches.

Applying this exercise to other tunes you're familiar with can help get your creative juices flowing and help you add interest to your playing.

Another exercise that's fun to experiment with involves taking a familiar tune and playing it in different time signatures. This will not only help you come up with some different variations on tunes, but will also help you develop an internal sense of rhythm and a feel different meters.

Let's take the old standard, "Soldier's Joy." We'll start with a straight, intentionally simple version.

SOLDIER'S JOY
Track 40

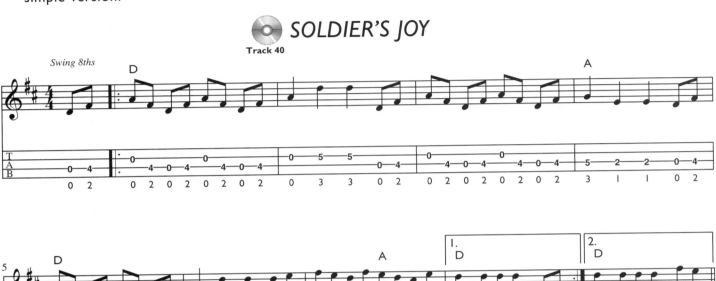

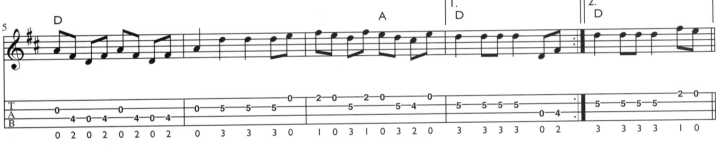

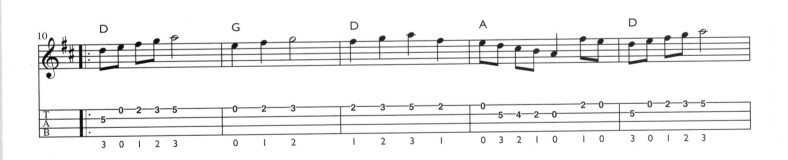

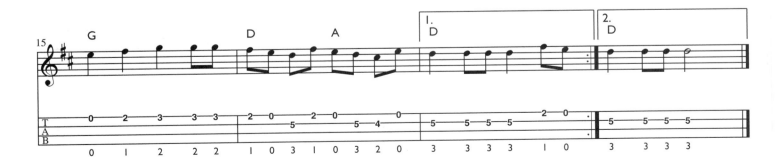

Now, let's turn "Soldier's Joy" into a waltz (in ¾).

SOLDIER'S JOY—WALTZ

Track 41

Let's try the same tune again, this time as a jig in $\frac{6}{8}$.

SOLDIER'S JOY—JIG

Track 42

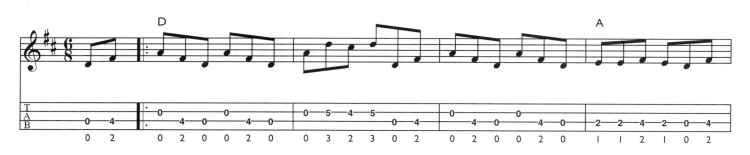

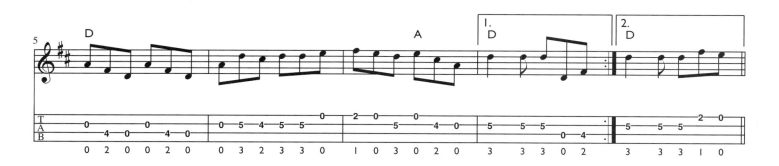

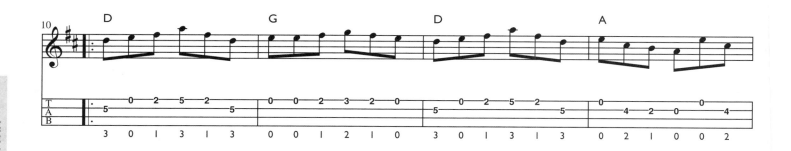

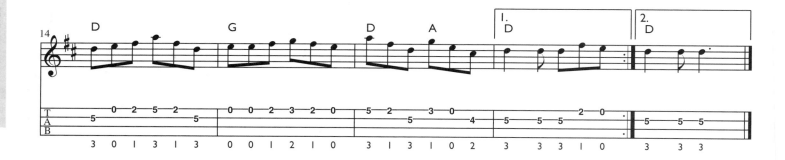

Hopefully, as you played through these different versions of "Soldier's Joy," you found yourself needing to focus with intensity on playing this familiar material in a new, different feel. Focusing in this way will help develop a powerful internal sense of rhythm and will prove invaluable to you. This exercise also serves as proof positive that rhythm is critical in defining the nature and feel of a piece.

PART THREE—RHYTHM

CHAPTER 8

Improvisation

By now you have amassed a great deal of harmonic, melodic and rhythmic material and have at least begun the process of putting this material into practice (no pun intended) in your playing. Using this knowledge to create new, spontaneous compositions and solos is perhaps the most rewarding part of the process in advancing your playing to that next level. This section of the book will offer some suggestions that might help you to minimize the challenges. First, let's dispel a few myths about improvisation.

- **The ability to improvise is not necessarily something you're born with.** Certainly, there are some incredibly gifted musicians whose improvisations seemed effortless in all regards, even at the outset. Those folks are in the minority though and that's good news for the rest of us who struggle to apply our musical knowledge to the creation of interesting, spontaneous solos. We can be taught to improvise!

- **You don't need to have perfect pitch to improvise,** although being able to hear different intervals is helpful.

- **You don't need to practice your instrument constantly.** In fact, many great improvisers recommend that you first use your voice and sing or hum your ideas before attempting them on your instrument. Since your voice is with you all the time and your mandolin is not, learn to put your voice to work in "virtual" practice sessions.

Like anything else you pursue in life, there are some bad habits to avoid. **Things you should avoid include:**

- **Continually trying to play higher, faster and louder.** This would ultimately lead you down a dead-end street. Remember the importance of tone; don't sacrifice for speed or volume.

- **Practicing too many new ideas** instead of building on some of the musical ideas you have already played. There is just so much your mind (and fingers) can absorb in any one practice session. Try to focus on mastering just a few ideas at a time.

- **Getting locked into the same ideas,** the same pitches, the same rhythms and the same expression (or lack of it). Avoid the comfort zone—challenge yourself with new material and ideas constantly and you will reap substantial rewards.

There are many books, recordings and videos that offer differing approaches to learning to improvise, all of them valuable. Let's look at one method for learning to improvise. This method consists of several distinct steps as part of the overall process and is derivative of a method taught by the great jazz saxophonist, Lee Konitz. He breaks down improvisation into these five steps:

Step 1. Create a skeleton of the melody out of quarter notes

Step 2. Expand this melody using eighth notes

Step 3. Apply some rhythmic variations to the melody

Step 4. Create a *countermelody* (a second melody that works when played simultaneously with the melody)

Step 5. Create a completely abstract variation on the melody

As you first begin to apply this method it might strike you that it isn't very spontaneous. You'll find yourself really thinking about the tune and analyzing it in ways you hadn't thought would necessarily be part of a spontaneous process. Be patient and consistent! Like most things in life, if you apply this process on a regular basis, it will become easier and easier and ultimately something that you can do unconsciously. It will *become* spontaneous.

Now that the disclaimers are out of the way, let's start the process using this tune in the style of the jazz standard "Autumn Leaves."

RAKING LEAVES NO. 1

Track 43

Step 1 says that you should first create a skeletal version of the melody using quarter notes. Try to determine the important notes that convey the overall sense of melody. We did this in our discussion of building chord solos in Chapter 4, so hopefully this part of the process won't be totally foreign to you. Here is a very simple, quarter-note melody made from "Raking Leaves No. 1" using the notes that best convey the melodic line.

RAKING LEAVES NO. 2

Track 44

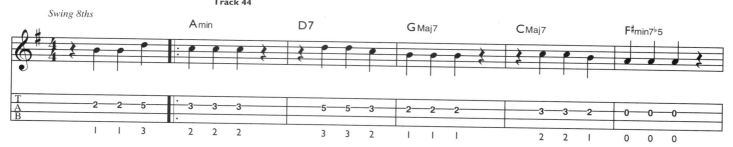

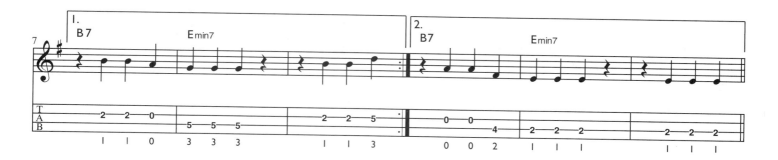

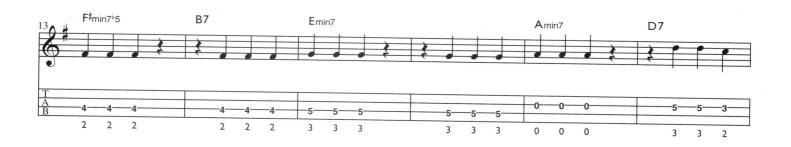

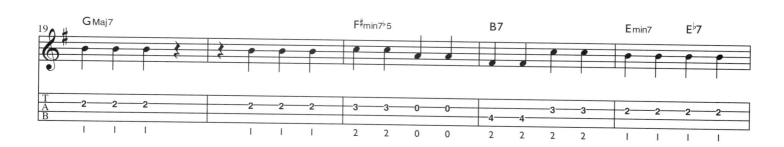

Now let's create a quarter-note melody that uses simple arpeggios of the chords.

RAKING LEAVES NO. 3

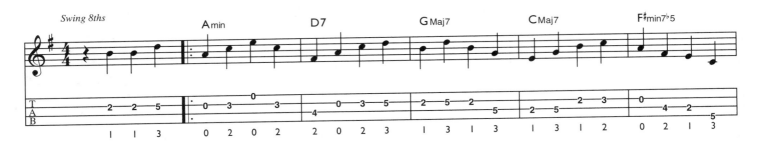

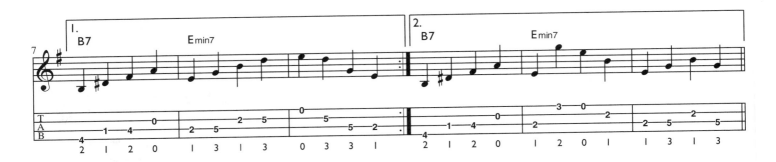

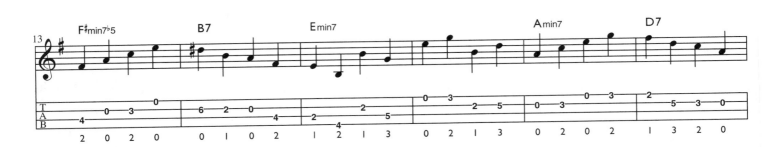

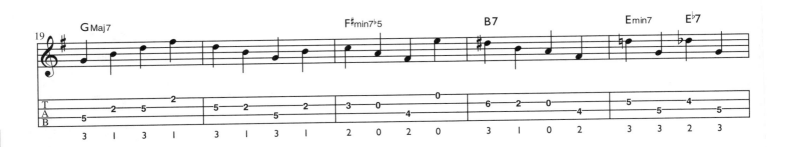

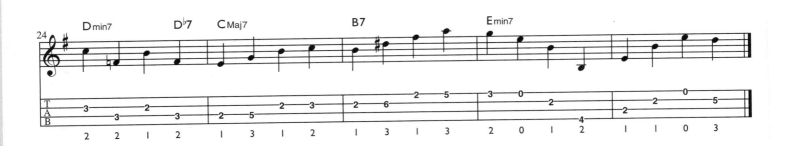

In the previous step, we established important tones that can act as a foundation for the next steps. We've also departed from the melody somewhat in favor of outlining the harmonic structure of the tune.

You can do many other things at this level. You might try arpeggiating the chords beginning on different chord tones in addition to the root of the chord; specifically the 3rd, 5th and 7th degrees in the chords. You could also create an arpeggiated line that would ascend through one chord and descend through the next. You could also make up a simple melodic line that connects the root of one chord to the root of the next.

Now let's continue and expand our quarter-note ideas into eighth notes. This is the level in which the most improvisation occurs, especially within the styles of bluegrass and jazz. In this step, we'll expand on our quarter note ideas and take a simple one-bar idea, make it a simple pattern and take it through the rest of the chord changes. There are many great books filled with melodic patterns and it would be a great idea for you to check them out.

Some great jazz improvisers to check out:

Together with bass guitarist Victor Lemonte Wooten (left), and his brother Roy "Future Man" Wooten (middle) on the drumitar, *an electronic drum shaped like a guitar, banjo virtuoso* **Béla Fleck** *(right) formed the Flecktones who recorded their landmark debut album in 1990. The group mixes many styles, including jazz and bluegrass.*

During the 1940s, vocalist **Ella Fitzgerald** *recorded a string of hits with the Ink Spots, Louis Jordan, the Delta Rhythm Boys and others.*

Saxophonist **John Coltrane** *first came to notice as a sideman at age 29 in 1955, formally launched a solo career at 33 in 1960, and was dead at 40 in 1967. He was among the most important, and most controversial, figures in jazz.*

As with Step 2 on page 275, this next version of "Raking Leaves" uses mostly eighth notes. This variation also employs a simple one-bar pattern starting on the 3rd of each chord, which is taken through all of the chord changes. You probably wouldn't want to construct an entire solo from a single pattern, but this device—working a pattern through a set of chord changes—can be very effective when used sparingly.

RAKING LEAVES NO. 4

Track 46

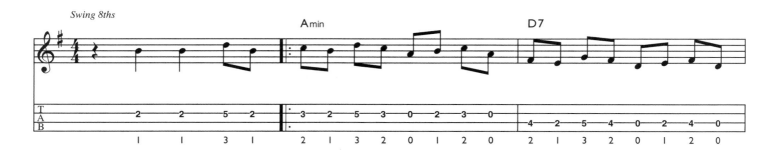

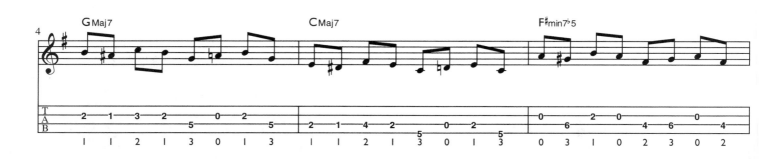

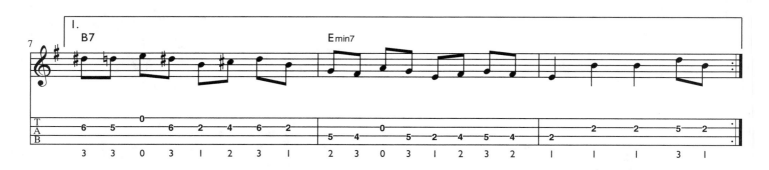

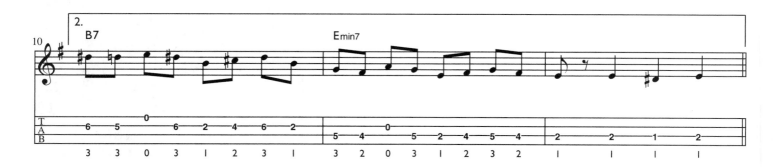

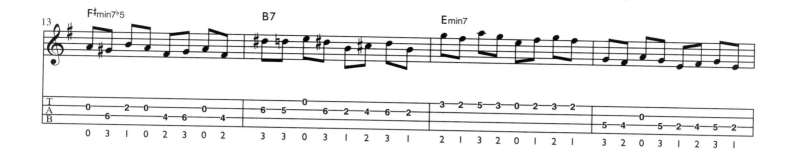

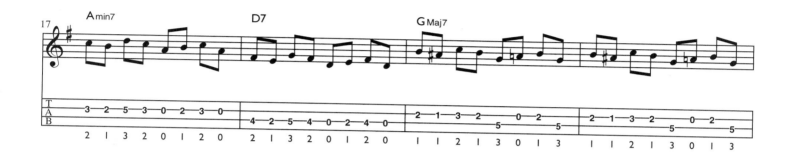

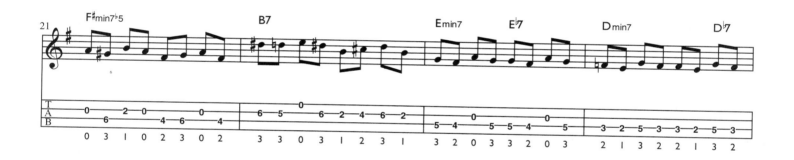

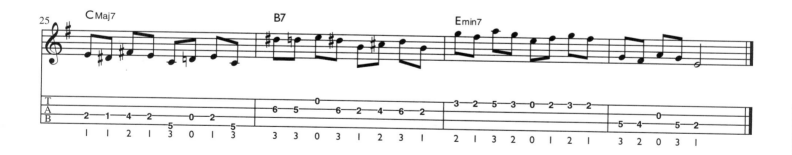

By shifting the melodic rhythm of the melody, as per Step 3 on page 275, we can come up with some interesting ideas that are closely tied to and yet different from the original melody.

RAKING LEAVES NO. 5

Track 47

In Step 4, we create a countermelody, which will weave around the original, sometimes accompanying the original melody and at other times filling in some of the blank spaces in the original melody.

A great way to begin is to record yourself slowly playing the original melody (page 276), then while playing back your recording, create a melody line that weaves nicely around the original. Ultimately, you will want to get to the point where you can hear the original melody in your head as you spontaneously create counterpoint. This will take time, so hang in there. A little practice at this each day and it will become natural for you. Record the original melody to "Raking Leaves," get a fellow musician to play it for you or play along with track 43 of the recording that is included with this book while you try this sample of a very simple melody.

RAKING LEAVES NO. 6
Track 48

In the final step of our process you will want to treat the tune as though it were a blank canvas of sorts. Create a melody here that doesn't necessarily resemble the original at all. Here, you can bring to bear any or all of the melodic and rhythmic techniques you've learned thus far. Don't be afraid to experiment but as always let taste be your guide. You should still respect the harmonic structure of the tune so that your note choices will make sense and have some appeal, but aside from that, let your imagination and creativity run wild and just go for it!

One final thought on this method for learning to improvise: Remember you must *be patient*. It will work for you. Your improvisations will move from a conscious process of deliberate thought to total spontaneity—but you will have to put time and patience into the process to get there.

More inspirational improvisers:

Chick Corea has been one of the most significant jazz pianists since the 1960s. He has been involved in quite a few important musical projects, and his musical curiosity has never dimmed. Along with Herbie Hancock and Keith Jarrett, he was one of the top stylists to emerge after Bill Evans and McCoy Tyner and is also one of the few electric keyboardists to be quite individual and recognizable on synthesizers. He has composed several jazz standards, including "Spain," "La Fiesta" and "Windows."

*There is no more influential jazz pianist than **Bill Evans**, who made his first recording in 1956. Only McCoy Tyner exerts nearly as much pull among younger players— and he has left his mark on such noted players as Herbie Hancock, Keith Jarrett, Chick Corea and Brad Mehldau.*

*Pianist John Lewis, vibraphonist Milt Jackson, bassist Ray Brown and drummer Kenny Clarke first came together as the rhythm section of the 1946 Dizzy Gillespie Orchestra and went on to form the **Modern Jazz Quartet**. While the MJQ has long followed John Lewis's musical vision, making jazz "respectable" by occasionally interacting with classical ensembles and playing concerts at prestigious venues, they always left plenty of space for bluesy and swinging improvising.*

CHAPTER 9

Finding Material from Around the World

The mandolin is truly the king of instruments. You can play virtually any type of music on it and your choices in repertoire are limited only by your preferences, tastes and imagination.

You can find mandolin repertoire almost anywhere. Recorded material and jam sessions are certainly great sources. Books can also be a treasure trove of great material. Since the mandolin shares the same tuning as a violin, virtually any violin book becomes a potential source of material for you! The downside of using violin books is that very few of them include any type of tablature. If you've gone through this series of books by reading the tablature, devote some time now to learning to read standard music notation. Being able to read music will open up entirely new doors for you and expose your ears to sounds and rhythms that you might not otherwise experience.

So far as finding music that works on the mandolin, in the United Sates and throughout the world the impact of bluegrass music on the mandolin cannot be overstated. Bill Monroe's mandolin playing defined the style and made it one of the best-loved, most widely played types of music in the world. There are bluegrass concerts, festivals, radio shows, jams, clubs and organizations, repertoire books, recordings and videos all waiting for you to discover them.

Another of the obvious sources involves anything in the classical literature composed or transcribed for violin. There is a wealth of wonderful material to be discovered in classical music.

If you find that you enjoy playing classical music, you should check to see if there is a mandolin orchestra in your area. A quick search for "mandolin orchestras" on the Internet would be a good place to start. Mandolin orchestras flourished in the 1900s in large part because of a stroke of marketing genius on the part of the Gibson Company. When they introduced the other members of the mandolin family around 1910—the mandola, mandocello, and mandobass—they also began marketing the idea of a mandolin orchestra that could play regular orchestral string music using these instruments. To support their idea, Gibson created a carefully planned program that involved music teachers in the actual sale of mandolin family instruments by getting them to organize mandolin orchestras. As a result, hundreds of mandolin groups were formed all over the country. In fact, mandolin orchestras became so popular with both professional and amateur musicians that they dominated the music scene in the United States for nearly a decade.

Yet another way of finding good material is to take a virtual trip around the world with the mandolin. In so doing, you will discover that the mandolin is so popular in so many countries that lots of music exists for it in places you might not have thought to look: the British Isles, Balkans, Russia, Italy, Greece, Brazil, Sweden—all have wonderful mandolin music waiting for you to explore.

The Internet can be a great tool for discovering mandolin related music from these countries. A search with one of the popular "search engines" or a visit to some of the Usenet newsgroups out there can help you begin your journey with relative ease.

Here are two tunes that you can use as a springboard in your search for international mandolin music. They illustrate the diversity to be found in mandolin music from other countries. The first is a popular French-Canadian fiddle tune that works very well on the mandolin and sounds much like some American fiddle tunes. The second is from Greece. It features a melody that is still accessible and yet a departure from what you're probably used to hearing.

OLD FRENCH (CANADA)
Track 49

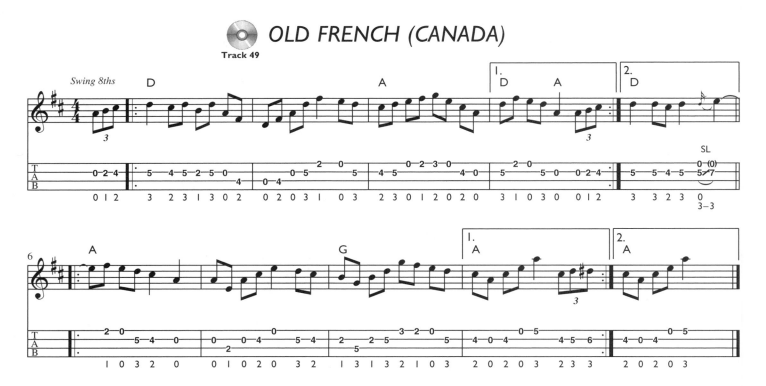

SIMO LIGERI
Track 50

WRAPPING UP

Final Thoughts and Suggestions

We sincerely hope that you've found this book helpful in understanding some of the key areas that will allow you to gain mastery of the mandolin. The wonderful thing about music is that it's a lifetime study; the more you learn, the more there is yet to learn. Here are a few final thoughts and suggestions for you to consider as you continue your study of music in general and the mandolin in particular.

- **Listen!** There is a wealth of recorded material featuring the mandolin. We are blessed to live in an age where music from around the world is easily accessible and the talents of the musicians making it are astounding. Listen to recordings over and over and over again. Attend concerts. Take part in jam sessions. Go to workshops. Listen! Inspiration and the answers to your musical questions are there if you listen closely, often enough.

- **Always try to find people to jam with who are better than you.** They will push you to improve.

- **Practice consistently.** Charlie Parker practiced 11–15 hours per day over a period of about three to four years. While you may not have that kind of time, dedicate yourself to practicing every day without fail.

- **Avoid getting stuck in a practice rut**, covering the same musical ground in every practice session. Strive to learn new material frequently.

- **Music is supposed to be fun!** Try to always allow yourself some fun whenever you practice.

- **Focus on the sound you and your instrument make together.** Experiment with your right hand close to and farther way from the bridge. Try attacking notes with different velocity. Good musical ideas are wonderful but if your sound is weak or monotonous who will want to listen?

- **Think about music as often as you possibly can** during the day, even when you are without your instrument. Use your drive time, time in the shower, and so on, to listen to great musicians, review in your head material you're trying to memorize, sing solos to yourself, etc. This type of "virtual practice" and focus on music will pay off!

- **Don't be afraid to take chances in your playing.** If you've advanced through the three books in this series you should be well equipped technically, so go for it.

- Good teachers, books and instructional materials are all tremendously helpful but always remember, *in the end it's all up to you!*